OLD HATE – NEW HOPE

VOLUME TWO • 1825 to 1876

By Ira Peck with Steven Deyle

HISTORICAL CONSULTANTS

Elaine Tyler May
*Professor of American
Studies and History
University of Minnesota
Minneapolis, Minnesota*

Susan Levine
*Historian
University of North Carolina
Chapel Hill, North Carolina*

IRA PECK is a professional writer. Born in New York City, he attended public schools there and Harvard College, where he majored in history. As a journalist, he worked as a newspaper reporter and a magazine editor. He has written numerous biographies and historical books for young people.

STEVEN DEYLE is a professional historian and teacher. He has received degrees in American history from the University of California—Santa Cruz and Columbia University. He was a historical consultant and contributing writer for Scholastic's *African American History: Four Centuries of Black Life*.

ON THE COVER

The painting called *The Right to Know* appeared as an illustration in *Look* Magazine on August 20, 1968. Printed by permission of the Estate of Norman Rockwell. Copyright © 1968 Estate of Norman Rockwell. The following caption appeared with the painting: "We are the governed, but we govern too. Assume our love of country, for it is only the simplest of self-love. Worry little about our strength, for we have our history to show for it. And because we are strong, there are others who have hope. But watch us more closely from now on, for those of us who stand here mean to watch those we put in the seats of power. And listen to us, you who lead, for we are listening harder for the truth that you have not always offered us. Your voice must be ours, and ours speaks of cities that are not safe, and of wars we do not want, of poor in a land of plenty, and of a world that will not take the shape our arms would give it. We are not fierce, and the truth will not frighten us. Trust us, for we have given you our trust. We are the governed, remember, but we govern too."

For reprint permission, grateful acknowledgement is made to:
Joan Daves, agent to the estate of Martin Luther King, Jr., for the excerpt from I HAVE A DREAM by Martin Luther King, Jr., copyright © 1963 by Martin Luther King, Jr.

Scholastic Inc. ISBN 0-590-35701-8

12 11 10 9 8 7 6 5 4 3 2 1   7 0 / 9 1 2 3 4 5 / 9

PUBLISHER
ELEANOR ANGELES

EDITORIAL DIRECTOR
CAROLYN JACKSON

PROJECT EDITOR
DEBORAH GORE

SKILLS EDITOR
MOLLIE COHEN

MANAGING EDITOR
KEVIN GILLESPIE

ASSISTANT EDITOR
LISA KEATING

EDITORIAL ASSISTANT
LISA CRAWLEY

PRODUCTION
CLAUDIA BRUCE
VIRGINIA DUSTIN
MIDGE MARONI

◆

DESIGN DIRECTOR
CAMPION PRIMM

ART DIRECTOR
JUDITH ORLICK

PHOTO & ILLUSTRATION
RESEARCHERS
PHOTOSEARCH, INC.

CARTOGRAPHER
DAVID LINDROTH

ILLUSTRATOR
CHIP WASS

COVER DESIGN
ROSEMARY INTRIERI

CONTENTS

APPENDIX

MAPS

CHARTS AND GRAPHS

OLD HATE – NEW HOPE

JACKSON'S

1820   1825   1830

1821

Sequoyah
invents written
Cherokee alphabet.

1828

Andrew Jackson
elected seventh
U.S. president.

1829

First commercial
railroad, the Baltimore
& Ohio, begins service.

1830

Congress
passes Indian
Removal Act.

1831

Nat Turner's
Rebellion

In 1831, a young French nobleman toured the United States. The visitor, Alexis de Tocqueville (ah-lek-SEE deh TOHK-vil), had come primarily to study the American prison system. He traveled through all parts of the country and observed the workings of American democracy.

What de Tocqueville saw led him to believe that the United States was the most democratic country on earth. Even the "humblest citizens" had political rights. Yet in many ways, he felt that American democracy was incomplete.

De Tocqueville's perception of America was in many respects correct. The United States was

The 1800s brought widespread change to Americans' lives —from the political reforms of Jacksonian democracy to the Industrial Revolution witnessed by these mill workers.

AMERICA

1835   1840

1835

Indian removals
to west of the
Mississippi begin.

1836

Mill workers go on
strike in Lowell,
Massachusetts.

1838

Cherokee
Trail of Tears

UNIT 1

more democratic than ever before. Yet women, blacks, and Native Americans were still denied the rights of citizens. In the early years of the republic, only white male citizens who owned a certain amount of property could vote. This meant that poor citizens, even if they were white and male, were left out of government.

Vermont was the first state to change this law. When it entered the Union in 1791, it gave all adult white males the vote. Other new states did the same. In the 1820s, even the 13 original states began to change their laws about the right to vote. The poorer man's vote counted just as much as the richer man's vote.

The Rise of Jackson

This change in the voting rights of white males brought other changes in American politics. Earlier, Americans had turned to wealthy men for leadership. Now they began looking for leaders who claimed to be average citizens. In 1828, just such an average man, Andrew Jackson, was elected president.

Jackson was not a poor man

when he took office, but he came from a poor family. Like many Americans, he had migrated west. Jackson became a wealthy Tennessee planter. He was a man who refused to let anyone tell him what to do.

In his speeches, Jackson emphasized how much he admired the "common people." As a rule, he distrusted Eastern bankers. He thought the bankers cheated people out of their money and often acted as if they were better than everyone else.

Jackson appealed to farmers, factory workers, and the poor. Their support enabled Jackson to win the **electoral college** (a group of people chosen by voters to elect the president and vice-president) votes of every Western and Southern state in the election of 1828. His opponent, President John Quincy Adams, won votes only in his native Northeast.

The rise of Andrew Jackson changed the nature of American politics. The Federalists and Democratic–Republicans would never again be the two major political parties. The followers of Jackson became known as Democrats.

Democrats fa-

"BORN TO COMMAND."

OF VETO MEMORY.

HAD I BEEN CONSULTED.

KING ANDREW THE FIRST.

Although considered an average citizen by "the common man," Andrew Jackson's forceful leadership led some critics to dub him "King Andrew."

vored states' rights and a limited federal government. Their opponents, such as Henry Clay, called themselves Whigs. Whigs supported a strong federal government. The Democrats and the Whigs would remain the two major parties for the next 25 years.

Politics became an important part of American life. Its importance was reflected in the sharp rise in voter participation. In 1824, only 27 percent of those eligible voted. In 1828, this figure jumped to 56 percent. And by 1840, an incredible 78 percent of all eligible voters went to the polls. (In 1988, only about 50 percent of those eligible voted in the presidential election.) Also, many aspects of modern political campaigns came into being during this period. Among the new creations were political conventions, campaign slogans, and large outdoor rallies.

The country was changing rapidly and the two parties fought over how to handle these changes. One important issue was local improvements.

Political power, once limited to rich landowners, was now open to every white male in the United States.

The Whigs thought the national government should help pay for the building of new roads, bridges, and railroads. The Democrats believed this was best left up to the states.

Industrializing America

The American economy was also changing. In the 1700s, a great change in manufacturing and industry, which would also affect the U.S., swept Great Britain. Early each morning, men, women, and children took their places behind noisy machines. The machines could turn out cotton cloth, farm tools, or rifle barrels much faster than individual workers. The process of becoming an industrial society was called industrialization.

This system was fairly new in the 1830s—but it was growing fast. More and more factories were being built in such Northeastern states as Massachusetts and Connecticut.

Industrialization also affected American politics. Factory owners in the North needed to sell their goods. To protect themselves from cheap British imports, they asked Congress to impose a high tariff. The rural South did not become industrialized and objected to the tariff. Southern farmers needed to buy manufactured goods, such as farm tools and clothing, from Britain and other European countries. A high tariff made imported goods more expensive than before.

The debate over tariffs caused a national crisis in the early 1830s. High tariffs passed in 1828 and 1832 angered many Southerners. The state government of South Carolina said it would not collect the tariff duties. If the U.S. government forced South Carolina to obey, it declared it would leave the country. In reaction to the tariff, Vice-President John C. Calhoun anonymously wrote a pamphlet arguing that a state had the right to **nullify** (declare illegal) an act of Congress. However, Calhoun did not take a public stand on the issue, in order to avoid embarrassing President Jackson.

Although Jackson was a Southerner, he believed the nation's laws were more important than the rights of states. He convinced Congress to pass a lower tariff. Then he threatened to send in the Army if South Carolina refused to obey the law. Finally, South Carolina agreed to collect the lower tariff duties. Jackson's action during the Nullification Crisis shows how persuasive he was.

Jackson also got his way in the "bank war." In 1832, Jackson decided to destroy the national Bank of the United States. He believed that it served Eastern businesses and cheated Western and Southern farmers. He asked Congress not to renew the bank's charter. When Congress refused, Jackson vetoed the new charter. Then he withdrew government funds from the bank and deposited them in smaller banks run by his supporters.

Dreams of Democracy

On the frontier, Native Americans were being forced from their lands and their ways of life. As European American settlers moved into Indian homelands,

Canals, 1825–1840

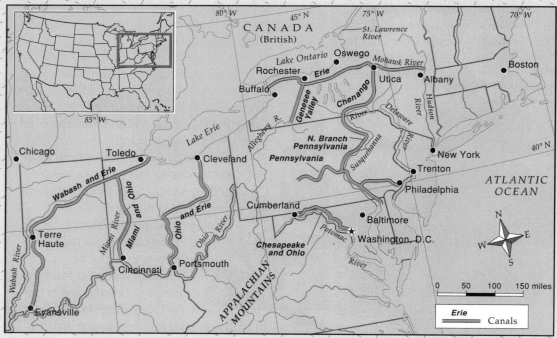

What canal(s) and/or rivers would you have used to travel from Buffalo to New York in 1831? If you were traveling from Buffalo to Evansville, what water route(s) might you have taken?

AMERICAN ADVENTURES

Eager for new lands to settle, whites forced tribe after Native American tribe from their homelands. In 1843, representatives of 16 tribes met with U.S. officials, hoping to solve conflicts raised by the forced move.

many Indians were forced to move further west. While Jackson was president, Congress passed a law forcing Native Americans like the Cherokee and Creek tribes of the Southeast to move west of the Mississippi River. Many members of these tribes did not survive the move. Many settlers did not seem to care about the suffering or death of Indians.

African Americans were also discriminated against. In the North, slavery was against the law, but whites would not mix with blacks or treat them as equals. Blacks were kept out of white churches, schools, jobs, and hotels.

The expansion of the "cotton kingdom" in the South and the factory system in the North fed regional tension. In the South, two million blacks were slaves. Slaves weren't needed on the smaller farms of the North, but the cotton-growing South required a large supply of cheap labor, which slavery gave them. By the 1830s, many white Southerners believed their way of life depended on slavery. In many areas, black slaves greatly outnumbered white farmers and planters. White Southerners often worried that their slaves might rise up and revolt against them. In 1831, their fears came true during a slave uprising called **Nat Turner's Rebellion**.

The United States in Andrew Jackson's day was more democratic than ever before. But there were still large groups of people who did not share in this democracy. During his travels through the United States, de Tocqueville noticed the gap. American democracy was strong and growing—but far from complete.

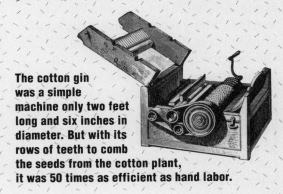

The cotton gin was a simple machine only two feet long and six inches in diameter. But with its rows of teeth to comb the seeds from the cotton plant, it was 50 times as efficient as hand labor.

1 "OLD HICKORY"

When Andrew Jackson promised to be a president of the people, they took him at his word. Butchers, bakers, settlers, and other commoners flocked to his inauguration, tossing formality out the window —or trampling it underfoot.

No one had ever seen anything like it before. Woodsmen, who lived in log cabins west of the Appalachian Mountains, were pouring into Washington, D.C. Many wore coonskin caps and muddy boots. Their mouths were full of chewing tobacco. They were real pioneers, farmers, and hunters.

There weren't enough rooms for them in the hotels. So four or five of them slept together in a bed. Some slept on floors or on pool tables.

What were they all doing in Washington? They had come to see their hero,

Andrew Jackson, sworn in as president. Wasn't Andy "one of the boys"? Wasn't he born in a log cabin, just as they had been? Didn't his folks have to chop down trees to make way for a farm, just like theirs? Jackson wasn't one of those gentlemen fellows from the East, no sir.

No question about it—Jackson was their man. And now it was March 4, 1829, the day Jackson was to be sworn in. He took the solemn **oath** (pledge to be honest and keep promises) of office and then rode on horseback to the White House. He was going to have a party there for important government men and their wives. The tables were all set up with good food and punch.

Jackson's supporters didn't want to go home. They wanted to see Jackson in the White House. So they followed him to the building and pushed their way in. Inside, some of them stood on fancy, velvet chairs to see their hero. Others pushed toward the food tables to eat. Plates were broken and food and drink was spilled on the beautiful carpets. Ladies in fine silk dresses fainted. President Jackson was shoved against a wall. Friends kept him from being crushed by the crowd. Finally they helped him to escape. Jackson spent his first night as president in a hotel.

Growing Up in the Carolinas

Andrew Jackson—hero of the "common man"—was born in the western part of the Carolinas in 1767. At that time, it was Indian territory covered with forests of pine trees. The few houses or cabins were made of logs. Jackson's father, a Scotch Irish farmer, died a few days before Andy was born. His father had hurt himself pushing a heavy log.

Jackson wasn't a good student in school. He was too busy wrestling, racing, and jumping. But he did learn to read well. Few people in those parts could read or write. So Jackson used to read the newspaper out loud to the farmers. One day in 1776, he read to them about the Declaration of Independence. It had just

been signed in Philadelphia.

When he was 13, Jackson joined the South Carolina militia in the American Revolution. Soon after, he was taken prisoner by the British. Jackson was ordered to polish the shoes of a British officer, but he had a hot temper and refused to shine the officer's shoes. The officer hit Jackson hard on the face with his sword. Jackson had a scar there for the rest of his life.

After the Revolutionary War, Jackson studied to become a lawyer. No one understood how he made it. He seemed to spend most of his time playing cards and making bets on horse races. But he did become a lawyer and then traveled to Nashville, Tennessee. This was the "Wild West" in those days. Jackson's temper continued getting him into trouble. While fighting a duel with one man, he was hit by a bullet two inches from the heart. Then Jackson fired his pistol and killed the other man.

Jackson moved to Nashville in 1788. He bought his own plantation, "The Hermitage," in 1795 and grew wealthy as a cotton planter and slave owner. Jackson was elected to the United States Senate and later served as a justice on the Tennessee Supreme Court. However, it was not politics, but the War of 1812 that first made Jackson a national hero.

In 1813, Jackson led riflemen from Tennessee in a fight against the British and their Indian allies. They marched 500 miles through wilderness. "He's as tough as hickory," said one soldier. His men nicknamed him

Andrew Jackson (1767–1845) was a new kind of leader—an outspoken man of action and a staunch defender of everyday Americans.

Old Hickory. In 1814, Jackson led his fighters into Florida and captured Pensacola. A year later, he commanded an American army against the British at New Orleans. This army was made up of Tennessee and Kentucky riflemen, Frenchmen, free blacks, pirates, and some Indians. It was a tough fighting force, and won a complete victory over the British. By the end of the Battle of New Orleans, the British had suffered 2036 killed or wounded. Jackson's army lost only 8 dead and 13 wounded.

But news from Europe that the war was over had not arrived yet. If America had known sooner, the Battle of New Orleans would not have taken place. As it turned out, Jackson became a great hero in America because of the victory at New Orleans.

A year later, Jackson's forces fought the Creek Indians at the Battle of Horseshoe Bend in Mississippi Territory (present-day Alabama). The Creeks had earlier killed hundreds of nearby villagers. Jackson let the Creek Indian women and children leave, but then killed all of the 800 remaining Creek men. He later signed a peace treaty with the Creeks, who gave up 23 million acres of land.

Three years later, in 1818, Jackson led another army into Florida. At that time, Florida was Spanish territory. But before long, Jackson and his men had captured almost all the Spanish towns and forts in the area. They also crushed the Seminole Indians. The following year, 1819, Spain signed a treaty and gave up all of Florida to the United States.

Seventh President

Jackson was elected president of the

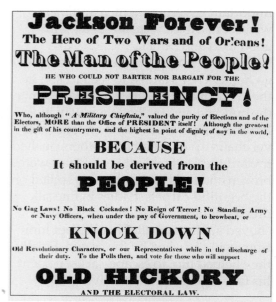

Jackson certainly had his critics, but those who loved him gave him overwhelming support.

United States in 1828. He was supported by the rich and the common people everywhere.

During Jackson's presidency, he fought hard against any group that seemed to be working for its own good ahead of the nation's good.

"The Federal Constitution must be obeyed, state rights preserved, our national debt must be paid, direct taxes and loans avoided, and the Federal Union preserved," said Jackson in his 1829 **inaugural address** (speech made at time of being sworn in to office). He also rewarded many of his supporters with jobs in government. This came to be known as the **spoils system.** His followers worked on many different state reforms such as the right of workers to form labor unions, secret-ballot elections, and inspection of banks.

Above all, Jackson gave all white men the feeling that they had a voice in government. He was especially popular with the farmers of the West and the factory workers of the East. To these people, Jackson was not only a voice, but the living proof of a new idea. He stood for the idea that, in a democracy like the United States, a poor white man could rise to the top—and become president. The struggle for equal rights for women, blacks, and Native Americans was still to come.

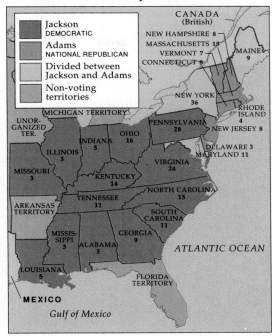

Electoral Vote, 1828

Jackson
DEMOCRATIC

Adams
NATIONAL REPUBLICAN

Divided between
Jackson and Adams

Non-voting
territories

CANADA
(British)

NEW HAMPSHIRE 8
MASSACHUSETTS 15
VERMONT 7
CONNECTICUT 8
MAINE 9

MICHIGAN TERRITORY

NEW YORK 36

RHODE ISLAND 4

UNOR-GANIZED TER.

PENNSYLVANIA 28

NEW JERSEY 8

OHIO 16

INDIANA 5

DELAWARE 3
MARYLAND 11

ILLINOIS 3

VIRGINIA 24

MISSOURI 3

KENTUCKY 14

NORTH CAROLINA 15

ARKANSAS TERRITORY

TENNESSEE 11

SOUTH CAROLINA 11

MISSIS-SIPPI 3

ALABAMA 5

GEORGIA 9

ATLANTIC OCEAN

LOUISIANA 5

FLORIDA TERRITORY

MEXICO

Gulf of Mexico

Study the key. Which candidate was most popular in the South? Which candidate was most popular in the North? How many total electoral votes did each candidate receive?

CHAPTER CHECK

WORD MATCH
1. Battle of Horseshoe Bend
2. spoils system
3. Battle of New Orleans
4. oath
5. inaugural address

a. pledge to tell the truth and keep promises
b. giving political supporters government jobs
c. speech made at time of being sworn in to office
d. led to Jackson's becoming a hero
e. led to a peace treaty and the acquiring of 23 million acres of land

QUICK QUIZ
1. Why was Andrew Jackson not considered a gentleman by Easterners?
2. Name some things Jackson did to become a national hero.
3. What were some of the ideas Andrew Jackson favored as president?

THINK ABOUT IT
1. If you had been alive during Andrew Jackson's time, do you think you would have supported him for president? Why or why not?
2. Do you think someone like Andrew Jackson could be elected today? Why or why not?

2 THE TRAIL OF TEARS

This painting shows the Cherokees traveling the bitter "Trail of Tears." The Indian Removal Act authorized the U.S. Army to force Cherokees out of their homes and onto reservations west of the Mississippi River.

Doublehead was a prosperous businessman. He owned a plantation and several stores. Doublehead was also a Cherokee Indian chief. In his hunger for wealth, he accepted money from European American settlers for part of his land. This deal violated the **sacred** (holy or regarded with great respect) Cherokee Blood Law. It was a very serious crime to sell Cherokee land to whites. The punishment for breaking this law was death.

One night Doublehead entered a Cherokee tavern. An Indian named Ridge was waiting for him. Doublehead had broken the Blood Law, so Ridge shot and killed him.

The Cherokee Indians lived on valuable farmland in the hills of Georgia. They had lived on this land for hundreds of years. Now, in the early 1800s, white settlers wanted this land for themselves.

The Cherokees adopted some European ways. The Cherokees wrote their own constitution in 1820, which they based upon the U.S. Constitution. They declared their land an independent nation. They wanted to live by their own laws. Georgia's state government ruled that the Cherokees were not a real nation. The state wanted to give Cherokee land to white Georgians in a lottery.

When some settlers discovered gold on Cherokee land, whites urged the removal of the Cherokees. Settlers could become wealthy only if they owned the land. President Andrew Jackson wanted the Cherokees to move to less valuable land on a **reservation** (public land set aside for special use) west of the Mississippi. He believed whites and Indians could not live together in peace.

Congress Acts

Congress passed the Indian Removal Act in 1830. This law gave the government the right to exchange lands west of the Mississippi for Indian lands in the East. The government set up an Indian Territory in Oklahoma. The land was to belong to the Indians "as long as grass grows or water runs."

The Choctaws (CHAHK-taws) of Mississippi were forced to move to Oklahoma in the winter of 1831 to 1832. In the next few years, the Creeks and Chickasaws (CHIK-uh-saws) of Alabama and Louisiana followed them west. Along the way, many Indians died of cold, disease, and starvation. The Cherokees did not want this to happen to their own people. They wanted to stay on their land.

John Ross, the leader of the Cherokees, traveled to Washington to win support from the federal government. Ross argued and won the Cherokee case before the Supreme Court. Still, Jackson ordered the Cherokees to move. When Ross came back from Washington, settlers stole horses and other belongings from the Cherokees. Some settlers beat and killed Indians, hoping this would drive the rest away.

Many Cherokees now believed that going west was the only way they could live in peace. To survive, they had to sign a treaty with Georgia, selling their land to the state. Several hundred Cherokees belonged to this group called the Treaty Party. In 1835, the Treaty Party signed an agreement with Georgia. Others did not agree with the Treaty Party because it did not represent all Cherokees. According to the agreement, the Cherokees would leave in two years. They would go west to Oklahoma. In return, Georgia would pay them $5 million.

Leaving the Land

The deadline for leaving was May 1838. By this time the Treaty Party and several thousand others had already gone west. But most of the Cherokees stayed on their land, tending their farms and businesses.

Georgia troops came and forced the Cherokees from their homes. Hundreds of Cherokees escaped from the soldiers

A Cherokee leader named Sequoyah created the first written version of an Indian language. He believed that the ability to read and write helped give whites their power.

and fled to the hills of North Carolina. One Cherokee named Charley killed a soldier during the escape. The army offered to leave the Indians alone in North Carolina if they would bring back Charley for punishment. Charley voluntarily surrendered, and was shot. Because of his sacrifice, the rest of the Indians were allowed to stay in North Carolina.

The other Cherokees were packed into **internment** (confinement) camps. The camps were like prisons. They were dirty and the Cherokees did not have enough food and clean water. The Indians had to wait in the camps until everything was ready for them go west.

It was the hottest time of the year. Because of the heat and the filth in the

Indian Removals, 1820–1840

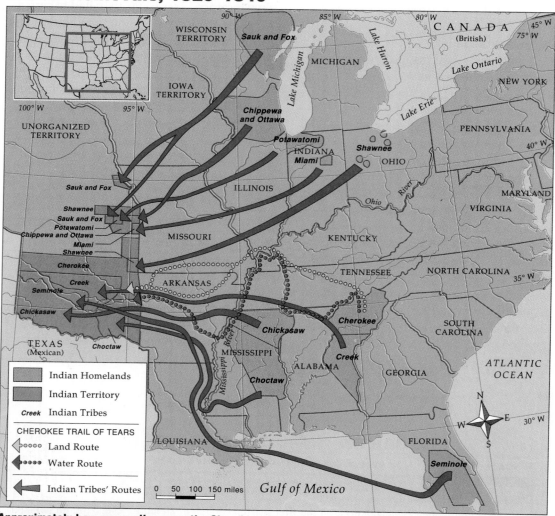

Approximately how many miles were the Cherokees forced to travel from their homeland to what is now Oklahoma? Which tribe was forced to travel the greatest distance?

AMERICAN ADVENTURES

camps, many Indians got sick. Some died, and others became too ill to travel. Ross feared that if his people began to head west now, most would not survive the journey. He asked the U.S. Army to let them wait until the fall. General Winfield Scott, who was supervising the removal, agreed.

Over the summer, about 2000 Cherokees died in the camps. In October 1838, the great move finally began. Soldiers loaded thousands of Indians onto wagons. Others were forced to walk. It was more than 800 miles to their new homeland and it took most of the winter to get there. It was a miserable journey. Along the way, disease and bitter cold took the lives of 2000 more Cherokees. By the time they reached their strange, new home in March of 1839, one-fourth of the Cherokee nation had perished.

Many of the survivors swore vengeance against the leaders of the Treaty Party. John Ross begged them to be merciful. There had been enough death already. But the Blood Law had been broken. At a secret meeting, it was decided that the guilty must be punished. Murderers killed Ridge, Ross's son, and two other leaders of the Treaty Party.

Despite the hardship in getting there, the Cherokees survived on the reservations in Oklahoma. The land was much worse than what they had left. The Cherokees farmed the land and built new schools and houses. But they will always remember those who died on the path to the new land. They call this path the Trail of Tears.

CHAPTER CHECK

WORD MATCH
1. sacred
2. internment
3. reservation
4. John Ross
5. Doublehead

a. public land set aside for special use
b. holy, or regarded with great respect
c. sold Cherokee land to whites
d. won the case for Cherokees keeping their land
e. confinement

QUICK QUIZ
1. What was the sacred Cherokee Blood Law?
2. What was the Indian Removal Act?

THINK ABOUT IT
1. Why did President Jackson want the Cherokees to move from their land? Do you think this was fair? Why or why not?
2. The Cherokees declared themselves an independent nation within Georgia; they wanted to remain on their own land. The state of George said they were not a nation. The state wanted to take Cherokee land and give it to white settlers. Can you think of any solutions to this conflict?

ᴄʜᴀᴘᴛᴇʀ 3 LOWELL'S MILLS

The hours were long and the work hard, but getting a job at a cotton mill was the dream of many a young girl in the mid-1800s. These young women proudly display spindles of cotton thread.

Dear Mary:

I went into the mill to work a few days after I wrote to you. It looked very pleasant at first, the rooms were so light, and spacious, and clean, the girls so pretty and neatly dressed, and the machinery so brightly polished or nicely painted....They set me to threading shuttles, and tying weaver's knots, and such things, and now I have improved so that I can take care of one loom. I could take care of two if I only had eyes in the back part of my head....

At first the hours seemed very long, but I was so interested in learning that I endured it very well; and when I went out at night the sound of the mill was in my ears.... After that it seemed as though cotton-wool was in my ears, but now I do not mind at all. You know some people learn to sleep with the thunder of Niagara in their ears, and a cotton mill is no worse....

Yours as ever,
Susan

In a set of letters written in 1844, "Susan" described life as a worker at the cotton mills in Lowell, Massachusetts, to her friend "Mary" back home in New Hampshire. The real author of these letters was Harriet Farley, a mill worker. The letters were printed in *The Lowell Offering*, a magazine for mill workers, which Harriet edited.

Like thousands of other young women, Farley came to Lowell to work in the mills. Her family was poor and she had been working to help support them since she was 14. She had made straw hats, stitched shoes and even taught school, but none of these paid very well. The mills of Lowell seemed to hold a chance for her independence.

The work was hard and unfamiliar. The noise could be deafening—as "Susan" quickly found out. And the hours were long. The machinery clanged into action at 5:00 in the morning and did not stop until 7:30 at night. The mill workers got only two half-hour breaks during that whole long day—one for breakfast, and one for lunch. Standing for 13 hours a day, 6 days a week, left them with sore legs and aching feet.

For many of the young women in Lowell's mills, the pay made all the discomfort worthwhile. Many earned about $2.25 for a week's work. This may seem like very poor pay, but it was fairly high

The Lowell Offering was a literary magazine written by and for "factory girls" working in the cotton mills of Lowell, Massachusetts.

by the standards of the day. The girls at Lowell were glad to get it. It meant that they had money for themselves, or for their families to save or to spend.

Independence

Until the 1830s, most women depended on their families for support until they married. Some, like the young Harriet Farley, worked for **wages** (payment made for work done) at home or taught school to support themselves. Another mill worker, Harriet Robinson, explained what this meant to women: "After the first payday came, and they felt the jingle of silver in their pockets, their bowed heads were lifted. They looked you in the face."

The women who came to Lowell from the farms of New England were pioneers. They were beginning something new in American life—an experiment in large-scale manufacturing modeled after that in Great Britain. They produced cotton cloth in a way that had never been tried before in the United States.

Cotton Mills

The new system for making cloth took several steps. At one end of the factory, the women received shipments of raw cotton from Southern states. Then, with the help of giant machines, they twisted it, spun it, and wound it into cotton thread. Next, they placed the thread on huge power looms and wove it into yards of cotton cloth. Finally, the cloth was shipped and sold all over the country.

What was so new and different about this? People had been making cotton cloth for thousands of years. The difference was that before this, cloth was spun and woven at home for family use. Families still had spinning wheels and hand looms in their homes in the 1830s. But Lowell's mills made producing cloth faster and cheaper and in larger quantities easier than doing it the old way.

Cotton, the **raw material** used in these mills, came from Southern plantations. The workers who grew, cleaned, and shipped the cotton were slaves. The mills at Lowell and other new factory towns helped make slavery more profitable in the South. Northern mill owners depended on slave-grown cotton to make money.

One of the first Americans to try manufacturing on a large scale was a Boston merchant, Francis Cabot Lowell. He built a cotton mill in Waltham in 1813, near Boston. It soon made so much money that Lowell and his partners looked for a place to build a larger mill. Lowell found a village of 200 people on the Merrimack River. But before he could build there, Lowell died at the age of 42. His partners started the mill in the river town, renaming it Lowell. They mostly hired young women because they believed it was fair to pay them less than men. The women, they thought, had no families to support, so they would not demand higher wages.

In its early years, the village was a worker's dream-come-true. It had canals, orderly mills, and good living conditions. The mill owners planned neat, well-run boarding houses for the women to live in. Soon Lowell grew into a town. Then the town became a city. In 1836, there were 17,633 people, most of them young women, living in Lowell.

Labor Troubles

But as the town grew, the workers' lives became harder. The mill owners cared less about the mill workers' welfare, (well-being) and more and more about making money. The manager explained his attitude. "I regard my work people just as I regard my machinery. So long as they can do the work for what I choose to pay them, I keep them, getting out of that all I can."

In 1834, the girls in the Lowell mills received shocking news. The price of cotton was dropping and the mill owners wanted workers to increase production. The owners announced that each worker's weekly wages would be cut by one dollar. That meant that many workers would be getting only pennies a week. Hundreds of workers walked off the job and paraded up and down the streets of Lowell. It was one of the first **strikes** (workers' refusal to work) in American history.

Workers circulated a petition among themselves with the headline "Union Is Power." In it, they promised to support each other, refusing to go back to work until wages were restored. The petition also accused the mill owners of being greedy, and of treating the women like slaves.

The owners did not listen. They cut wages anyway. Their goal was to earn money by making cotton cloth faster and cheaper than it had ever been made before. Lowell's women workers did not forget the need to stand united. Nine years later, a Lowell worker, Sarah Bagley, organized the Female Labor Reform Association. This group was formed to campaign for a 10-hour workday.

Industrialization made it easier for business owners to make money, but forced others to give up their independence in order to earn a living.

What was happening in Lowell was only an early chapter of a much larger story. By the 1840s, other industries were also growing in the Northern states. Men, women, and children were going to work in factories, for better or for worse. Often they were made to work long hours in dingy rooms for very little pay.

Industrialization (the process of developing large factories) brought changes both good and bad to the lives of working people. Factory work was hard and often boring. It was especially so for children, a large part of the work force at this time. Children in factories lost their chance to get an education, and often lost their health as well.

Because it took so much money to start a factory, fewer people could run their own businesses. Instead, they had to work for factory owners. On the other hand, industrialization added to the wealth and power of the Northeast. It provided jobs to unskilled workers and to new immigrants who took the jobs, despite low pay and unhealthy working conditions. Mass production made many kinds of manufactured goods less expensive.

CHAPTER CHECK

WORD MATCH
1. raw material
2. strikes
3. welfare
4. wages
5. industrialization

a. well-being
b. payment for work done
c. a natural product that is used in manufacturing
d. the process of developing large factories
e. workers' refusal to work

QUICK QUIZ
1. Name some conditions of the cotton mills like the ones in Lowell.
2. What were the two major improvements cotton mills had over home spinning?
3. Who were the main employees of the cotton mills? Why?

THINK ABOUT IT
1. The factories of the 19th century caused many changes in American society. Compare the benefits and disadvantages they brought to the working people.
2. How did the mill owners and managers treat their employees? Were they fair or unfair to the workers?

4 NAT TURNER'S REBELLION

Slavery was a harsh way of life. These slaves worked in a field of sugarcane, under the watchful eye of an armed overseer. The slaves, whose clothing makes them easy to spot, were expected to work without weariness or complaint.

"Remember that ours is not war for robbery nor to satisfy our passions; it is a struggle for freedom. Ours must be deeds, not words." On August 21, 1831, a black slave named Nat Turner spurred on an excited group of followers in a forest in Southampton County, Virginia.

Little is known about Turner's life before the rebellion. His parents and grandparents had been slaves. He learned to read and write at an early age. Turner claimed he saw visions from God, and believed he had a per-

sonal mission to lead others out of **bondage** (slavery).

Turner had a plan—to march from one plantation to another, killing slave owners and their families. He wanted the slaves to join him in an attack on Jerusalem, the county seat. If they could capture the town, he felt their revolt would become famous and it would lead more slaves to rebel. If the attack failed, the rebels would retreat to a swamp and fight on. Soon they would attract more followers, said Turner, and one day take over the entire state of Virginia.

No accurate account exists of what became known as **Nat Turner's Rebellion**—except perhaps Turner's own famous book, *Confessions*. After dark, Turner and seven followers entered the house of his owner, John Travis, and murdered each member of the family. Then, taking all the guns they could carry, the rebels invaded other neighborhood houses and plantations, killing people as they slept. Only a few slaves—perhaps 60 to 80—joined the revolt. Most were too frightened or felt some loyalty to their masters.

That night, Turner and his band killed 57 men, women, and children. The next morning they headed for

Nat Turner (1800–1831) was a deeply religious man whose harsh life led him to violence. But instead of freeing slaves, his revolt led to a sharp crackdown on blacks both slave and free.

Jerusalem, but ran into a group of armed white men. After some fighting, the slave band broke up. Turner himself escaped into a swamp two miles from the Travis home.

Turner's uprising shook the South. Newspaper reports fueled rumors that as many as 150 to 800 slaves had slaughtered hundreds of whites. People demanded to know: Who was Nat Turner? What events led to such a blood-bath (killing of many people)? When would the revolt be put down?

Crisis Over Slavery

Two million African Americans lived in slavery in the South. In the Southern states, laws gave blacks little protection. A white person could go to jail for beating up another white person. But white owners almost never were punished for whipping or even killing their slaves. Black slaves and their children also belonged to their masters—like any other personal property. All slaves could be bought and sold as their masters saw fit.

From Colonial days, slavery divided Americans. Even before 1800, most Northern states enacted laws to abolish slavery. In 1808, the U.S. Congress passed a law against bringing any more slaves into the country. After that, slaves were **smuggled** in illegally from Africa and the West Indies.

The debate raged on. Some people, called **abolitionists,** insisted slavery was a terrible evil that must end. Others demanded that slaves be freed slowly, to avoid a national crisis. Still others started a "Back-to-Africa" movement, asking that slaves be returned to Africa to start a new homeland of their own.

In the South, many rich people believed slavery was an important part of a prosperous society. John C. Calhoun, a leading South Carolina politician, insisted that slavery was a "positive good," and that blacks were well taken care of by their masters. Throughout their lives, he argued, blacks were given food, housing, and medical care.

Calhoun failed to mention that the slaves' food was usually poor and fatty. Their clothing was rough and ragged. Few of them wore shoes, except in the winter months. Most died much younger than their masters. The majority of slaves (men, women, and children) worked in the fields, though some worked in homes.

In the late 1820s, an **economic depression** (slump or collapse) caused the prices of both cotton and slaves to fall in the South. An anxious society passed harsh laws against blacks. The state of Virginia, for example, enacted laws that forbade any free blacks from learning to read or write.

Blacks resisted slavery every day. Some broke tools as they worked in fields. Some slaves expressed their anger by destroying crops or burning forests. Others ran away. If caught, they might be whipped or even burned on the face with

In the South, slaves were highly valued—but as possessions, not as people. The most talented slaves earned high prices at slave auctions.

a red-hot iron.

Such events enraged Turner, who became convinced the only way blacks could free themselves was through bloodshed. After his rebellion, the Virginia state militia took terrible revenge.

Blacks Punished

More than 100 innocent blacks were murdered in cold blood. Dozens of others were tortured to make them "confess." Finally, 53 slaves were put on trial. Some were hanged, others were let go.

Turner was caught in October and tried for murder. In his *Confessions,* he calmly described the bloody events of the massacre. In addition, Turner explained the religious beliefs that caused him to lead the revolt. Nat Turner was executed on November 11, 1831.

Turner's uprising shook the whole South. After the rebellion, the Southern states passed even harsher laws against blacks, free or slave. They were forbidden to meet in groups, drink liquor, have guns, or travel freely. The laws did not solve the problems of slavery. In fact, they made the problems worse than before. The laws did reinforce the ability of many white Southerners to control blacks, both slave and free. In the years to come, arguments about slavery would divide Americans deeply. In the end, slavery would lead the nation into the worst war in its history—the Civil War.

After his arrest, Nat Turner dictated his *Confessions* to Thomas Gray, a white lawyer. The book later sold widely among whites who were terrified of similar revolts close to home.

THE
CONFESSIONS
OF
NAT TURNER,
THE LEADER OF THE LATE
INSURRECTION IN SOUTHAMPTON, VA.

As fully and voluntarily made to

THOMAS R. GRAY,

In the prison where he was confined, and acknowledged by him to be such when read before the Court of Southampton; with the certificate, under seal of the Court convened at Jerusalem, Nov. 5, 1831, for his trial.

ALSO, AN AUTHENTIC

ACCOUNT OF THE WHOLE INSURRECTION,

WITH LISTS OF THE WHITES WHO WERE MURDERED.

AND OF THE NEGROES BROUGHT BEFORE THE COURT OF SOUTHAMPTON, AND THERE SENTENCED, &c.

CHAPTER CHECK

WORD MATCH
1. bloodbath
2. abolitionists
3. smuggled
4. economic depression
5. bondage

a. slavery
b. killing of many people
c. slump or collapse
d. believed slavery was wrong and tried to stop it
e. taken from one place to another secretly

QUICK QUIZ
1. What did Nat Turner want? How did he think he could succeed?
2. Why did Southern states pass harsh slave laws in the late 1820s?
3. What arguments were made by Southerners in defense of slavery? Were they accurate? Explain.

THINK ABOUT IT
1. Describe Nat Turner's plan. Do you think it was right for him to use violence? Why or why not?
2. John C. Calhoun insisted slavery was a "positive good" because slaves were given food, housing, and medical care throughout their lifetime. What do you think of his argument?

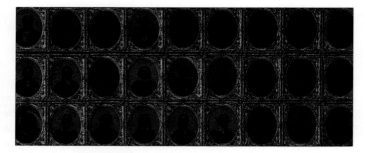

JACKSON'S AMERICA

History Detective

1. I am the piece of legislation that made it possible for the government to exchange land west of the Mississippi River for Indian lands in the East. What am I?

2. The women who worked my machines made me one of the most famous of the new factories that turned cotton into cloth in record time. What am I?

3. I led a group of slaves in a bloody raid on the houses and plantations of slave owners. Who am I?

4. As industrialization spread, American factory owners needed me to keep cheap imports from coming in from Britain. What am I?

5. By becoming president, I showed that America was the land where the "common man" had a fair chance to develop into a leader of the entire nation. Who am I?

Voices From the Past

Sojourner (SO-jurn-er) Truth is famous as one of the leaders in the fight for the rights of African Americans. But she also fought hard for women's rights. In May 1851, Ms. Truth gave an unprecedented speech to a national conference on women's rights. Read the excerpt from her speech, below, and answer the questions that follow.

[Some people] say dat womin needs to be helped into carriages, and libted ober ditches, and to hab de best place everywhar. Nobody eber helps me into carriages, or ober mud-puddles, or gibs me any best place! And a'n't I a woman? Look at me! Look at my arm! [She bared her right arm to the shoulder, showing her tremendous muscular power.] I have ploughed, and planted, and gathered into barns, and no man [beat] me! And a'n't I a woman?

1. Sojourner Truth felt women were not treated fairly in America. What examples from American society in the 1800s can you think of to prove her point?

2. Why do you think Sojourner Truth wanted her listeners to recognize her physical capabilities? How could this recognition affect lawmakers' feelings, and thus, legislation on women's rights?

Hands–On History

Expressing a Viewpoint—You are a member of the jury in the trial of Nat Turner. You are an abolitionist. In your own words, explain what you believe drove Turner and his followers to kill 57 people. What do you think would be the effect nationally if your jury decided to let Turner go free?

AMERICAN ADVENTURES

YESTERDAY'S NEWS

The American Adventures' Newspaper

1.

Philadelphia, Penn., March 6, 1823—In recent months, Americans have continued to discuss the rights of slaves and free black men. One of the most controversial issues has been religion. After some slave revolts in the early 1800s, many communities would not allow their slaves to assemble for worship. African religious rituals of any kind were forbidden, as were the aspects of religion blacks had adopted from America. Many slave owners also feared slaves' use of the Bible. They were afraid slaves might interpret it to say that all men are equal, including blacks. In addition, the Bible is a book. Many slave owners believe that if slaves learn to read the Bible, they might go on to read books with ideas that will lead them to revolt.

On the other hand, many abolitionists point to the Bill of Rights and disagree with the slave owners.

2.

3.

Bethel African Methodist Episcopal Church was founded in Philadelphia in 1794.

Black Baptists in the South

Prior to slave rebellions, which caused Southern whites to prohibit slaves from worshiping, the Baptist religion had been popular with slaves in the South. A slave named Andrew Bryan built the first Baptist church for black worship in Savannah, Georgia, in 1776.

In setting up churches, blacks began to establish their own culture in America. Excluded from politics and schools, they made the churches the center of their communities. Slave owners knew this. For a brief time, owners felt that worshiping made the slaves better workers. But when the owners felt their control slipping, they immediately revoked the slaves' right to religion.

There are some blacks who live in the North as "free men." In most ways, they live a free life. Yet they have also had problems establishing churches. In the past, free blacks seldom formed separate churches until they were forced out of existing ones by pressure from whites. Richard Allen founded an African Methodist Episcopal church in Philadelphia. Peter Williams did the same in 1796 in New York. Today, their churches are part of what is known as the A. M. E. Zion Church.

These churches are popular among blacks, and are not affected by the wishes of southern slave owners. Still, the A.M.E. Zion members do not forget their brothers and sisters, whom they remember with songs like "Go Down, Moses."

You Be the Reporter

Match each question with its news item above.
1. What would you call this article?
2. Using what you have learned about the Bill of Rights and what it says about religion, finish this paragraph.
3. How would you title this story?

YEAR	TITLE	AUTHOR
1776	Common Sense	Paine
1852	Uncle Tom's Cabin	Stowe
1906	The Jungle	Sinclair
1939	Grapes of Wrath	Steinbeck
1962	Silent Sping	Carson

TABLE SKILL

USING INFORMATION FROM TABLES

In his *Notes on the State of Virginia*, Thomas Jefferson said that "those who labor in the earth are the chosen people of God." He cautioned the nation against getting too heavily involved in manufacturing. When Jefferson died in 1826, the United States was still basically a nation of farmers, but times were slowly beginning to change.

To understand how the labor force was changing in the years between 1820 and 1840, you can study the following tables. Like most tables, these organize numbers or other facts in neat columns and rows so you can find and compare information easily.

Study the title and column headings of the table on this page. On a separate sheet of paper, complete each statement by writing the letter of the best choice.

1. According to the title and subtitle, this table shows people in the labor force who were at least **(a)** 10 years old. **(b)** 16 years old. **(c)** 21 years old.

2. For the period between 1820 and 1840, the table gives totals for every **(a)** year. **(b)** fifth year. **(c)** tenth year.

3. Each number shown in the table stands for **(a)** the total number of persons. **(b)** thousands of persons. **(c)** millions of persons.

Use facts from the table to answer the following.

4. In 1820, the labor force consisted of more than 3 million persons. **(a)** How many in the labor force were slaves? **(b)** How many were free?

5. By 1830, the total labor force had climbed from 3,135,000 to 4,200,000, or about 25 percent. Which segment of the labor force had increased the most?

6. Over the 20-year period from 1820 to 1840, **(a)** what was the general trend (direction), in the total number of workers? **(b)** how was the trend for free laborers different from that for slave laborers?

Between 1820 and 1840, most U.S. workers made their living in **agriculture** (farming). Yet the numbers of workers in manufacturing jobs was increasing at a very rapid rate. You can

Labor Force: 1820 to 1840

(In thousands of persons 10 years old and over)

Year	Free	Slave	Total
1820	2185	950	3135
1830	3020	1180	4200
1840	4180	1480	5660

see this from the table opposite. The 12 columns in this table list numbers of workers in different industries. Notice especially the facts for wage earners in "Cotton Textiles," "Iron and Steel," and "Other Manufacturing Industries."

Use facts from the table below to answer the following questions on your answer sheet.

7. Note the figures for agriculture in 1820. **(a)** Had the number employed in this industry increased or decreased in 1830? in 1840? **(b)** Based on this information, would you expect the number employed in agriculture to go up or down in 1850?

8. Based on this table, what new industries existed in the 1840s that had not existed before?

9. Between 1820 and 1830, the number of cotton textile workers increased from 12 thousand to more than four times that number! **(a)** By 1840, was the total in this category about five times, six times, or seven times the 1820 figure? **(b)** How many times did the number of iron and steel wage earners increase between 1820 and 1840?

10. From the two tables together, you can see that several trends were ocurring in the U.S. labor force between 1820 and 1840. **(a)** Make one general statement that explains what the trends were in both the numbers of free and slave workers and the numbers of manufacturing wage earners. **(b)** Then explain how these trends might have been related.

Employment by Industry: 1820 to 1840

(In thousands of persons 10 years old and over)

Year	Agriculture	Fishing	Mining	Construction	Cotton Textile Wage Earners	Primary Iron and Steel Wage Earners
1820	2470	14	13	—	12	5
1830	2965	15	22	—	55	20
1840	3570	24	32	290	72	24

Year	Other Manufacturing Industries	Trade	Ocean Vessels	Railway	Teachers	Domestics
1820	NA	—	50	—	20	110
1830	NA	—	70	—	30	160
1840	500	350	95	7	45	240

NA = Not available

Source Note: *Historical Atlas of the U.S.*, Bureau of the Census, 1975.

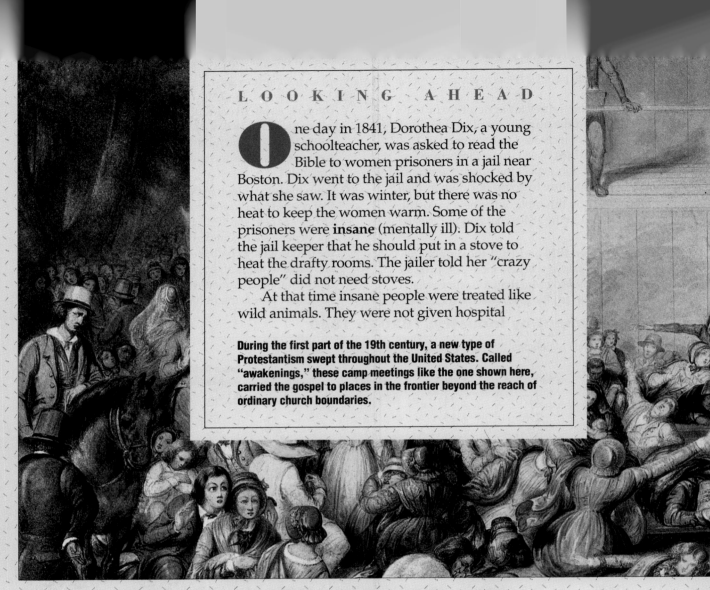

One day in 1841, Dorothea Dix, a young schoolteacher, was asked to read the Bible to women prisoners in a jail near Boston. Dix went to the jail and was shocked by what she saw. It was winter, but there was no heat to keep the women warm. Some of the prisoners were **insane** (mentally ill). Dix told the jail keeper that he should put in a stove to heat the drafty rooms. The jailer told her "crazy people" did not need stoves.

At that time insane people were treated like wild animals. They were not given hospital

During the first part of the 19th century, a new type of Protestantism swept throughout the United States. Called "awakenings," these camp meetings like the one shown here, carried the gospel to places in the frontier beyond the reach of ordinary church boundaries.

REFORM AND

1815	1820	1825	1830	1835	1840

1817
Gallaudet founds first school for the deaf.

1826
American Society for the Promotion of Temperance founded.

1831
The Liberator published.

1833
Anti-Slavery Society founded.

1837
Massachusetts legislature creates Board of Education.

CULTURE

1845   1850

1848   **1850**

Bill of Women's   Hawthorne's   Dorothea Dix
Rights adopted at   *The Scarlet Letter*   begins hospital
Seneca Falls, N.Y.   published.   reform movement.

UNIT 2

care. Instead, they were often locked up in jails and poorhouses, or even in dark cages, closets, or cellars. Cruel or ignorant keepers whipped them. They had little or nothing to wear and often went hungry.

Dix was outraged by what she saw. She felt she had to do something to help the insane. For the next two years, she went to every jail, poorhouse, and home where insane people were kept. She urged Massachusetts lawmakers to **allocate** (set aside for a specific purpose) money for a hospital for the mentally ill.

Dix traveled more than 60,000 miles throughout the United States to visit the insane. As a result of her efforts, in almost every state she visited, money was allocated for new hospitals for the mentally ill.

Dorothea Dix was not the only person at that time helping those who needed special care. Many Americans were also trying to make life better for everyone. These people were called reformers. Women were in the forefront of reform efforts, even though they couldn't vote. The period from the election of Andrew Jackson in 1828 to the eve of the Civil War, became one of the greatest periods of reform activity in American history. As the population boomed and cities sprang up almost overnight, Americans wanted to create a better world.

From Religion to Education

Why did some people become reformers? First of all, many changes were tak-

Dr. Benjamin Rush developed this chair to help calm the mentally ill.

ing place in American society. People were hopeful about the new opportunities in the West and in the growing cities of the East. Second, the tremendous changes brought by industrialization made people think that any type of progress was possible. Third, there was a great renewal of religious faith. Revivalist preachers such as Charles Finney encouraged many Americans to do good works for the love of God. This made many people believe it was their duty to help others.

Many of the reforms dealt with changing peoples' lifestyles. Some reformers wanted to give up all forms of money. Others, such as the Shakers, quit their jobs and homes to live in special communities apart from the rest of society. Here they tried to create their own **utopia** (ideal place).

Some reformers wanted to change the type of clothes people wore. A few women began wearing loose-fitting "bloomers," made popular by Amelia Bloomer. Others tried to change what people ate. The most famous health reformer was Sylvester Graham. He told people to give up meat, coffee, and sweets. Instead, he told them they should eat fruits, vegetables, and his new creation—the Graham cracker.

Many reformers tried to correct serious societal problems. Some worked for women's rights. Others wanted people to stop drinking alcohol. In the cities, reformers tried to make conditions better for laborers, especially those in factories.

Important changes were taking place in education. A young lawyer named Horace Mann fought for the right of every child to attend a public school. Catherine Beecher helped many women become teachers in the West. A doctor in Boston, Samuel Gridley Howe, set up the first center for the teaching of blind children. Others established schools for children who were deaf or could not speak.

Opposing Slavery

By far, the largest group of reformers were those who opposed slavery. By the

William Lloyd Garrison was one of the nation's most spirited abolitionists.

This is Dorothea Dix, crusader for the mentally ill.

1830s, some Northerners became convinced that slavery was immoral. These people, abolitionists, wanted to eliminate it everywhere.

The most famous abolitionist was William Lloyd Garrison. In 1831, he began criticizing slavery in his Boston newspaper, *The Liberator*. For the next 30 years, Garrison remained one of the most vocal opponents of slavery.

Two leading abolitionists did not come from the North. Sarah and Angelina Grimké (grim-KEE) were the daughters of a wealthy South Carolina slave owner. The two sisters moved North to campaign for abolition. Large crowds came to hear the Grimké sisters give first-hand accounts of the evils of slavery. The sisters drew attention for another reason. They were the first women to speak in public meetings. At that time, most people thought women should cook and clean for their families and keep out of public matters.

The actions of the abolitionists made many people angry. Some white Southerners felt threatened by the abolitionists, because they thought the abolitionists were trying to destroy their way of life. In response, they began defending slavery more forcefully. At first, many Northerners preferred not to think about slavery because they did not believe it concerned them. They thought the abolitionists were just troublemakers. However, as the economic influence of the South became stronger, particularly in the newly-opened western territories many Northerners began to think of slavery as a national problem.

Women played a major role in the abolitionist movement. They often signed petitions and wrote letters to public officials. But many male abolitionists did not want women to be members of their anti-slavery societies. Women abolitionists were hurt by the treatment they received from some male abolitionists. They noticed important similarities between the position of blacks and the status of women in the United States. While helping to give black slaves their freedom, many white women realized they were not as free as white men. In most states, women could not vote, hold public office, or even own property.

Female abolitionists started a women's rights movement. Among the leaders were Sarah Grimké, Elizabeth Cady Stanton, and Lucretia Mott. In 1848, women held their first national convention in Seneca Falls, New York. There, they drafted the Declaration of Sentiments, a statement of their goals modeled after the American Declaration of Independence. It said: "We hold these truths to be self-evident: that all men and women are created equal; that

they are endowed by their Creator with certain inalienable rights; that among these are life, liberty, and the pursuit of happiness."

Art and Literature

The desire to perfect American society was also expressed by American artists. During this period of rapid change, many Americans felt a need to understand who they were. Artists began capturing scenes which described American life and ideals.

A group of painters known as the Hudson River School began painting romantic scenes of the American countryside. George Catlin made numerous paintings of Native Americans.

Many of the writers, such as Ralph Waldo Emerson, examined the

An early type of photograph shows an unknown black woman around 1850.

positive aspects of American society. Others, like Nathaniel Hawthorne and Edgar Allan Poe, explored the darker sides.

The one idea that united many Americans at this time was a strong faith in change and the hope in progress. They believed that anything was possible. And many thought it was their duty to make things better.

These unadorned oval boxes and chests show the Shaker passion for sturdy and useful objects.

School Enrollment Rates, 1850–1900

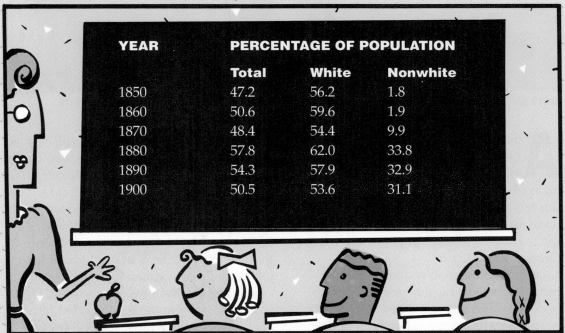

YEAR	PERCENTAGE OF POPULATION		
	Total	White	Nonwhite
1850	47.2	56.2	1.8
1860	50.6	59.6	1.9
1870	48.4	54.4	9.9
1880	57.8	62.0	33.8
1890	54.3	57.9	32.9
1900	50.5	53.6	31.1

How did the enrollment rates of whites and non-whites compare between 1860 and 1870? Between 1880 and 1890? In what ways might the Civil War have affected school enrollment rates for each group?

LOOKING AHEAD,

5 THEY WOULD BE HEARD

Sarah and Angelina Grimké, former South Carolina slaveholders, lectured on the evils of slavery.

An angry mob dragged William Lloyd Garrison through the streets of Boston. They put a rope around his neck. The mob wanted to hang him. But the mayor of Boston was able to stop them just in time. He put Garrison in jail for a while to protect him. The date was October 21, 1835.

Why did the mob want to hang this man? Because he ran a newspaper that opposed slavery. It was called *The Liberator*.

Slavery had never taken hold in the North the way it had in the South. By this time all Northern states had laws against

it, but many white Northerners still discriminated against black Americans. They believed blacks should only have certain jobs—the hardest, lowest-paying ones. Although few Northerners defended slavery, many hoped that slavery in the South would die away by itself. Others thought the government might be able to get rid of it, slowly, step by step.

Garrison was not willing to wait. He wanted slavery in the South ended right away. He fought against slavery day and night. Even when he was in jail, he wrote these lines on the wall of his cell: "Keep me as a prisoner, but bind me not as a slave. Punish me as a criminal, but hold me not as a **chattel** [moveable property, or a slave]. Torture me as a man, but drive me not like a beast."

Many Northerners did not like Garrison. They said he was a trouble-maker. If people in the South wanted slavery, they said, that was the Southerners' business. Ignoring the immorality of slavery, many workers in the North were afraid they would lose their jobs if the slaves were freed. The blacks, they said, would come North and work for less money. Additionally, factory owners and other business leaders in the North made their money from cotton. They did not want to see an end to slavery, either.

Target of Mob Action

Northern mobs often attacked abolitionists. The people who wanted an immediate end to slavery were favorite targets of mobs. Their lives were not safe. But Garrison—and other abolitionists— would not wait. Garrison was not afraid of anyone. Nothing would stop him from talking and writing against slavery. When he started his newspaper, Garrison said:

"I am in earnest . . . I will not excuse [anyone]. I will not retreat a single inch. . . . And I will be heard."

Garrison made many enemies by tak-

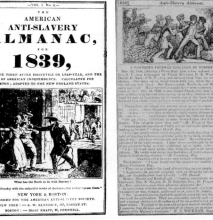

This copy of *The Anti-Slavery Almanac* was published in 1839 in both New York City and Boston. The almanac highlighted articles supporting abolition.

ing this stand. He also won many friends. Two of his most important friends were sisters from South Carolina, Sarah and Angelina Grimké.

William Lloyd Garrison and the Grimké sisters could not have been more different. Garrison grew up poor in a small town near Boston. His father, an alcoholic, abandoned the family when William was three. At nine, William had to leave school to find employment. In his teens, he began working for newspapers, and in 1831, he started an anti-slavery newspaper of his own, *The Liberator.*

Sarah and Angelina Grimké were the daughters of a wealthy slave owner. They were taught at home by private tutors. As children, they were surrounded by servants. But the servants were black slaves, and the Grimké sisters began to see how wrong slavery was.

Angelina wrote angrily in her diary about the cruel punishments slaves had to endure. Sarah secretly taught her maid to read. When her father found out, he threatened to punish both Sarah and the maid. Teaching a slave to read was against the law.

"No Neutrals"

Garrison's newspaper angered many, but it also attracted reformers like the Grimké sisters. Garrison used strong language. He called slavery "sinful." He called the South wicked for supporting it. Many people—even some who opposed slavery—did not like the tone of Garrison's paper.

Angelina Grimké agreed with Garrison. She read *The Liberator* and admired Garrison's strong stand against slavery. When Grimké read about the mobs who attacked him, she wrote a letter to encourage him.

"The ground upon which you stand is holy ground; never, never surrender it," she wrote. "If you surrender it, the hope of the slave is extinguished."

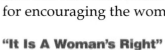

This banner proclaimed the publication of *The Liberator*, William Lloyd Garrison's anti-slavery newspaper.

Garrison thought her letter so powerful that he published it in *The Liberator*. Many of Grimké's friends were upset. Women were not supposed to have their letters printed in newspapers. Nor were they supposed to support people like Garrison with his radical ideas about freeing the slaves. Grimké should apologize for having hurt her family, they said.

But Garrison helped Angelina see that she could be a strong voice in the abolitionist movement. Because she had seen slavery first-hand, people would believe her when she talked about its cruelties.

Angelina kept writing against slavery. She even used quotations from the Bible to argue against slavery. Women might not be able to vote, she said, but they could still help change the laws. Grimké wrote a book which was published by the American Anti-Slavery Society that

Garrison had founded. Soon after the book came out, the society offered her a job talking to small groups of abolitionist women in New York City.

Angelina Grimké was an excellent speaker—tall, clear-voiced, and passionate. So many women wanted to hear her that she began to speak in churches instead of parlors. Sometimes, Sarah would speak as well. Soon men also began coming to hear them speak.

People were shocked. Respectable women did not speak in public before mixed audiences! A group of ministers published a letter saying that the Grimké sisters were breaking God's law. The ministers criticized Garrison for encouraging the women.

"It Is A Woman's Right"

The criticism made Angelina Grimké angry. She wrote more letters to *The Liberator* in reply.

"Human beings have rights, because they are moral beings," she argued. "Whatever it is morally right for a man to do, it is morally right for a woman to do. . . . I believe it is woman's right to have a voice in all the laws and regulations by which she is to be governed." A woman could even be president of the United States, she said. Angelina kept right on speaking about abolition. Both Grimké sisters also wrote pamphlets about women's rights.

In 1838, Angelina Grimké married Theodore Weld, another abolitionist.

She celebrated by speaking at an anti-slavery meeting in Philadelphia. While she was on the platform, a mob outside began throwing bricks and stones through the windows. The audience was frightened, but Grimké calmed them.

"What if that mob should now burst in upon us, break up our meeting and commit violence upon our persons — would this be anything compared with what the slaves endure?" she asked. The meeting continued, but the next day the mob burned down the building where she had spoken.

Sarah and Angelina Grimké and William Lloyd Garrison fought against slavery with words. They wrote articles and gave speeches trying to persuade people that slavery was evil. They succeeded in bringing many people to their side. When Garrison founded the American Anti-Slavery Society in 1833, people had laughed at him. But by 1840, the society had 200,000 members.

Garrison and the Grimkés opposed violence as a way to end slavery. They hoped words and the power of persuasion would be enough, but slavery endured. Finally, it took the Civil War and the Thirteenth Amendment to the Constitution in 1865 to end slavery in the United States.

CHAPTER CHECK

WORD MATCH
1. chattel
2. Angelina Grimké
3. William Lloyd Garrison
4. *The Liberator*
5. moral

a. anti-slavery newspaper
b. abolitionist who had anti-slavery letter printed in *The Liberator*
c. moveable property, later a term for slaves
d. having a system of values about what is just or right
e. abolitionist who published the newspaper *The Liberator*

QUICK QUIZ
1. Why did many Northerners attack William Lloyd Garrison?
2. The Grimké sisters became abolitionists. Name two differences between them and Garrison.
3. A group of ministers condemned the Grimké sisters for speaking against slavery in public. What did they say to defend themselves?

THINK ABOUT IT
1. Do you think the abolitionists would have brought an end to slavery even without the Civil War? Why or why not?
2. If you were alive at the time of William Lloyd Garrison and the Grimké sisters, would you be an abolitionist? Why or why not?

6 SCHOOLS FOR ALL

In this one-room school, there were students of many ages. Here, students on the left study, while those on the right recite their lessons from memory to the young teacher.

Picture a typical public school of the 1820s. It has just one room and the students are crowded together. They sit on "chairs" that are small, square pieces of wood attached to upright posts. The seats have no arms or backs or writing tops, and some are so high the children's feet do not touch the floor.

A stove in the center of the room provides the only heat in the winter. Near the stove, the temperature may be 90 degrees. But near the windows, which often have broken glass panes, the temperature may be below 30 degrees. Here the ink freezes in the pens used by the students. On rainy days, there are other problems. The roof leaks, water pours into the schoolroom, and the dirt floor turns into mud.

The teacher in this room is a man, for in those times it was believed that a woman's "place" was in the home. The teacher sits at a desk with several rods of hard wood on it. These rods are used to punish bad students, for the teacher believes in the motto, "Spare the rod, spoil the child." Often the teacher's own education is very poor. He may simply be a graduate of the grade school he is now teaching. Teachers' salaries are so low that communities cannot be too fussy about who they hire. No wonder that well-to-do parents send their children to private schools where conditions are much better.

Yet the students in this public school are lucky. At least they are getting some education. Hundreds of thousands of young people in the nation have no opportunity to go to school at all. Some have to work hard on the family farm. Others work 10 hours a day or more in city factories.

Horace Mann

In the 1830s, many **reformers** tried to improve public school education. Horace Mann was one of them. He was born in Franklin, Massachusetts, on May 4, 1796. As a child, he worked from morning to night on his father's farm. There was little time to play, and he never went to school for more than 10 weeks each year. But he loved books, and he read almost every one of the 116 volumes in the town library. These books were the gift of Benjamin Franklin, for whom the town was named.

Early in his life, Mann decided that he wanted to do "something for the benefit [betterment] of mankind." To accomplish this, he would need a college education. For six months he crammed for college entrance examinations and eventually was admitted to Brown University in Providence, Rhode Island. Despite poor health, he became one of the best students in his class.

After college, Mann became a successful lawyer and later served in the Massachusetts State Legislature. There, he **championed** (strongly supported) laws to help the sick and the poor. In 1837, the legislature created a state **Board of Education** to improve the public school system in Massachusetts. Mann became its secretary. The job paid much less than he earned as a lawyer and a senator, but he did not hesitate to take it. This was his great opportunity to "benefit mankind."

Improving Schools

Why was public education so important to Mann? He believed that in a democracy like the United States, everyone had to have schooling. He knew people could not rule themselves if they were ignorant. Without free public schools for all, the United States would become like European countries where only the rich and well-born received an education and rose to power.

Nineteenth-century textbooks attempted to instill the proper values in students, while teaching them to read.

Mann visited public schools throughout Massachusetts to see for himself where improvements were needed. He could not force the towns and villages to make improvements. He had to persuade them. Everywhere Mann went he told the parents why they needed good schools. He accused parents of spending more money on their cattle than on their children's educations. His speeches, magazine articles, and reports to the legislature began to get results. People voted to build better schools and to provide them with free textbooks and libraries. Next, Mann persuaded them to build public high schools so that children could continue their education.

But learning depends on more than buildings and books. Students must have good teachers. Under Mann's leadership, Massachusetts created the first state colleges to train teachers.

Mann often met strong opposition. Many people objected to paying higher taxes for public schools. Why should middle-class or wealthy people have to pay for the education of the poor? But Mann's crusade for public education would not be stopped. In fact, many other states began to copy his work in Massachusetts. He would become known throughout the country as the father of free public schools for all children.

Catharine Beecher

While Mann tried to improve schools in Massachusetts, another reformer, Catharine Beecher, reached out to children in the West. She was the daughter of a minister and the sister of Harriet Beecher Stowe, who would write the famous anti-slavery novel, *Uncle Tom's Cabin.* Catharine was born September 6, 1800, in East Hampton, New York. She became concerned not only with the lack of good schools and teachers, but also with the condition of women.

Beecher recognized that both poor and upper-class women were denied rights. She visited factories where women from poor families worked long hours for wages "that will not keep soul and body together." Educated women from upper-class families were denied useful work outside the home. Their suffering, Beecher said, was as great as that of working-class women. The difference was that their spirits were starved rather than their bodies.

Beecher's brilliant idea was to improve both the education of children and the condition of women. Out West only one child in six received any schooling, partly because there were so few teachers. In speeches and articles, Beecher urged working-class women to leave their factory jobs and become teachers in the West. Educated upper- and middle-class women could become teachers, or they could raise money for education and supervise schools in their communities. Women, she said, could elevate teaching to a "true and noble" profession.

Beecher traveled from city to city in the 1840s and organized women's committees to support her cause. Once she had run private schools for girls. Now she used her experience to train young women who wished to become teachers. She taught them how to deal with the lack of good schoolrooms and books. She also trained them to teach children moral habits and health care.

Beecher received many letters from these teachers about their problems in the West. One woman wrote that she had to teach 45 children aged 6 to 16 in a one-room log cabin. The parents were very suspicious, and watched her closely.

"I was told when I came," she wrote, "that they would not pay a teacher for more than three months in a year. But since then I have gained their good will and confidence. They have provided me with a good schoolhouse, with writing desks and a blackboard. They promise to support me all the year round."

From the 1840s on, more and more women were hired as teachers in the United States. Women would work for less money than men because they had fewer job choices. Beecher even used this argument for hiring women. If it would help them gain useful employment outside the home, she was willing to accept this unfair pay scale.

By 1860, the great majority of teachers in the United States were women. Beecher's goal, "to elevate those of my sex as educators of the young," had been accomplished.

Catharine Beecher promoted the status of women as teachers and homemakers.

CHAPTER CHECK

WORD MATCH

1. Horace Mann
2. reformers
3. championed
4. Catharine Beecher
5. Board of Education

a. trained young women to become teachers
b. strongly supported
c. lawyer who assisted in creating Board of Education
d. group created to improve the public school system
e. try to improve quality of life

QUICK QUIZ

1. How did Horace Mann learn so much when he only went to school a few weeks each year?
2. Why did Mann think public education was so important?
3. Catharine Beecher believed schools needed good teachers. She also saw rights and opportunities denied to both working-class and upper-class women. How did she connect these issues?

THINK ABOUT IT

1. Why were teachers' salaries so low? Was this fair? What did Beecher think of this situation?
2. What do you think might have happened to the United States if people like Mann and Beecher did not fight for better schools and trained teachers?
3. What does "Spare the rod, spoil the child" mean? Do you believe in it? Why or why not?

7 WOMAN'S RIGHTS CONVENTION

Here is Elizabeth Cady Stanton, who crusaded to free blacks from slavery and women from domination by men, with one of her six children.

A s a child, Elizabeth Cady loved to play in the attic of her family's large home in New York State. She and her sisters would nibble on cubes of maple sugar, crack open hickory nuts, and parade about in their great-grandmother's dusty ball gowns. Elizabeth enjoyed many games. She loved horses and became an accomplished rider. In winter, she built snow forts, and played hide-and-seek behind the apple barrels and washtubs in the family cellar.

But Elizabeth was also a serious and scholarly young woman who spent hours in her father's law office. She learned at a young age that women, married women, had few legal rights.

"You are entirely in your husband's power," Judge Daniel Cady would tell a female client as a distraught Elizabeth listened. "Your earnings are his. I can do nothing for you." Seated quietly in the corner, Elizabeth studied her father's legal texts. For a while she believed that if she cut out the page on which an unfair law was written, she could do away with the law altogether. Her father explained to her that such a simple solution was not possible.

"When you are grown up, and able to prepare a speech," he told his daughter, "you must go down to Albany and talk to the legislators; tell them all you have seen in this office—the sufferings of women, robbed of their inheritance, and left dependent on their unworthy sons."

Elizabeth knew firsthand the difficulties of being a woman. After she graduated from the local academy with a prize in Greek, she was left behind as her male classmates went off to college. In the early 19th century, few American colleges admitted women. Women were expected to be submissive wives and doting mothers. Like children, they were to be "seen and not heard."

Why was it that a woman who established a successful shop, for example, had no right to keep the money she earned? Why was she often denied **custody** (control or care) of her own children upon separation from her husband? Why was she not allowed to vote? Until her death in 1902, Elizabeth Cady Stanton publicly addressed these questions. Many people scorned and ridiculed her. Fortunately, she was not alone in her work.

The Anti-Slavery Convention

Elizabeth met the well-known abolitionist, Henry Stanton, about 1840. Although her father objected, the couple married in 1840 and spent their honeymoon at the World Anti-Slavery Convention in London.

The American Anti-Slavery Society had recently divided over the issue of women's rights. Still, Cady Stanton and the other American women expected to be welcomed as delegates to the London convention. They were outraged when full participation was denied them. Ministers quoted the Bible to prove female submission was "the will of God."

Most American male delegates, including George Bradburn, rushed to defend the women. "Prove to me, gentlemen," Bradburn said, "that your Bible sanctions [allows or approves of] the slavery of women—the complete subjugation of one-half the race to the other—and I should feel that the best work I could do for humanity would be to make a grand bonfire of every Bible in the Universe." Despite his efforts, women were not allowed to speak at the convention. They sat silently in a curtained gallery.

In London, Cady Stanton met another exceptional woman. Lucretia Coffin had grown up in Nantucket, Massachusetts. There, Lucretia's mother ran a small shop at home while her father was captain of a whaling ship. Nantucket was a whaling and fishing town. Men were often away at sea, and their wives enjoyed an equality with them that was unknown in other parts of the country.

The Coffins were Quakers, one of the few religious groups that gave equal roles to women. The Coffins believed that girls should be educated as well as boys. Lucretia was sent to a Quaker boarding school when she was 13. There, she later became a teacher and married one of her colleagues, James Mott. At 28, Lucretia Mott became a Quaker minister and a public lecturer against slavery. Public speaking was very unusual for women at this time.

Mott was a remarkably gifted, analytical, and independent thinker. Cady Stanton was immediately drawn to her and absorbed all she could of Mott's ideas. While walking the streets of London, the two women vowed to hold a woman's rights convention once they returned to America.

The Conference at Seneca Falls

The convention would not be held for another eight years. After the London convention, Cady Stanton returned with her husband to Seneca Falls. Although Cady Stanton was busy with her domestic duties, she did not forget her discussions with Mott. Cady Stanton was also dissatisfied with the slow progress of women's legal rights. The New York Married Woman's Property Act, passed in April 1848, gave women control of homes and property they purchased, but it denied them their wages, which still went to their husbands. Working women, especially, were still at an extreme disadvantage.

In July 1848, Cady Stanton was invited to a friend's home in nearby Waterloo. There she and Lucretia Mott were reunited. As Cady Stanton spoke of all her grievances, the two women were stirred to action. Together with Mary Ann McClintock, Jane Hunt, and Martha C.

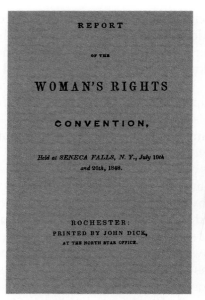

REPORT

OF THE

WOMAN'S RIGHTS

CONVENTION,

Held at SENECA FALLS, N. Y., July 19th and 20th, 1848.

ROCHESTER:
PRINTED BY JOHN DICK,
AT THE NORTH STAR OFFICE.

Stanton's Declaration of Sentiments mirrored the language and tone of the Declaration of Independence.

Wright, they hastily organized what was to be the First Woman's Rights Convention.

The women needed a platform for their grievances. Cady Stanton had a brilliant idea. She drew up a **Declaration of Sentiments** that used the language and form of the American **Declaration of Independence.** But she made a few important changes. For the name of King George she substituted the word "male." One passage reads: "The history of mankind is a history of repeated injuries and usurpations on the part of man toward woman, having in direct object the establishment of tyranny over her."

The women then drew up a list of 18 demands. Among these were the rights of women to share in the custody of their children, and the right to gain an education. But Cady Stanton recognized that without **suffrage** (the right to vote), women stood little chance of winning their demands.

Even Mott was stunned. "Thou will make us ridiculous," she cautioned. "We must go slowly." Cady Stanton prevailed, however, and when the two-day conference opened on July 19, the resolution to secure "the sacred right to the elective franchise" was hotly debated. Attending were three hundred people, including 40 men. Among them was Frederick Douglass.

Every resolution except suffrage was unanimously accepted. Many delegates feared that the demand for women to vote would destroy their credibility. The convention approved suffrage by a narrow margin.

Future Achievements

The press, dominated by men, ridiculed the women of Seneca Falls. Cady Stanton and Mott continued to fight on behalf of all American women. They were joined by many others, including Susan B. Anthony and Lucy Stone, who worked tirelessly to influence legislative decisions. Some gains, such as the right of women to sue in court, and keep their own wages, became law quickly. However, it would be 72 years before women would gain the right to vote.

Charlotte Woodward, at age 17, trembled with excitement as her carriage rode

Amelia Bloomer's innovative new garment offered women new freedom of movement in keeping with their freer outlook.

into the Wesleyan Church of Seneca Falls in July 1848. Of all the women attending the first Woman's Rights Convention, she was the only one who lived to cast the vote. In 1920, she was in her 90th year. "I am going to the polls," she said, "if they have to carry me."

CHAPTER CHECK

WORD MATCH
1. custody
2. sanctions
3. Declaration of Independence
4. suffrage
5. Declaration of Sentiments

a. allows or approves of
b. attacked men's treatment of women
c. control of or care of
d. attacked Britian's treatment of American colonists
e. the right to vote

QUICK QUIZ
1. Name some of the laws unfair to women during Elizabeth Cady Stanton's day.
2. What was unusual about Cady Stanton's platform of grievances?
3. Which grievance in the Declaration of Sentiments created the greatest controversy at the Seneca conference? Why?

THINK ABOUT IT
1. Do you think Cady Stanton hurt the women's movement by demanding the right to vote when she did? Why or why not?
2. Compare the fight for women's rights in the 19th century with the Women's Movement today. Do you see any similarities or differences?

CHAPTER 8 THE TRANSCENDENTALISTS

Thomas Cole captured the reverence of nature common to the Hudson River School in this painting, *Schroon Mountain in the Adirondacks.*

In Salem, Massachusetts, Judge John Hathorne condemned 20 people to death by torture and hanging for practicing witchcraft. Meanwhile, in nearby Concord, the Reverend Joseph Emerson preached love and tolerance.

Though these men lived in the 17th century, they influenced the lives of two great American writers of the 19th century—Nathaniel Hawthorne and Ralph Waldo Emerson. Hawthorne, who added the "w" to his last name as an adult, was fascinated by his cruel ancestor. Many of his stories take place during the years of the Salem witch hunts. Emerson, too, was swayed by his ancestor. He followed Joseph's footsteps and became a Unitarian minister.

Hawthorne and Emerson were part of a group of New England writers, led by Margaret Fuller. Known as **transcendentalists,** they believed that each person has a divine, or god-like, spirit. This spirit is the source of all truth and the guide for all our actions. Wisdom, they believed, comes from listening to our own thoughts and intuitions. They considered self-reliance the most important rule to live by.

Evil and Poetry

Like their forefathers, Hawthorne and Emerson were as different as night and day. American author Henry James described Emerson as a "sun-worshipper" who basked in the light of humanity's goodness. But he compared Hawthorne to a cat who can see in the dark because Hawthorne spent his life exploring the shadowy corners of the soul.

Despite their differences, they had many things in common. They were born within a few miles of each other, just one year apart. Emerson was born in Boston in 1803, Hawthorne in Salem in 1804. Both were young when their fathers died, and they each became shy, sensitive boys. Both endured periods of poverty. Both failed to earn enough from the sale of their books to support their families.

For many years, Emerson and Hawthorne were neighbors in the rural village of Concord, Massachusetts. They took walks together through the woods and along the banks of Walden Pond, but true friendship never blossomed. Their outlook differed too greatly. Emerson was optimistic and interested in new ideas. Hawthorne was pessimistic and stubborn. Even the forms their writing took were different. Hawthorne expressed himself through short stories and novels. Emerson wrote poems and essays.

Hawthorne was the first American author to explore in detail what happens to people who commit evil. Many of his characters suffer because of evil done by their ancestors. Hawthorne said he himself suffered from guilt over the cruel deeds of Judge Hathorne. The people in Hawthorne's stories exist in a strange, ominous world. They encounter haunted houses, secret passageways, blood-stained steps, and supernatural beings.

His most famous novel, *The Scarlet Letter,* takes place in the 1640s, the early years of Puritan settlement in New England. The story is about a woman named Hester Prynne (prin) who is accused of adultery. The man who punishes her bears a resemblance to Judge Hathorne.

Like his characters, Hawthorne led a troubled life. Yet there were good times. He found comfort in the home he shared with his wife Sophia, and their children Una, Rose, and Julian. Above all, his imagination provided relief. While he was writing, he could escape from his cares. Seeing his stories in print filled him

Despite Ralph Waldo Emerson's (1803–1882) hardships, his prose and poems often reflected optimism and individualism.

with a sense of pride and accomplishment. And he enjoyed the fame and praise that his four novels and more than one hundred short stories brought him.

But in his last years, his health declined. He grew too weak to write. Unable to do the one thing that made him feel worthy, his will to live faded. His death came two months before his 60th birthday.

The Nonconformist

Emerson, who outlived Hawthorne by 18 years, also lived in the shadow of his ancestors. By the time he was born, members of the Emerson family had been ministers in Concord for 167 years. As a boy, Waldo (as he preferred to be called) was expected to follow his ancestors into the clergy. Eventually, he graduated from the Harvard Divinity School and gained his license to preach. But one Sunday after five years in the pulpit, he shocked his congregation. He told them that his search for truth had led him to reject certain basic beliefs of the church. To be true to himself he must resign as their minister.

"Whoso would be a man, must be a nonconformist," Emerson wrote in an essay called "Self-Reliance." Dramatically, he had declared himself a **nonconformist** when he broke the long chain of Emersons in the ministry. And he declared it repeatedly in essays and poems that were often attacked in the

With works such as *The Scarlett Letter*, Nathaniel Hawthorne (1804–1864) psychologically probed human nature.

press by those who disagreed with his beliefs. Even Hawthorne scoffed at some of Emerson's ideas.

More than any other writer of his time, Emerson reflected the **idealism** (striving to higher goals and a better world) and independence of the New World. In one of his essays he wrote: "To believe your own thought, to believe that what is true for you in your private heart, is true for all men, that is genius."

Nine of the twelve books published in his lifetime were collections of essays. They cover many subjects, but they are mostly about love, friendship, and self-reliance.

Even in writing poems, Emerson was a nonconformist. Other poets set their words to strict patterns of rhyme and rhythm. But he wrote in a plain, conversational way. His style changed the course of American poetry. Two of the greatest poets of the 19th century—Emily Dickinson and Walt Whitman—imitated his poetry. And they, in turn, influenced many poets of the 20th century.

Like Hawthorne, Emerson had his share of sorrow. Tuberculosis robbed him of two brothers. It also claimed his first wife, Ellen, who died after they had been happily married for just 17 months. And his favorite child, Waldo, died young of scarlet fever.

Despite his sorrows, Ralph Waldo Emerson wrote this poem, called "What is Success," to help others:

To laugh often and much;

*To win the respect of intelligent people
and the affection of children;*

*To earn the appreciation of honest critics
and endure the betrayal of false friends;*

To appreciate beauty;

To find the best in others;

*To leave the world a bit better, whether by
a healthy child, a garden
patch or a redeemed social condition;*

*To know even one life has breathed
easier because you have lived;*

This is to have succeeded.

In addition to his poetry, Ralph Waldo Emerson gained a national reputation as a scholar and lecturer. Through his poems and his prose, he joined Nathaniel Hawthorne as one of America's classic authors.

CHAPTER CHECK

WORD MATCH
1. Salem, Massachusetts
2. Concord, Massachusetts
3. nonconformist
4. transcendentalists
5. idealism

a. follows personal beliefs instead of what may be popular
b. where the witch hunts took place in the 17th century
c. believe that each person has a divine spirit
d. home of Hawthorne, Emerson, and Walden Pond
e. striving to higher goals and a better world

QUICK QUIZ
1. Hawthorne and Emerson are both important American writers. List some differences between them, both in the forms of their writings, and their feelings about people.
2. The background of writers influences how they see the world. How was this true of Emerson and Hawthorne?

THINK ABOUT IT
1. Describe Emerson's definition of genius. Do you agree with it? Why or why not?
2. In your own words, describe Emerson's thoughts about nonconformists. Can you think of any ways this idea is connected to your own life?
3. Read Emerson's poem above. How do you describe success?

REFORM AND CULTURE

History Detective

1. Believers like Nathaniel Hawthorne and Ralph Waldo Emerson followed my tenet that self-reliance is the main requirement for personal happiness. What am I?

2. Because I argued that without free public schools, only rich and well-born Americans would receive an education and rise to power, I am known as the father of free public schools for all. Who am I?

3. Catharine Beecher believed that women could raise me to be a "true and noble" position. What am I?

4. With my newspaper, *The Liberator*, I published my opinions against slavery and became one of the most famous abolitionists in U.S. history. Who am I?

5. I received more argument than any other resolution at the First Woman's Rights Convention in 1848. What am I?

Voices From the Past

The nature of American women's work changed dramatically during the 1800s. Below, read what Edith Abbott writes in *Women in Industry* about women in factories at that time. Then answer the questions that follow.

> . . . it was questionable whether [enough] labor could be found to run the new mills when they were constructed. . . . This new work was identical with the work which women had long been doing in their own homes, and it was inevitable that the difficulties caused by the [lack] and high cost of male labor should [lead to] the employment of wo-men . . . The new system, it was thought, not only gave women a chance of earning their livelihood, but educated them in habits of honest industry. The rise of manufacturers was said to have "elev-ated the females . . . from a state of [poverty] and idleness to competence and industry." It was point-ed out that young women who, before the introduc-tion of the factory system, were "with their parents . . . bare-footed and living in wretched [homes]," had "since that period been comfortably fed and clothed, their habits and manners and dwelling greatly improved"; and they had in general become "useful members of society."

1. How did new industries affect women's lives in the 1800s?

2. Reformers in the mid-1800s thought it was unfair for women to be allowed to work but not to vote. Would you have agreed with them. Why or why not?

Hands–On History

Being Persuasive—If you were alive during the golden age of reform in America, which social concern of the time would be most im-portant to you? Write a speech about it in a way that would sway others to your view.

YESTERDAY'S NEWS

The American Adventures Newspaper

Boston, Mass., June 20, 1847—Americans have been hearing about the new ideas coming from a small group of writers and philosophers in Massachusetts. Their philosophy is called transcendentalism. Two of their experiments with transcendental ideas will end later this year. One experiment, near a Massachusetts pond, is testing transcendental beliefs in solitude; the other, in contrast, on a farm in the same state, is testing these beliefs in a community.

Thoreau Returns from Walden Pond

Walden, Mass., September 6, 1847—After spending two years by himself in the wilds of Massachusetts, transcendentalist Henry David Thoreau returned to civilization today. His experiment now over, *Yesterday's News* was able to interview him.

YN: You were alone for two years. Did you have trouble killing time?

HDT: As if you could kill time without injuring eternity.

YN: What luxuries of society did you miss the most?

HDT: Most of the luxuries, and many of the so-called comforts of life, are not only not [necessary], but positive hindrances to the elevation of mankind.

YN: You mean, without the luxuries we all enjoy, you still felt "alive"?

HDT: To be awake is to be alive.

YN: Really now, why did you leave civilization for two years?

HDT: I went to the woods because I wished to live deliberately, to [see] only the essential facts of life, and see if I could not learn what it had to teach, and not, when I came to die, discover that I had not lived.

YN: Many Americans think you are crazy for living alone for two years. How do you respond?

HDT: If a man does not keep pace with his companions, perhaps it is because he hears a different drummer. Let him step to the music that he hears. . . .

A portrait of Margaret Fuller, whom Emerson, in 1836, called "an accomplished lady."

West Roxbury, Mass., October 5, 1847—The first experiment with community transcendentalism ended this year. In 1841, transcendentalists set up Brook Farm in West Roxbury, Massachusetts, where men and women gathered to live under the transcendental doctrine. The members worked cooperatively, growing everything they needed. Among the leaders of the community was Margaret Fuller, one of quite a few women involved in transcendentalism. She edited the popular transcendentalist magazine, the *Dial*.

You Be the Reporter

Match each question with its news item above.

1. What overall title would you give these three articles?

2. What would be a good title for this story?

INTERPRETING A PRIMARY SOURCE

What did women want in 1848? As you learned in Chapter 7, that was the year of the Seneca Falls convention, where Elizabeth Cady Stanton drew up her famous Declaration of Sentiments. The account in your textbook is a **secondary source** or second-hand account, because it is told by someone who was not there. You can also study **primary sources,** such as letters and documents—the actual Declaration of Sentiments, for example—written by someone who was there.

Read the following excerpts from the Declaration of Sentiments. On a separate sheet of paper, answer the questions that follow.

Seneca Falls, New York,
July 19-20, 1848

When, in the course of human events, it becomes necessary for one portion of the family of man to assume among the people of the earth a position different from that which they have hitherto occupied . . . a decent respect to the opinions of mankind requires that they should declare the causes that impel them to such a course.

We hold these truths to be self-evident: that all men and women are created equal; that they are endowed by their Creator with certain inalienable rights; that among these are life, liberty, and the pursuit of happiness . . . . Whenever any form of government becomes destructive of these ends, it is the right of those who suffer from it to refuse allegiance to it, and to insist upon the institution of a new government. . . .

The history of mankind is a history of repeated injuries and usurpations on the part of man toward woman, having in direct object the establishment of an absolute tyranny over her. To prove this, let facts be submitted to a candid world.

He has never permitted her to exercise her inalienable right to the elective franchise. . . .

He has taken from her all right in property, even to the wages she earns. . . .

He has monopolized nearly all the profitable employments, and from those she is permitted to follow, she receives but a scanty remuneration. . . .

He has denied her the facilities for obtaining a thorough education, all colleges being closed against her. . . .

Now . . . in view of the unjust laws above mentioned . . . we insist that they [women] have immediate admission to all the rights and privileges which belong to them as citizens of the United States.

. . . we shall use every instrumentality within our power to effect our object. We shall employ agents, circulate tracts, petition the State and National legislatures, and endeavor to enlist the pulpit and press in our behalf. . . .

1. Each of the words below is included in the Declaration of Sentiments. Match each word on the left with the correct definition. Use a dictionary if you need to.

   (a) tyranny — to take exclusive ownership of
   (b) allegiance — incapable of being given up
   (c) monopolize — complete power
   (d) remuneration — loyalty
   (e) inalienable — things seized wrongfully
   (f) usurpations — wages paid for a job or service

2. Why was the Declaration of Sentiments necessary? Choose the reason best expressed by the first two paragraphs. (a) Women should be able to express their ideas freely. (b) Women should explain why their position in society must change. (c) Women were not included in the Declaration of Independence

3. According to the Declaration of Sentiments, which of the following rights should all women have that were denied them?
   (a) to vote
   (b) to attend college
   (c) to own property
   (d) to form their own government and laws
   (e) to follow any profession they choose
   (f) to refuse to pay taxes

4. Read the last two paragraphs of the Declaration. (a) What was the author demanding for women? (b) How did she propose that women achieve their goals?

Compare the language of Elizabeth Cady Stanton's Declaration with that of the Declaration of Independence on page 196 of your textbook. Answer the following on a separate sheet of paper.

5. Compare the first paragraph of both documents. (a) What specific phrases or ideas are similar in the two paragraphs? (b) Describe one way that the paragraphs differ.

6. Compare the first sentence of the second paragraph of both documents. What phrase has been added in the Declaration of Sentiments?

7. Both the Declaration of Independence and the Declaration of Sentiments describe forms of tyranny. (a) Who is the tyrant mentioned in the Declaration of Independence? (b) Who is the tyrant referred to in the Declaration of Sentiments?

What is your opinion of the Declaration of Sentiments and its message? Answer the following.

8. If you had read the Declaration in 1848, would you have agreed with its goals and grievances? Explain why or why not.

9. Why do you think the author based this document on the Declaration of Independence? Do you think it was a good idea? Explain.

10. If the Seneca Falls convention were convened today, would women have the same grievances they had in 1848?

Lavinia Porter clearly remembered the hardships her family suffered on their overland journey to California. Many years later, she said it was still "a constant source of wonder" how they were able to endure it. Her family suffered both physically and mentally. Leaving friends and family members behind was especially painful. Porter said, "I never recall that sad parting from my dear sister on the plains of Kansas without the tears flowing fast and free."

Lavinia Porter was only one of thousands of Americans who migrated to the Pacific Coast in

During the early 1800s, thousands of Americans packed what they could, sold the rest, and risked everything for new lives in the strange and dangerous Wild West.

FROM SEA TO
SHINING

1820	1825	1830	1835	1840	1845

1821
Mexico gains independence from Spain.

1834
Santa Anna becomes leader of Mexico.

1836
Battle of the Alamo fought.

1844
James Polk elected President.

1845
United States aquires Texas.

SEA

1850

1846

Mexican
War
begins.

1848

Gold discovered
at Sutter's Mill,
California.

UNIT

3

A wagon train of Mormon pioneers heads west from the Missouri River in the spring of 1847. Poor conditions and disease had already killed hundreds of them.

the mid-19th century. Between 1841 and 1866 some 350,000 people made this trip. Most took a 2000-mile path known as the Overland Trail.

This dirt trail went from Missouri all the way to the Pacific Ocean. The first 700 miles led through land as flat as a football field and as broad as an ocean. Then the trail climbed slowly upward through the Rocky Mountains. There it divided into two trails. One led down into Oregon. The other went off towards California.

The pioneers usually traveled in families and rode in covered wagons. Oxen pulled the wagons through mud, across rivers, and over mountains at a rate of two miles an hour. The travelers suffered from disease, hunger, and cold. Many

died along the way.

Some pioneers had encounters with Native Americans that occasionally led to conflict. At first, the Indians were helpful to the inexperienced travelers. Sometimes they gave them directions, food, and other necessary supplies. However, tensions soon developed between the two groups. The Native Americans began to resent all the new people moving onto their land. Many travelers treated the Indians poorly. Sometimes they even killed the Indians.

Eventually, some fighting broke out between Native Americans and European American settlers. Between 1840 and 1860 an estimated 400 pioneers were killed by Indians, equal to the number of Indians who were killed by settlers. These dangers did not stop other families from heading west. Every year more wagons rumbled through—mile after weary mile.

Reasons for Moving

Why did the settlers head to the West? Some went for health reasons. Others moved because of religious concerns. But most people trekked west because they thought it would improve their lives. They could own their own land. There would be new jobs. According to one Ohio woman, "going to the Far West seemed like the entrance to a new world, one of freedom, happiness, and prosperity."

But did the area of the West really belong to Americans? In 1835, the western border of the United States was the Rocky Mountains. Beyond these mountains, the British claimed Oregon. Texas and California were part of Mexico. And the people who lived on all these lands were Indians.

Many Americans believed the area west and south of the Rockies should belong to the United States. They thought the United States had a "natural right" to it. Some European Americans thought that the people living there—the Native Americans and Mexicans—were not as "civilized" as they were. By spreading American culture and democracy, they believed they would improve the quality of life for these "less fortunate" people.

In 1845, an article by John L. O'Sullivan in the *Democratic Review* put their thoughts into words. It said God had set aside America from the Atlantic to the Pacific for the United States. It did not matter what the people living there thought. European Americans were destined to settle the country. In fact, the article said the United States had a right, which became known as **Manifest Destiny**, to expand to the Pacific Coast.

O'Sullivan wrote: "the fulfillment of our manifest destiny [is] to overspread the continent allotted by Providence for the free development of our yearly multiplying millions."

Within three years after this article appeared, the United States had done just that. Between 1845 and 1848, the United States gained almost a million square miles of Western land. The United States **annexed** (added on to its territory) Texas in 1845. It gained Oregon a year later and California in 1848. How did this come about?

Pioneers, looking for a better way of life, put their faith in guidebooks like this one which promised safe routes west.

Gaining Territory

Before the 1830s, mostly Native Americans lived in Oregon. Only a handful of British and American fur traders

Population Growth by Region, 1820–1850

	1820	1830	1840	1850
Northeast	4,360,000	5,542,000	6,761,000	8,627,000
North Central	859,000	1,610,000	3,352,000	5,404,000
South	4,419,000	5,708,000	6,951,000	8,983,000
West	—	—		179,000
TOTAL	9,638,000	12,860,000	17,064,000	23,193,000

PRESENT DAY REGIONS ARE AS FOLLOWS:

- **NORTHEAST:** New York, New Jersey, Pennsylvania, Maine, New Hampshire, Vermont, Massachusetts, Connecticut, Rhode Island
- **NORTH CENTRAL:** Ohio, Indiana, Illinois, Michigan, Wisconsin, Minnesota, Iowa, Missouri, North Dakota, South Dakota, Nebraska, Kansas
- **SOUTH:** Delaware, Maryland, District of Columbia, Virginia, West Virginia, North Carolina, South Carolina, Georgia, Florida, Kentucky, Tennessee, Alabama, Mississippi, Arkansas, Louisiana, Oklahoma, Texas
- **WEST:** Montana, Idaho, Wyoming, Colorado, New Mexico, Arizona, Utah, Nevada, Washington, Oregon, California, Alaska, Hawaii

Which region's population grew the most between 1820 and 1830? Between 1830 and 1850?

were there. Then, beginning in 1836, European Americans started arriving over the Oregon Trail.

Both Britain and the United States had strong claims to Oregon. In the 1840s, some U.S. leaders demanded that the British give up their claim. The British refused. It looked as if Britain and the United States might fight another war. But in 1846, the two nations signed a treaty that divided the Oregon lands between them.

The problems with Mexico were not as easy to solve. Mexican cowboys had been living in the American Southwest and present-day Texas for hundreds of years.

In the 1820s, U.S. farmers began moving into these Mexican territories. Soon there were more U.S. citizens than Mexicans living in Texas. The Mexican government passed laws preventing U.S. citizens from settling there. Despite the laws, U.S. citizens continued to move in. In 1836, some settlers revolted and set up their own government. They refused to recognize Mexico's sovereignty in Texas.

In the United States, many Southerners wanted to make Texas part of the United States. For almost 10 years, Texas had been an independent republic. But people in the Northeast were opposed to admitting another slave state to the Union. They wanted Texas to remain independent. In 1845, after several years of bitter argument, Texas was annexed by an act of Congress.

Many Americans, including President

James K. Polk, wanted more land from Mexico than just Texas. They wanted New Mexico, Arizona, and California as well. President Polk sent U.S. troops to the southern border of Texas, territory Mexico claimed. He wanted to start a war with Mexico.

In 1846, war broke out. Some U.S. army troops invaded Mexico from Texas. Other U.S. troops landed at Veracruz on the Gulf of Mexico. They fought their way inland to Mexico City, the Mexican capital. After two years of fighting, the Mexican government surrendered in 1848. In the peace treaty, all of California and much of the present Southwest were sold to the United States for $15 million.

By war and by treaty, the United States gained Oregon and California on the Pacific Coast. The United States also claimed Texas, Utah, Nevada, and much of New Mexico and Arizona. In 1848, the nation stretched "from sea to shining sea."

Rising Conflict

Expansion was supposed to bring unity to Americans, but it raised many problems concerning the issue of slavery. From the 1820s onward, the new land increasingly divided the nation and led to regional conflict.

In 1848, the discovery of gold in California set off a mad dash of settlers who hoped to strike it rich. Within a year, the population of California soared from 14,000 to almost 100,000. When California tried to become a state, a great question arose. Should slavery be allowed there? Southerners said yes. Northerners said no. The problem threatened to tear the nation apart.

Then an influential senator, Henry Clay, came up with ideas to settle the quarrel. After long and fierce debates, his ideas were passed into law as the Compromise of 1850. One law made California a free state where slavery was outlawed. Another law, the Fugitive Slave Act, required Northerners to help Southerners capture their runaway slaves. No one was truly happy with the compromise, but it did settle the immediate problem.

Would Clay's compromise work? Would it settle the question of slavery and hold the country together? Only time would tell.

The westward expansion was a boon for European Americans—but a disaster for Native Americans, who were driven from their traditional homelands.

9 PIONEER LIFE

This painting by Samuel Colman shows a wagon train crossing at a shallow point in the Medicine Bow River in present-day Wyoming. It may have been weeks since they had seen anyone other than themselves.

The sky turned red and clouds of dust began to sweep across the prairie. From inside the tiny Kansas schoolhouse, India Harris Simmons and her frightened students watched as a black, funnel-shaped cloud moved straight toward them. They were miles away from the nearest house, in one of the first schools on the Kansas frontier.

Suddenly a child standing in the doorway, his face drained of color, cried out, "It's done turned, teacher. It's going straight north." The tornado had shifted its course.

The children opened their books and returned to work. Having journeyed with their families into a vast new land where schools, papers, and books were scarce, they desperately wanted to learn.

New Beginning

In the early 1840s, restless young people, many of them farmers with families, saw westward settlement as an adventure. They wanted to escape heavy taxes, and sometimes debts, for a new life away from what they thought of as the crowds back East.

The typical farm family's dreams were

60

simple. They would build a log cabin or house made of packed earth and roots on new land. All day long, fathers and sons would toil on the windswept prairie, tending to crops or hunting for buffalo, rabbit, and deer. Women would gather buffalo chips for fuel. They would clean houses, cook, and garden. At night, after a supper of corn bread and roasted hen, the family would listen to fiddle music beneath a sky filled with stars.

But settling the frontier presented serious hardships for men and women alike. Not everyone undertook the dangerous and demanding expedition with enthusiasm. Women left behind, usually forever, relatives, neighbors, and most of their possessions, to be near their husbands and keep their young families together.

Since the Plains Indians did not build upon the land they had inhabited for centuries, European Americans considered Indian territory to be free land. Plains Indians roamed over a wide area searching for buffalo and carrying most of their possessions with them. The early pioneers were often frightened by the Indians and traveled in large groups for protection. But most Indians, while resentful, were curious about the intruders. They readily exchanged salmon and buffalo meat for blankets, cash, and clothing.

In later years, Congress passed laws that enabled the **homesteaders** to claim frontier property if

Trees, and thus firewood, were scarce in the open plains. This woman gathers the only readily available fuel—cow chips.

they established residency and made improvements on the land. Gradually, white settlers took most of the Indian lands.

For many families, Kansas represented only the beginning of the western frontier. About 350,000 men, women, and children crossed the Overland Trail between 1841 and 1866. The trail began in small towns, called jumping-off places, on the western border of the Missouri River. The southern route led to California. The northern route went to the Oregon Territory.

Guidebooks and early settlers' accounts romanticized (gave an appealing quality to) the Pacific Coast. One man who traveled to the Oregon Territory in 1834 described it as a "terrestrial paradise." But the journey was difficult. Women hiked up steep mountains, sometimes carrying small children in their arms, while men hoisted the covered wagons up rocky cliffs with ropes and pulleys. Together they crossed arid deserts and traversed rolling streams in canoes with the help of Indian navigators. Women nursed children and husbands through illness after illness.

Clean water was not always accessible and diseases spread rapidly. Cholera and typhoid, carried across the continent by **emigrants** (people who leave one country to settle in another), proved to be the most deadly illnesses. Many Indians were not immune to these European diseases and died after catching them. During the height of the cholera epidemic, one traveler wrote: "The road from

Independence [Missouri] to Fort Laramie [Wyoming] is a grave-yard."

Travel Diaries

Some pioneers recorded their thoughts and experiences in diaries. They tell of treacherous journeys, many of which lasted over eight months. Amelia Stewart Knight described how she carried her young son across mountains while she was nine months pregnant. When that same child got scarlet fever, she nursed him tenderly while riding in the back of a cramped and stuffy wagon.

Countless families experienced the grief of losing a child—whether to illness or accident. Abigail Malick journeyed with her family to the Oregon Territory in 1848. It was a year and a half before she could bring herself to write about her 17-year-old son Hiram's drowning in the Platte River. In a letter to her daughter back home, Malick wrote: "It has Almost kild Me but I have to bear it. And if we Are good perhapes then we can meete him in heven." Over the next 17 years, in the letters the Malick family wrote home, Hiram's drowning was always mentioned.

Frontier Life

The life that greeted these pioneers, once they settled on the open land, was not an easy one. They worked from dawn to dusk. Women lugged pails of water from nearby streams, swept out the dusty cabins, cooked meals over open fires, and made clothes from sheep's wool they had woven and dyed

Trails to the Far West, 1835–1850

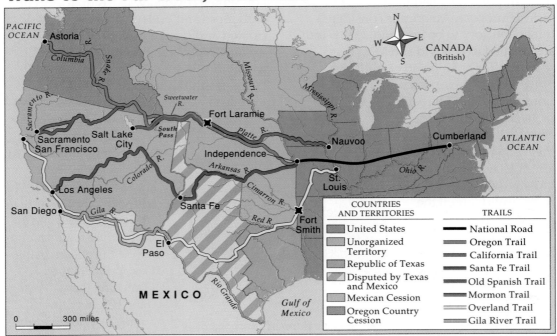

Along which trail(s) would you travel if you were going in Missouri from Independence to Astoria in 1840? From Independence to Los Angeles?

AMERICAN ADVENTURES

themselves. Men plowed the hard soil with crude farm tools, spending endless hours in the hot sun. Women and children helped out in the fields when there was much work to be done. Prairie fires, cyclones, and blizzards posed a constant threat.

The nearest doctor could be miles away, and hospitals were almost nonexistent. Young Theodore Potter, growing up on the Michigan frontier, waited hours with a broken leg while his father trudged through the snowy woods at night to find a doctor. Woman after woman described giving birth in a lonely room while her husband rode frantically in search of a doctor or a **midwife** (one who assists women in giving birth).

Despite the hardships, many who sought out the wilderness and the prairie found a "beauty and mystery over all"

For supplies, news, and refuge from danger, settlers traveled to the nearest fort, which might be days away. This one is Fort Laramie, Wyoming.

that sustained them. Lydia Murphy Toothaker, a Kansas settler, described how she felt living on the vast and peaceful plains: "It was such a new world, reaching to the far horizon without break of tree or chimney stack; just sky and grass and grass and sky. . . . The hush was so loud."

CHAPTER CHECK

WORD MATCH
1. romanticized
2. homesteaders
3. epidemic
4. midwife
5. emigrants

a. assists women in giving birth
b. people who leave one country to settle in another
c. looked at some situation or event in an appealing way
d. widespread illness
e. people who claimed frontier property by settling there

QUICK QUIZ
1. What hardships did pioneers face?
2. Name some reasons the early pioneers and farmers moved to the western frontier.
3. Why did American settlers consider Indian territory to be free land?

THINK ABOUT IT
1. If you had been a western pioneer, you would have faced hardships. What do you think would have been the greatest danger you faced?
2. Think about what life was like for a boy or girl on the frontier. If you had lived at that time, would you have wanted to grow up in a pioneer family? Why or why not?

CHAPTER 10 VAQUEROS

The vaqueros were a tough, proud breed of men who herded cattle on the grazing lands of the Southwest. Here, a vaquero catches a wild mustang with his lariat. Next, he will saddle it and break it in.

The wide, flat plains of New Mexico lay silent in the sunset. For a long moment, all seemed empty and calm. Then, as the sun sank down, the earth began to tremble.

A low, rumbling sound came out of the west. Slowly it grew louder. Hoofbeats! A herd of wild cattle thundered across the land. Their feet trampled everything on the ground. Then, as they passed, the roar returned to a rumble. Soon the plains were silent once more.

This scene took place in the 1700s, when the first cowboys rode. In those days, the dry plains rumbled often to the hoofbeats of great cattle herds. The cattle had been brought to North America by the Spanish. Cowboys rode the ranges of Texas and New Mexico long before any settlers from the United States moved into these lands.

These early cowboys were Mexican Indians. They worked the ranches of the Spanish **missions** (centers for a religious group setting up churches, schools, and hospitals). They had not become cowboys by choice. In the 16th century, Mexico had been conquered by the Spanish. The

Spanish brought Mexican Indians by force to what is now the Southwestern United States. At the missions, they were taught how to ride and to rope. Many of the Indians had been branded on the cheek with the letter G—for *guerra* (GEH-rah), the Spanish word for war.

Cowboy Life

These Mexicans became excellent cowboys. They took great pride in their work and in the special outfits they wore. Around their heads were bright kerchiefs. Wide-brimmed hats protected them from sun and rain. Their knee-length pants buttoned on the sides and folded into buckskin shoes. Each man had a long knife fastened to his right leg. He also wore great slabs of cowhide down his legs, called *chaparreras* (chap-uh-REH-rus). These protected his legs when he rode through heavy brush.

The Mexican cowboy was called a *vaquero* (vah-KEH-roh), or mounted herdsman. He carried no gun. His main weapon and tool was the *lariat*, a strong rawhide rope. With it, a vaquero could bring a wild bull to the ground—or a man, if necessary.

Vaqueros lived with their families in huts on ranches. They started most of the traditions picked up later by American cowboys. One of their jobs was to round up long-horn cattle that roamed the prairies.

This figurine—called a *bulto*—of the Virgin Mary is just one reminder of the rich traditions left behind by the Spanish, who settled the American Southwest.

Spanish Settlers

In the early 1800s, about 3000 Spanish settlers lived in present-day Texas. Many were clustered around the missions. But some had their own ranches. Other settlers lived in towns such as San Antonio, Goliad, and Nacogdoches. San Antonio was the largest town.

What is today the state of New Mexico was the most important northern outpost of New Spain. In 1800, about 20,000 Spanish settlers lived there, most of them along the Rio Grande Valley. The town of Santa Fe was the capital. The settlers raised cattle and sheep and grew corn. Some mined gold or copper. Fighting between settlers and Indians was a constant danger.

The people of New Mexico lived on their own for many years. Many did not go to Mexico City because travel was slow and difficult. They had almost no contact with citizens from the United States. The Spanish would not allow trade with their neighbor to the east, and any American who came to New Mexico was turned away or put in prison. The New Mexicans developed into very independent people.

Mexican Independence

The vaquero way of life came to an end in the early 1800s. In 1821, Mexico threw off

Spanish rule and became independent. The new Mexican government opened the vast mission lands of the Southwest to settlers. The vaqueros were let go from the missions. They became free men and their way of life came to an end. More and more settlers moved into the Southwest, dividing the land into many separate ranches. Soon the vaqueros had no place to ride.

Many other things changed under Mexican rule. People from the U.S. were invited to settle in Texas. American traders were suddenly welcome in New Mexico. An American named William Becknell opened a new trading route between Santa Fe and Independence, Missouri. Household goods and tools were shipped to New Mexico. Gold, silver, and furs were sent back to Missouri. For many years, wagon trains loaded with goods rolled over the well-worn path of the Santa Fe Trail. The trail also became one of the major routes for settlers heading west.

The Spanish brought the first cowboys to the region. They also brought their language, religion, and architecture. Many places in the region still have Spanish names. Some of the old Spanish mission churches have survived to this day. People still build houses in the old Spanish style with white plaster walls and red tile roofs.

Today, great highways wind where cattle trails used to be. Large cities stand

Spanish missions offered food, clothing and housing to the Indians of the American Southwest. In return, the Indians took instruction in Christianity, observed Spanish customs, and worked for the mission. These missions thrived from the 1500s to the 1800s when the American Southwest was under Spanish rule.

where many of the missions once ruled. The plains still roll out toward the horizon, but wild herds of cattle no longer thunder across these lands. The men who spent their days following the herds under the hot western sun were part of western expansion. They live now in our legends of the West—legends that endure in the movies and on television.

This cook at a California ranch rolls out flour for tortillas. The women who cooked for the cattle owners and vaqueros were usually Mexican Indians.

CHAPTER CHECK

WORD MATCH
1. chaparreras
2. vaquero
3. lariat
4. guerra
5. missions

a. Spanish word for mounted herdsman, or cowboy
b. Spanish word for war
c. Spanish word for leather pants worn to protect cowboys' legs
d. Spanish word for a strong, rawhide rope
e. headquarters of religious group setting up churches, schools, and hospitals

QUICK QUIZ
1. Who were the first cowboys in the American Southwest?
2. When Mexico became independent from Spain, life changed for the people in Spanish territory. Name a few changes that took place.
3. Spain ruled the Southwest for centuries. What are some reminders of Spanish rule?

THINK ABOUT IT
1. How different do you think life would have been if Spain had continued to rule the Southwest? Would the United States be as powerful as it is today? Why or why not?
2. Describe how the vaqueros started a tradition that American cowboys followed. Would you like to have lived the life vaqueros lived? Why or why not?

Built as a chapel in the 1700s, the Alamo served as a fortress for Texas revolutionaries in the 1830s. This historical site was later restored.

A blood-red flag flew from the steeple of the parish church in San Antonio, Texas. It was hoisted there by soldiers of the army of Mexico's dictator, General Antonio López de Santa Anna, on February 23, 1836. The meaning of this flag was clear to the 186 Americans holed up in the Alamo, an old Franciscan mission that had been turned into a fort. The flag stood for "no quarter." Unless the Americans surrendered, they would be slain to the last man.

From the walls of the Alamo, a defiant cannon shot was fired. This was the answer of Colonel William B. Travis, the 27-year-old commander at the Alamo. The next day, Travis appealed "to the people of Texas and all the Americans in the world" for help. "I shall never surrender or retreat," he said. "I am determined to sustain myself as long as possible and die like a soldier who never forgets what is due to his own honor or that of his country—victory or death."

Texas, Mexico

With these words, the stage was set for the historic battle of the Alamo. What brought it about? The answer goes back to events that began in 1821, the year that Mexico won its independence from Spain. At that time, Texas was a vast, almost empty province of Mexico. Fewer than 7000 Mexicans inhabited it. Comanche (cuh-MAN-chee) Indians roamed and hunted on horseback at will.

To help protect and develop Texas, the government of Mexico invited Americans to settle there. They were offered land at only 10 cents an acre, compared to $1.25 an acre for land in the United States.

Americans poured into Texas. By 1835, there were 30,000 of them, while the Mexican population barely reached 7800. As long as the Mexican government left them alone, the American settlers gave little thought to independence.

The Mexican government believed at first that the Americans would be absorbed into the Mexican community. To promote **integration** (uniting ethnic and racial groups to function together) it passed a number of laws. **Immigrants** (people who come into a new country or region) for the United States had to be Roman Catholics and had to obey Mexican law. All official business had to be carried out in the Spanish language.

But these attempts at peaceful integration failed, and tensions rose between the Mexican population and the Americans. Most of the American colonists were not Roman Catholics. Very few bothered to learn Spanish, and many scoffed at Mexican laws.

The Mexican government had still another grievance against Americans. A number of adventurers from the United States invaded Texas with private armies.

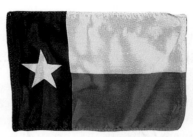

Santa Anna's siege of the Alamo stirred patriotic fervor among American Texans, who adopted the Lone Star symbol that today serves as the Texas state flag

Their goal was to annex Texas to the United States. These adventurers were defeated, but many Mexicans feared the U.S. was bent on taking over Texas. Their fears were increased by frequent demands in the U.S. Congress and in the press for annexation of much or all of Texas.

Mexico Reacts

Alarmed by these threats, the Mexican government began taking steps to strengthen its hold on Texas. The first was to outlaw slavery throughout Mexico in 1829. This was clearly aimed at Texas, where many American settlers brought their slaves with them. The next year, Mexico banned all future immigration from the United States and encouraged more Mexicans to settle in Texas.

The final blow for the Americans came in 1835. That year, Mexican President Santa Anna threw out his country's democratic constitution and declared himself a military **dictator** (a ruler with absolute power and authority). He abolished state governments. Until then, the American settlers had little voice in how they were governed. Now they would have none at all.

Many people in the United States urged the American settlers to overthrow Santa Anna's dictatorship. So did a number of Mexican **liberals** (people belonging to a political party that favors reforms), who detested his rule. By this time, the settlers needed no prompting. In November 1835, they set up a **provisional** (temporary) government with Sam Houston as commander-in-chief of the Texas army. Houston was an adopted son of the Cherokee Indians.

Infuriated, Santa Anna led a Mexican army of 6000 men north across the Rio Grande River to put down the uprising. Reaching San Antonio in late February 1836, he found that a small group of Texans had taken refuge inside the Alamo. Besides Colonel Travis, they were led by Jim Bowie (BOO-ee), inventor of the Bowie knife, and Davy Crockett, a famous adventurer. Among those in the Alamo were several friendly Mexican men, women, and children who sided with the American settlers.

Defending the Alamo

The defenders of the Alamo were greatly outnumbered, but their fort was strong. Its stone walls were at least ten feet high and two feet thick. The walls were bolstered with wooden stakes and earth until at some points their thickness was five feet. The defenders had about 20 mounted cannons. The largest fired an 18-pound cannonball. This was a powerful array of weapons in the 1830s.

For several days, Mexican cannons pounded the Alamo, but with little effect. Then, on the morning of March 6, thousands of Mexican soldiers charged. Hundreds were cut down before they even reached the walls. Others toppled from ladders as they tried to climb over. Two charges were driven back, but a third smashed through a number of openings made in the walls.

The fighting continued inside the

Texas Goes to War, 1836

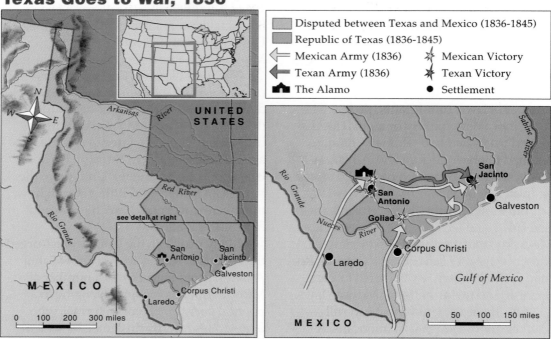

What natural feature formed the southern boundary of the area between Texas and Mexico that was disputed? Where did the Texans finally defeat and capture Santa Anna?

Alamo, where the defenders resisted against great odds. Before long, Travis and Crockett were dead. In the Alamo's chapel, Bowie lay sick on a cot. When the Mexicans rushed in, he fired two pistols until he too was shot. The Mexicans killed most of the Alamo's defenders. Five were executed as prisoners after the fighting ended.

A Costly Victory

Santa Anna had carried out his threat. But his victory was a costly one. He had lost about 1500 soldiers, killed and wounded.

The Mexicans strongly disapproved of the slaughter of the defenders. One general later wrote: "In our opinion, the blood of our soldiers as well as the enemy was shed in vain for the mere vanity of reconquering the Alamo by force of arms."

The Alamo aroused the Texans under Sam Houston. On April 21, 1836, they caught Santa Anna's army off guard at the San Jacinto River near the present-day city of Houston. Crying "Remember the Alamo!" they routed the Mexican force and captured Santa Anna. Santa Anna signed a treaty agreeing to end the war against the Texans and recognizing their independence. Then he was released and sent back to Mexico.

Texas remained independent as the Lone Star Republic until 1845. There were many people in Texas who favored immediate annexation by the United States. But annexation was opposed by members of Congress from the Northern states. They did not want to see Texas enter the Union as a slave state. Many also feared that annexation would lead to war with Mexico, which still claimed Texas as its territory. When Congress finally voted for annexation in 1845, their fears proved to be correct. Mexico and the United States were soon swept into a major conflict.

CHAPTER CHECK

WORD MATCH

1. dictator
2. immigrants
3. provisional
4. liberals
5. integration

a. uniting racial and ethnic groups to function together
b. temporary
c. people who come into a new country or region
d. ruler with complete power and authority
e. people belonging to a political party that favors reforms

QUICK QUIZ

1. Santa Anna led his army across the Rio Grande to put down an uprising. What was the uprising about?
2. Why did Santa Anna give Texas its independence from Mexico?

THINK ABOUT IT

1. Think about the reasons the Texans revolted against Santa Anna's dictatorship? Would you have followed Colonel Travis' "Victory or death" decision? Why or why not?
2. Think about some of the laws the Mexican government passed for Americans to follow. Do you think any were fair? If so, which ones? Why?

12 WAR WITH MEXICO

Texans were not the only Americans concerned about the war with Mexico. This painting shows a few other U.S. citizens catching up with the latest news of battles and losses.

A Mexican army of 15,000 men was marching north. Its aim: to destroy a much smaller United States army at a mountain pass in Mexico. Its leader: Santa Anna, the man who had captured the Alamo.

The date was February 1847, more than a year after Texas had become a state. The United States and Mexico were at war. How had this come about?

Texans gained independence from Mexico in 1836. They set up their own nation, nicknamed the Lone Star Republic, during the same year. But the future of the republic never looked very certain. For one thing, Mexico refused to accept the loss of Texas. For another, many Texans hoped that their republic would soon become one of the United States.

Sam Houston, their president, shared their hope. But Congress kept Texas waiting to become a state for nine long years. Why? The delay was due to the debate over slavery in the United States. Many Texans, including Houston, owned slaves. If Texas were admitted to the Union, slavery would spread to the Southwest. Many white Southerners hoped that this would happen. But Northerners did not want another slave state. Leaders of Congress were afraid of making Northern voters angry. They were also afraid of starting a war with Mexico, so they left Texas to struggle on its own.

Texas statehood was a main issue in the 1844 U.S. presidential election. Democrats demanded that Texas be admitted to the Union as a state. The Democratic candidate, James K. Polk, won the election. His victory set events in motion. The outgoing Whig president, John Tyler, now persuaded Congress to allow Texas to join the Union.

Polk's Demands

Once Polk took office, he made it clear he wanted more territory than Texas. The idea of Manifest Destiny influenced Polk, and he hoped Mexico would turn over the entire area from Texas to the Pacific Ocean. This area included what are now the states of New Mexico, Arizona, Nevada, Utah, and California. In November 1845, Polk sent a representative to discuss this with Mexican leaders. The following month, Texas became the Union's 28th state. At this point, Mexico broke off all ties with the United States. Any hope of obtaining more land from Mexico now seemed at an end.

Polk became impatient. General Zachary Taylor had already assembled an army at Corpus Christi in southern Texas. In January 1846, Polk ordered this army to march to the banks of the Rio Grande. Texans said the Rio Grande was their border with Mexico. But the Mexicans claimed the Rio Grande was well inside the Mexican border. Soon Mexican and U.S. troops were fighting. On May 12, 1846, the United States declared war on Mexico.

Taylor's March

The United States carried the war to the heart of Mexico. Taylor and his men captured Monterrey, Mexico, in September 1846. The next February, Santa Anna sent Mexican forces to hold back Taylor at Buena Vista (BWAY-nuh VEES-tuh). Taylor had an army of fewer than 5000 men. Most of them were untrained volunteers. Santa Anna decided to attack. Taylor, called Old Rough and Ready by his men, welcomed another fight. Since he was outnumbered about three to one, he placed his men in position at a mountain pass. There they would have an edge over Santa Anna's larger force.

On February 22, Santa Anna attacked at Buena Vista. All that day, U.S. riflemen and cannons beat back the Mexicans. As they fired, bands played *Hail, Columbia.* When darkness came, the fighting stopped. Both armies shivered through a night of rain.

The next day, Santa Anna lined up his troops for an all-out attack. Mexican bands played sacred music. The Mexican soldiers and horsemen wore uniforms with bright colors—green, yellow, crimson, and blue. Some carried silk banners and long, handsome feathers. As a battle cry, they shouted, "Viva!" (long live) to their leaders.

Soon the battle was on. The Mexicans hit hard and fought bravely, but U.S. troops drove them back. Late in the afternoon, another Mexican force opened a powerful attack. Bullets could not stop it. Many Mexicans fell. But others swept forward, shouting, "Viva! Viva!"

The cannons blasted the Mexicans at short range. Soon Santa Anna's men could stand the pounding no longer. They fell back into the mountains, and the firing stopped. It was a hard-fought battle, and the Mexicans had lost twice as many men as the Americans.

Scott's Truce

On September 14, 1847, U.S. troops under General Winfield Scott entered Mexico City. Scott arranged a **truce** (agreement to stop fighting) with Santa Anna. Four months later, Mexican and U.S. agents met in the village of Guadalupe Hidalgo (gwah-duh-LOO-pay ee-DAL-goh), near Mexico City. The Mexican agents signed a peace treaty with the United States government.

According to the **Treaty of Guadalupe Hidalgo,** Mexico signed over to the

The Mexican War, 1846–1848

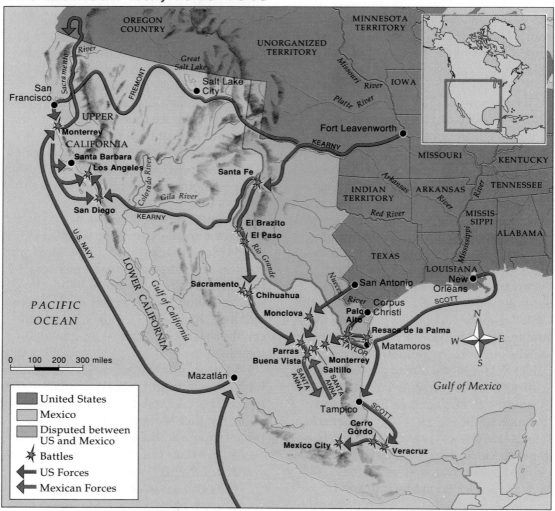

Which American general took a water route to Mexico? Which battles took place in cities along the Gulf of Mexico?

AMERICAN ADVENTURES

Victorious in battle, General Winfield Scott leads his men into Mexico City on September 14, 1847, to seek a truce with Santa Anna.

United States a huge territory. This became known as the **Mexican Cession.** It included all of what is present-day California, Nevada, and Utah. It also included parts of Arizona, New Mexico, Colorado, and Wyoming. Mexico agreed that the Rio Grande would be the boundary of Texas. In return for all this land, the United States paid Mexico $15 million. The United States also agreed to pay all the money that Texas citizens said Mexicans owed them.

Five years later, the United States paid Mexico $10 million for another piece of land. It was named the **Gadsden Purchase,** after the U.S. agent who arranged the sale. The Gadsden Purchase was much smaller than the Mexican Cession. But it finally settled the boundary between the two countries. Today the land obtained in the Gadsden Purchase includes the parts of southern Arizona and New Mexico.

CHAPTER CHECK

WORD MATCH
1. truce
2. viva
3. Treaty of Guadalupe Hildago
4. Mexican Cession
5. Gadsden Purchase

a. Spanish word for long life
b. Mexico signed over four Western states and parts of four others
c. Mexico gave up the southern parts of Arizona and New Mexico
d. agreement to stop fighting
e. set boundary between Texas and Mexico at Rio Grande

QUICK QUIZ
1. What were two major reasons it took so long for Texas to become independent?
2. How much Southwest territory did President Polk want?
3. Although Santa Anna's troops outnumbered the American troops at Buena Vista, the Mexicans were at a disadvantage. What was it?

THINK ABOUT IT
1. Think about the western boundary that James Polk wanted. Why do you think he felt so strongly about this?
2. Do you think the U.S. war with Mexico is a period of history America is proud of? Why or why not?

This man, an immigrant from China, was just one of the hundreds of thousands of people who poured into California from around the world after gold was discovered at Sutter's Mill.

J ames Marshall was shaking with excitement. He was dripping wet. He had just ridden through the rain to John Sutter's house in California. Sutter had sent Marshall to build a sawmill on his large property. Now Marshall wanted to see Sutter—alone. Marshall made Sutter lock the door to the room.

Inside, Marshall pulled a bit of cloth out of his pocket. In it were small bits of yellow metal. Marshall had found them in the sawmill stream on January 28, 1848. "It looks like gold," Sutter said. "Let's test it." The tests proved the yellow metal really was gold. And, Marshall told him, there was a great deal more where it came from.

At first Sutter tried to keep the news a secret. He did not want groups of **prospectors** (people who look for gold) on his property. But a storekeeper found out. He saw a chance to make money by selling supplies to gold miners. In May, he went to San Francisco with a bottle of gold dust. He went around shouting, "Gold! Gold!

Gold from Sutter's Mill!"

Soon San Francisco was burning with gold fever. Men, women, and children dropped everything and rushed to Sutter's Mill, about 100 miles northeast of the city. The fever spread to other California towns. The Gold Rush had begun.

By September, the news reached the Midwest and the East Coast. By the end of the year, it spread to Europe. Tens of thousands of people from all over the world set out for California—to strike it rich.

Routes to the West

In 1849, there were three ways to get to California from the Eastern United States. All of them were dangerous. One way was to sail from the Atlantic Coast, around South America, and north to San Francisco. This trip took six to eight months. Usually the ships were crowded, and the food was bad. Many ships were rotten and leaky, and some sank during storms.

Another way was the "shortcut" across Panama. Travelers went by ship to the Atlantic Coast of Panama. From there, they crossed over 75 miles by mule through steaming jungle to the Pacific Coast. Some travelers were left stranded by mule drivers. Others suffered or died because of poor food, bad water, or disease. Once travelers reached the Pacific, their trip was not finished. They had to wait for weeks or months for a ship to California.

The third way was by wagon train on overland trails. This way, across snowy mountains and sizzling deserts, was not much easier. Those who chose this route faced food and water shortages and disease.

What happened when the miners reached California? They had to work harder than ever. Gold mining was backbreaking work. The miners shoveled dirt from streams all day and then washed it out in tin pans. Sometimes they got only an ounce or two of gold. A few miners did strike it rich. Some dug as much as $1500 worth of gold in a single day. But most just broke even or lost money.

Many of the forty-niners who rushed to California, hoping to strike it rich, had no idea that pursuit of their dreams would mean backbreaking work. Dreams came true only for a lucky few.

Forty-Niners

In 1849, more than 100,000 people called **forty-niners** rushed to California. By 1850, people were still coming. Most were U.S. citizens, but several thousand were Mexicans, and a few thousand were South Americans. In time, news of the Gold Rush even reached China. The num-

Almost overnight, fortune seekers turned the relatively quiet port of San Francisco, California, into a booming town. This photograph shows the hustle and bustle of San Francisco in 1850.

ber of Chinese coming to America suddenly increased. Before 1850, fewer than 1000 Chinese had arrived in America. Then, in 1852 alone, more than 18,000 Chinese entered California. Many were recruited to work on the new railroads.

Several employment agencies sent women to California. Some came as domestic helpers, teachers, or dance-hall entertainers. Others intended to find husbands in the mining camps. One woman advertised in a local newspaper: "HUSBAND WANTED —By a lady who can wash, cook, scour, sew, milk, spin, weave, hoe (can't plow), cut wood, make fires, feed the pigs, raise chickens, rock the cradle (gold rocker, I thank you, Sir!), saw a plank, drive nails . . . and you can see she can write."

Not all the forty-niners went to California to mine for gold or to find spouses. Some of the most successful came with other ideas. One, for example, was a German Jewish merchant named Levi Strauss. Strauss arrived in San Francisco with large rolls of canvas. He hoped to sell the canvas to miners for use in making tents. But he quickly learned that many miners needed work pants most of all. So he began making pants out of the canvas. The pants were warm, rugged, and perfect for hard work. Strauss called them Levi's. Soon he was selling as many of them as he could produce.

Rattlesnake Diggings

By the early 1850s, northern California was swarming with miners. They gave strange names to their camps. They called one place Hangtown. A second was named Rattlesnake Diggings. The forty-niners were recognized easily by their clothes—broad-brimmed hats, red shirts, and knee-high boots. Many slept with weapons at their sides because they did not have police to protect them

AMERICAN ADVENTURES

from robbers or murderers. Outside of San Francisco, there was not yet much local government or law enforcement.

In fact, California's future was still undecided. During the war with Mexico, a U.S. soldier, John C. Frémont, had led a revolt of American settlers in California. They had fought Mexican troops—and won. After the Treaty of Guadalupe Hidalgo, California stayed in the hands of the United States. But the nation's law-makers could not decide what to do with the territory. The problem was a hard one to solve.

The root of this problem was slavery. Could slave owners from the South bring their slaves to California? Most North-erners believed that admitting more slave states into the Union would be wrong. Most Southern leaders thought that own-ing slaves was a person's natural right. The two groups bitterly argued. Some Southerners threatened to leave the Union if the issue was not decided in their favor.

California could not become a state until this quarrel was settled. But some Americans said that the problem could not be settled without violence and war. Then Henry Clay, a U.S. senator from Kentucky, stepped forward with propos-als to end the argument. Clay's plan set the stage for one of the most dramatic debates in the U.S. Congress.

CHAPTER CHECK

WORD MATCH
1. John Sutter
2. forty-niners
3. prospectors
4. Henry Clay
5. John C. Frémont

a. people who moved to California during the gold rush
b. owned sawmill in California where gold was first found
c. people who look for gold
d. leader of U.S. settlers in Mexican California
e. U.S. senator who tried to resolve conflict blocking California statehood

QUICK QUIZ
1. All routes from the East to California were dangerous. List each route and describe some of the dangers.
2. Who were the forty-niners? Where did they come from?
3. On what issue did the status of California's statehood rest? How did it look as if it might be settled?

THINK ABOUT IT
1. Do you think most people who rushed to strike it rich in California knew how hard it was to mine gold? What made gold mining so difficult?
2. If you had been alive in 1849, would you have tried your luck in the California gold rush? Why or why not?

14 A PLAN TO SAVE THE UNION

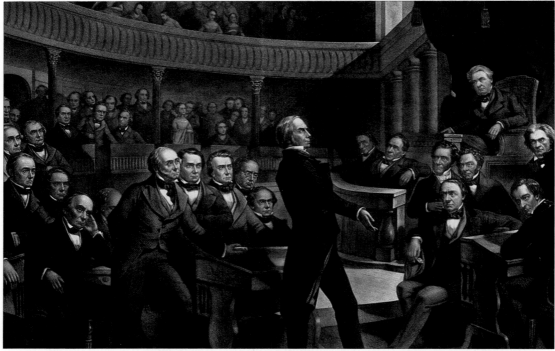

A long-respected member of Congress, Henry Clay of Kentucky went before his fellow senators in 1850, hoping to convince them to compromise on the matter of slavery—and preserve the Union.

Henry Clay sat at his desk in the United States Senate and looked around the room. He noticed an old friend with bushy gray hair. This man was so weak he could hardly walk. Clay knew that his colleague was dying. Yet the man still held great political power. He was Senator John C. Calhoun from South Carolina.

Clay noticed another senator walk into the room. It was his old friend from Massachusetts, Daniel Webster. Webster's brows were shaggy and black. His eyes were set deep into their sockets. His balding forehead seemed to be twice the size of

an average person's. Webster was the greatest speechmaker in American history—even greater than Clay himself. Friends of the Massachusetts senator called him the "godlike Daniel".

Clay had known Calhoun and Webster for many years. All three remembered when the British had set fire to the Capitol back in 1814. Then they had been young men with high ambitions. Each had hoped to be president. Each had been disappointed. Now all three had grown old.

Henry Clay still had one ambition. He wanted to save the Union from breaking

AMERICAN ADVENTURES

up over slavery. Clay had helped to save the Union once before—30 years ago, in 1820. The question then centered on whether or not Missouri should be allowed to enter the Union. If Missouri was admitted to the Union, the slave states would have control of the U.S. Senate.

Missouri Compromise

Northerners and Southerners had argued fiercely over this question. In 1820, Clay and other senators had finally worked out a compromise. They suggested that slaves be allowed in the new state of Missouri. At the same time, the senators said, Maine should enter the Union as a free state. Then the number of slave states and the number of free states would remain the same. The North and the South would still have about equal power.

What would happen with slavery in new Western states that might be added after 1820? The senators pointed to a line on the map running through the territory of the Louisiana Purchase. This line ran along the **parallel** (an imaginary line, or circle on the globe, which runs in the same direction as the Equator) 36° 30', or 36 degrees, 30 minutes. The parallel marked the southern border of Missouri.

The senators proposed that slavery be made illegal north of this line, except in Missouri where it would be permitted. This proposal would allow slavery south of this line. The idea passed the House and the Senate. It was known as the **Missouri Compromise.** For a while, it ended the angry talk about slavery.

California's Constitution

Now in 1850, Californians asked to come into the Union as a new state.

Missouri Compromise of 1820

How many free states were in the Union in 1820? How many slave states?

California's constitution outlawed slavery anywhere within its borders—even south of the 36° 30′ parallel. This angered white Southerners. They felt the North was trying to cheat them out of an opportunity to develop plantations in the West.

Southern leaders said they would fight for their rights. If they lost the debate over California they warned, they might **secede** (leave) from the United States. The South threatened to become an independent country.

Henry Clay wanted to prevent this. He hoped part of his plan would satisfy the North, and that the other part would satisfy the South. On February 5, 1850, the old senator climbed the steps of the Capitol. He had come to make the most important speech of his life.

Clay's Compromise Plan

Clay spoke for hours about his ideas. First, he said, California should be admitted to the Union as a free state. Second, Utah, Nevada, and the other territories obtained in the Mexican Cession could be either slave or free. The question there, he said, should be decided by a vote of the settlers themselves. Third, Northerners should help the South to enforce laws about runaway slaves. A federal law should strictly punish any Northerner who helped a slave gain freedom. Fourth, the slave trade in Washington, D.C., should be stopped, but slave ownership in the district would not be affected.

Some senators applauded Clay's plan. But the dying Senator John C. Calhoun attacked it. He thought it was unfair to the South. Southerners believed the South

The Compromise of 1850

Free State or Territory
Slave State or Territory
Territory Open to Slavery

How many free states were in the Union in 1850? How many slave states? What new territories were opened to slavery in 1850?

needed slavery to maintain its cotton-based economy. Calhoun was too weak to read his own speech about Clay's plan, so another Southern senator read it for him. It explained why the South could not compromise. It said: "The South asks for justice, simple justice, and less it should not take." The sick man's eyes blazed as his speech ended.

A few days later, people again crowded into the Senate balcony. They had come to hear Webster's booming voice. He told the audience he wished to save the Union "not as a Northern man, but as an American." For three hours, Webster gave reasons why the Senate should vote in favor of Clay's plan.

The Debate Heats Up

People quarreled over Clay's compromise for months. Northerners accused Webster of being a traitor. They hated the part of Clay's plan punishing Northerners for helping runaway slaves. How could Webster defend such a plan, they asked. Many people in both the North and the South attacked Clay's plan. But finally, in September 1850, Congress voted the plan into law. The law concerning runaway slaves was called the **Fugitive Slave Act.** The entire plan became known as the **Compromise of 1850.**

For the moment, Henry Clay had saved the Union from breaking up. California now joined the Union as the 31st state. But strong feelings about slavery in the territories lingered.

Slavery and what to do about it worried Americans throughout the 1850s. In the end, the problem led to the worst crisis in the nation's history. But this time neither Henry Clay nor Daniel Webster could help to solve the crisis. The two old friends died in the year 1852.

CHAPTER CHECK

WORD MATCH
1. Missouri Compromise
2. parallel
3. Compromise of 1850
4. secede
5. Fugitive Slave Act

a. imaginary line on globe that runs in same direction as Equator
b. made slavery illegal north of, and legal south of, a certain line
c. to enforce laws concerning runaway slaves
d. leave, quit
e. Clay's plan to deal with differences between slave and free states

QUICK QUIZ
1. Describe the main idea of the Missouri Compromise.
2. Why did the South oppose admitting California as a free state?
3. How did Clay's compromise attempt to satisfy both sides in the conflict over California statehood? What was the reaction in the North? In the South?

THINK ABOUT IT
1. Do you think Clay's compromise was a good plan? Would you have supported it? Why or why not?
2. The Compromise of 1850, which admitted California to the Union, avoided a crisis temporarily. Discuss the main issue of the day, which led to the worst crisis in the nation's early history.

FROM SEA TO SHINING SEA

History Detective

1. About 350,000 Americans traveled along me from Missouri to the Pacific Coast and a new life between 1841 and 1866. What am I?

2. My troops cried, "Remember the Alamo!" as they waged and won an attack on the Mexicans at the San Jacinto River. Who am I?

3. I was torn between British and U.S. ownership before an 1846 treaty divided me between the two nations and prevented a war. What am I?

4. Named for the year in which we traveled, we were 100,000 hopeful Americans following the news of gold to California. Who are we?

5. After Senator Henry Clay proposed me and Congress passed me, California joined the Union as a free state. What am I?

Voices From the Past

The land was the prize that drew pioneers to the West, but it was also the land that often tested them with terrors like prairie fires. Below, read what J.C. Ruppenthal wrote about how his mother fought off such fires in Kansas. Then answer the questions that follow.

> *The last act at night, after seeing that the children were asleep . . . was to sweep the entire horizon for signs of flame. . . . At times the flames were visible up to 20 or 25 miles away . . .*

> *Mother . . . seized the "American extra-heavy" white grain sacks, dipped them into water to wet them well, and then hastened toward the fire. . . . Fear [gave] power to mother and she fought without stopping. . . . She wet sacks and carried sacks and smote the flames . . . even as any of the men, and ventured to . . . where the fire ate steadily into the dry grass . . . She saw nothing but to exert every ounce of strength to beat the fire.*

1. Give three bits of evidence from the excerpt that suggest that J.C.'s mother battled a raging fire.

2. Imagine you are J.C.'s mother. In your own words, tell how you fought the fire and how you felt while doing it.

Hands–On History

Thinking About Alternatives—Pioneers had to contend with hardships including fierce weather, disease, and homesickness. How and why did they do it? Imagine you are living in the late 1830s. You have heard stories of successful pioneers, but you have also heard terrifying stories of failure on the plains. You have good, steady work in a factory in Philadelphia, Pennsylvania, but you can only hope to remain in the same job for the rest of your life. Will you go West? What frightens you most about going? Write an essay answering these questions and explain your feelings.

YESTERDAY'S NEWS

The American Adventures Newspaper

1.

"GOLD!" The word was no sooner said than thousands of men and women struck out for California to get their share. It started out as a local phenomenon. People from all over California dropped whatever they were doing to seek their fortunes. But before very long, the news spread all over the country. Risking everything including life itself, Americans have responded to the lure of the yellow nuggets. It is believed that, by year's end, over 100,000 people will have made the long journey to the West to strike it rich.

2.

A Whisper of Gold

Coloma, Calif., January 28, 1849—It started out quietly. When James Marshall showed John Sutter gold he discovered near Sutter's sawmill, Sutter was worried. He loved his land and he knew that gold could ruin everything. Marshall agreed with Sutter to keep the discovery quiet.

It was greed—but not greed for gold—that spread the news. A store owner in the area reportedly could imagine his business prospering if people came to mine the gold. He ran through the streets of San Francisco shouting, "Gold! Gold from the American River!" Almost everyone who could walk left the city to dig at Sutter's Mill. The Gold Rush had begun.

Fools of '49?

San Francisco, Calif., September 18, 1849—Whether the forty-niners travel by land or by sea, the trip to California is long and dangerous, taking months to make. In addition, a forty-niner needs a minimum of $750 just to pay his fare and buy clothing, supplies, and food.

If gold rushers survive the long journey, they face entirely new obstacles in California. Sickness and crime are major problems. And the truth about gold digging is the first lesson for most speculators—only a very few find enough gold to make the journey worthwhile.

Experts are trying to explain what makes people willing to risk their lives to make the trip.

3.

You Be the Reporter

Match each question with its news item above.
1. What would be a good title for this article?
2. Write a caption for this photo.
3. You are an expert on American culture. Why would Americans rush to California? Finish the article with your own ideas.

MAP SKILLS

UNDERSTANDING HOW BOUNDARIES CHANGE

What would it be like to live in a place where national boundaries keep changing? If you had lived in the American Southwest between 1820 and 1850, you could have answered this question. During a span of just over thirty years, about a million square miles changed hands two or three times between three or four different countries. The map on the opposite page shows some of the changes over one eight-year period from 1845 to 1853.

Refer to the map, its title, and key. Complete each statement below by writing the letter of the best choice on a separate sheet of paper.

1. According to its title, the purpose of this map is to show territory that was **(a)** ceded (given up) by Mexico. **(b)** granted to Texas. **(c)** gained by the U.S.

2. Dotted lines on this map stand for boundaries **(a)** today. **(b)** in 1845. **(c)** in 1853.

3. In 1845, the U.S. gained a considerable amount of territory from **(a)** the **cession** (giving up) of land by Mexico. **(b)** the **annexation** (attachment) of Texas. **(c)** the addition of the Gadsden Purchase.

Write the answers to the following questions on a separate sheet of paper.

4. Use the map's scale to estimate distances. **(a)** How far is San Antonio from Corpus Christi? from Los Angeles? **(b)** How long was the Pacific coastline ceded by Mexico?

5. Many political boundaries follow the courses of rivers. What river marked the northern boundary **(a)** of Texas in 1845? **(b)** of the Gadsden Purchase in 1853? **(c)** of Mexico in 1853?

6. The Mexican-American War was fought in part over a dispute about where the southern boundary of Texas should be. What river marked the southern border of Texas **(a)** in 1845? in 1850? **(b)** What country controlled the strip of land between the two rivers in 1845? in 1850?

7. Look at the area labeled "MEXICAN CESSION." **(a)** How many present-day states are entirely inside this area? **(b)** How many states are partly within it? **(c)** Name the states with land that was once part of this area. (Refer to the modern political map of the United States on page 812.)

8. The political identity of some places changed several times between 1845 and 1853. Imagine that you were a Pueblo Indian who lived at Taos. **(a)** What country controlled your area in 1845? in 1849? **(b)** In which state would you have been located in 1849? **(c)** Check the map on page 285. What country had controlled your area 30 years earlier, in 1819?

9. Imagine that you lived in Corpus Christi in the 19th century, and you wanted to visit someone in San Antonio. What boundary or dividing line would you have had to cross if it was the year **(a)** 1840? **(b)** 1849? **(c)** 1851?

10. Compare this map with the one on page 286 showing the Compromise of 1850. **(a)** What new states and territories were created in 1850 from the land that had been part of the Mexican Cession? **(b)** How did the land gains of the U.S. affect the balance between slave and free states and territories in 1850?

For Extra Credit: Make a timeline showing when boundaries of the American Southwest changed between 1820 and 1853.

AMERICAN ADVENTURES

U.S. Territorial Gains, 1845–1853

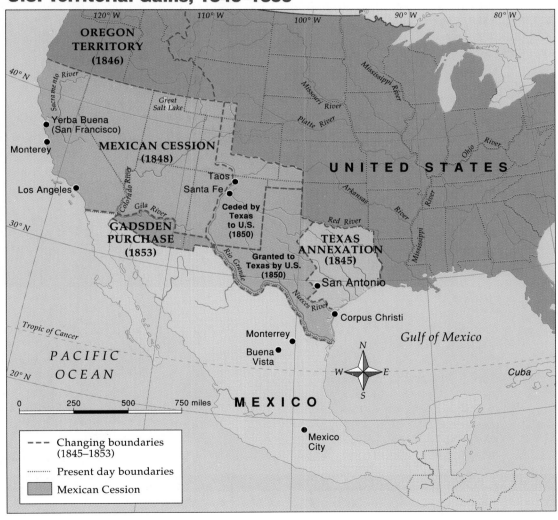

OREGON
TERRITORY
(1846)

40° N

Sacramento River

Great
Salt Lake

Yerba Buena
(San Francisco)

Monterey

MEXICAN CESSION
(1848)

Taos

Santa Fe

Los Angeles

Gila River

Colorado River

30° N

GADSDEN
PURCHASE
(1853)

Ceded by
Texas
to U.S.
(1850)

Granted to
Texas by U.S.
(1850)

Rio Grande

120° W

110° W

100° W

90° W

80° W

Missouri
River

Platte River

Mississippi River

UNITED STATES

Arkansas

Ohio River

Red River

River

Mississippi

TEXAS
ANNEXATION
(1845)

San Antonio

Nueces River

Corpus Christi

Tropic of Cancer

PACIFIC
OCEAN

20° N

0   250   500   750 miles

Monterrey

Buena
Vista

N

W   E

S

Gulf of Mexico

Cuba

MEXICO

Mexico
City

- - - Changing boundaries
(1845–1853)

.... Present day boundaries

Mexican Cession

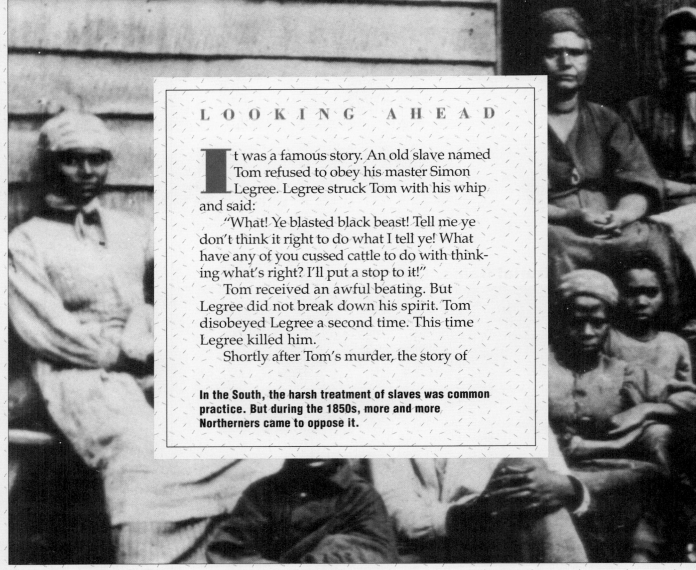

It was a famous story. An old slave named Tom refused to obey his master Simon Legree. Legree struck Tom with his whip and said:

"What! Ye blasted black beast! Tell me ye don't think it right to do what I tell ye! What have any of you cussed cattle to do with thinking what's right? I'll put a stop to it!"

Tom received an awful beating. But Legree did not break down his spirit. Tom disobeyed Legree a second time. This time Legree killed him.

Shortly after Tom's murder, the story of

In the South, the harsh treatment of slaves was common practice. But during the 1850s, more and more Northerners came to oppose it.

THE
ROAD TO

1846	1848	1850	1852	1854

1849
Harriet Tubman escapes to Philadelphia.

1850
Compromise of 1850 becomes law.

1851
Harriet Beecher Stowe publishes *Uncle Tom's Cabin.*

1854
Kansas–Nebraska Act allows settlers the choice of whether or not to have slaves.

WAR

1856   **1858**   **1860**

1857   **1859**

Dred Scott   John Brown found
decision   guilty of treason
                  and hanged.

UNIT 4

Uncle Tom's Cabin ended. It was not a true story, but it was based on real people and events. This novel was written in 1851 by a woman living in Maine—Harriet Beecher Stowe.

An immediate success, *Uncle Tom's Cabin* sold more than 300,000 copies in its first year. And it was reprinted again and again.

Why was *Uncle Tom's Cabin* so popular? The book had a powerful effect. For the first time, many Northerners saw the terrible results of Southern slavery. This story made many Northerners angry. Suddenly, those who had no opinion about slavery disapproved of it.

Southerners also became angry when they read *Uncle Tom's Cabin.* But they were upset because they thought the story gave the wrong picture of slavery. They said it only showed the harmful effects of slavery and not enough of its "benefits."

Uncle Tom's Cabin aggravated tensions between the North and South. In the

Frederick Douglass, an escaped slave, became a powerful voice in the anti-slavery movement.

1850s, more and more people began to wonder whether the Union could hold together.

King Cotton

The dispute between the North and South centered on the slavery question. But there were other tensions between the regions which were different in so many ways. In fact, these areas were beginning to seem like two separate nations.

There were differences in the way the people of the two regions made their living. Most of the South's wealth came from farming. Many crops were raised, but cotton was the most important. "Cotton is king," Southerners said. The South's cotton was sold to cloth factories in the North and in Europe.

Cotton and other crops were raised on large farms or plantations. Plantation owners felt they needed cheap slave labor to make a profit. Many white people in the South accepted slavery—even if they did not own slaves themselves. They believed black slaves and "king cotton" were part of the Southern way of life.

Most Southern whites did not own slaves. Only about one white Southerner in four was a slave owner. Yet many of the two million black men, women, and children lived on large plantations. The owners of large plantations were very powerful. They controlled government and ran things their way.

Northern Abolition

Life in the North was strikingly different from that in the South. Most Northerners lived on small farms. Farmers ran their own farms with the help of their families and sometimes hired hands.

At the same time, major changes were taking place in the North. Gradually, more of its wealth was coming from manufacturing than from agriculture. The North already had far more mills, factories, and railroads than the South. These mills and factories turned out 10 times as many goods as Southern factories. Manufacturing and business were becoming the Northern way of life. This way of life depended on free labor—not slavery.

Another difference between North and South was slavery. The Northern abolitionist movement began in the 1830s. For 20 years, most Northerners were not con-

cerned with slavery. But two events in the early 1850s made many Northerners change their minds. One was the publishing of *Uncle Tom's Cabin*. The other was the Fugitive Slave Act passed by Congress. The Fugitive Slave Act was part of the Compromise of 1850. The Act said Northerners had to help capture slaves who had escaped from the South. Northerners were forced to support Southern slavery whether they liked it or not. Many were angered by this.

The problem of runaway slaves troubled many Southerners. Not that many slaves escaped, but those that did were proof that some blacks would risk everything to escape the bonds of slavery.

Some former slaves became leaders in the anti-slavery movement. Frederick Douglass spoke against slavery in many parts of the North. Another famous runaway, Harriet Tubman, took more direct action. After her own escape from slavery, she risked death to help hundreds of other slaves escape from the South.

Western Slavery

Southerners continued to defend slavery as a way of life and as an economic system. Many of them wanted to

COLORED PEOPLE
OF BOSTON, ONE & ALL,
You are hereby respectfully CAUTIONED and advised, to avoid conversing with the
Watchmen and Police Officers of Boston,
For since the recent ORDER OF THE MAYOR & ALDERMEN, they are empowered to act as
KIDNAPPERS
AND
Slave Catchers,
And they have already been actually employed in KIDNAPPING, CATCHING, AND KEEPING SLAVES. Therefore, if you value your LIBERTY, and the *Welfare of the Fugitives* among you, *Shun* them in every possible manner, as so many *HOUNDS* on the track of the most unfortunate of your race.
Keep a Sharp Look Out for KIDNAPPERS, and have TOP EYE open.
APRIL 24, 1851.

In the North, sometimes free blacks as well as escaped slaves were stolen and forced into slavery.

see slavery spread into the western territories. The Compromise of 1850 prohibited slavery in California. But it left the question unsettled elsewhere.

In 1854, Congress reopened the slavery issue in western lands. The **Kansas–Nebraska Act** allowed settlers to choose for themselves whether or not to allow slavery. Fighting broke out in Kansas between those who favored slavery and those who opposed it. The conflict became known as Bleeding Kansas.

The possible spread of slavery into Kansas outraged abolitionists. It also angered a group of Northerners called **Free-Soilers.** Like abolitionists, Free-Soilers opposed slavery, but they did not demand that slavery be abolished in the South. They only wanted to keep it from spreading into new territories.

Now the struggle in Kansas united the Free-Soilers and abolitionists against the South. In the mid-1850s, they formed a new political party called the Republican party. Its major goal was to keep slavery from spreading into western territories.

Conflict Spreads

In 1857, the U.S. Supreme Court tried to put one legal question regarding slavery to rest. In the Dred Scott case, it ruled that Congress could not keep slavery out of the territories. This made Northerners even angrier than before.

Harriet Beecher Stowe's *Uncle Tom's Cabin* was one of the most talked-about novels of the 1800s. It added fuel to the fiery slavery debate that eventually split the nation.

Two years later, a white Northerner named John Brown led an unsuccessful slave revolt in Virginia. Northerners hailed Brown as a hero, while Southerners feared that most of the North was now against them.

In 1860, the Republican candidate for president was Abraham Lincoln. Lincoln was a Free-Soiler, not an abolitionist. But Southerners thought all Republicans threatened their way of life. Lincoln did not win a single Southern state, but he swept the North and was elected president.

Angry Southerners decided that they had had enough. On December 24, 1860, a few weeks after the election of Abraham Lincoln, South Carolina declared its independence from the Union. Other Southern states followed and formed the Confederate States of America. Then, on April 12, 1861, Southerners fired cannons at Fort Sumter in Charleston, South Carolina. They were the first shots of a long and terrible civil war.

Black slaves bring their "whole weeks picking" in carts and barrels to the plantation owner in this mid-19th century American primitive painting. Children often worked alongside men and women of all ages in the field.

15 SHE RAN A RAILROAD

Harriet Tubman [far left] posed for this photograph with a few of the hundreds of slaves she led to freedom on the Underground Railroad. Tubman risked her life every time she ventured South.

A poster in a Southern railroad station read:

WANTED—dead or alive—
Harriet Tubman.
A reward of $40,000 is offered for capture.

Who was Harriet Tubman, and why was such a large reward offered for her capture? The answer is in the story of her life. Harriet Tubman was born a slave on a Maryland plantation in 1821. As a child, she was whipped constantly. Harriet had scars on her neck from these beatings. Once when she was 14, she tried to save a slave

from a whipping. She stood in the way of the overseer with the whip. The slave started to run. Then the boss picked up a heavy iron weight. He threw it at the slave, but it struck Harriet's head instead and she fell to the ground. For days Harriet lay near death. Finally Harriet grew stronger, but she never got completely well. She had a deep scar where the iron weight had hit her. For the rest of her life, Harriet had strange spells of suddenly falling asleep.

Dash to Freedom

Tubman dreamed of escaping to the

AMERICAN ADVENTURES

North where there was no slavery. One night, sometime around 1849, she and two of her brothers made a break for freedom and headed North. Her brothers soon became frightened and turned back, but Tubman went on alone. She hid by day and moved north by night, guided by the North Star. She was also helped by the **Underground Railroad.** This was not a railroad at all. It was a secret escape route to the North. But the "railroad" did have many "stations." These were the homes of people who hid slaves by day and sent them on to other homes after dark. This secret **network** (connected group) stretched from the South to the North and then on to Canada. With its help, Tubman finally reached Philadelphia.

Slavery had long been outlawed in Pennsylvania. Tubman was free at last. But she was not content. She wanted to help her family and other slaves to escape. Soon she became a "conductor" on the Underground Railroad. She made trip after trip to the South to lead groups of slaves to freedom. In all, she helped free more than 300 slaves. Among them were her aged parents and the rest of her family. Southern slave owners tried again and again to capture her. Finally they offered the $40,000 reward.

Rescue Work

On one trip, Tubman led 11 slaves

The promise of freedom was important enough for even this handicapped, elderly gentleman to risk the hardships of the long dangerous escape through the Underground Railroad.

through the woods. They were cold and hungry. It was so dark they couldn't see each other. Yet Harriet Tubman led them as if the sun were shining. The slaves spoke in whispers. They were frightened, and they could hear dogs barking. They knew that **slave catchers** (people who made money catching escaped slaves) were after them.

Tubman knew of a stream nearby. It was icy cold, but she told the slaves to go into the water. Tubman knew the dogs could not smell them in the water and track them down. The slaves stayed in the water until they no longer heard the dogs barking.

They walked for days and weeks, and still they were far from freedom. Their goal on this trip was Canada. Why

Canada instead of one of the Northern states? Congress passed the Fugitive Slave Act in 1850. This law was part of Henry Clay's compromise of that year. It said that any runaway slaves caught in the North would have to be sent back South. So after 1850, the Underground Railroad ended in Canada.

The group went on together, hiding in swamps when danger was near. One day while they were hiding, Tubman began to wonder where the man from the next "station" was. He was very late. She prayed that the Underground Railroad had not let her down. Finally a man did come. He told Tubman he had a horse and wagon and food in his barn. That night Tubman went to the barn. There

Underground Railroad Routes, 1840–1860

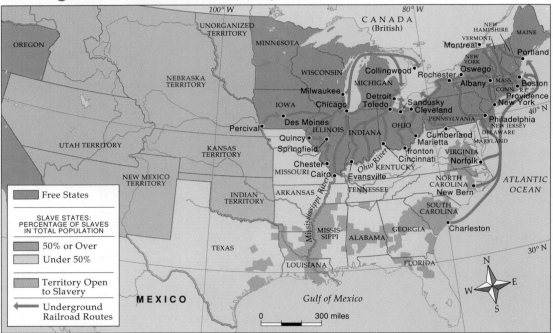

Imagine you are a slave traveling along the Underground Railroad in 1850. Through what states and cities would you travel if you were going from Cairo, Illinois to Collingwood, Canada? From New Bern, North Carolina to Montreal?

AMERICAN ADVENTURES

was everything the man had promised. "Praise God," the slaves said. They were another step closer to freedom.

Tubman's journeys were almost always dangerous. They took careful planning and great skill. There was usually a danger of being arrested. To reduce this danger, Tubman had one important rule. No slave should think of surrender or of returning South. Any slave who did was threatened with death.

In time, Tubman became known as the Moses of her people. Now and then she spoke to Northern anti-slavery groups of the hazards she had faced. Among her own people, she was considered a true heroine. She knew the hardships of slavery and had the courage to help others overcome them.

Harriet Tubman fought slavery in every way she could. During the Civil War, she served Union troops as a nurse and spy.

CHAPTER CHECK

WORD MATCH
1. slave catchers
2. Underground Railroad
3. "conductor"
4. network
5. "stations"

a. homes of people who hid slaves by day and sent them north at night
b. people who make money catching escaped slaves
c. connected group
d. secret escape route for slaves
e. person in charge of slaves during transport on the Underground Railroad

QUICK QUIZ
1. How did Harriet Tubman escape slavery, and what did she do after she gained her freedom?
2. What was Tubman's one important rule?

THINK ABOUT IT
1. By helping slaves to escape, Tubman broke the law—The Fugitive Slave Act of 1850 forbade it. Do you think Tubman was wrong for breaking this law? Why or why not?
2. If you were alive during her time and met Tubman, would you have helped her? Why or why not?

Frederick Douglass utilized his precious education by helping others learn of the evils of slavery. In this painting by Jacob Lawrence, a modern black artist, Douglass is shown putting out his antislavery newspaper, *The North Star*.

"I will run away. I will not stand it," said Frederick Douglass about his early life. "I would rather be killed running than die as a slave." He was making a speech in Nantucket, Massachusetts, in August of 1841. The audience was shocked. This tall, handsome young man had once been a slave!

This man, who became one of the greatest leaders of the fight against slavery, had been born a slave on a Maryland plantation in 1817. While still a boy, Frederick was sent to live with his master's relatives in Baltimore. The wife of his new master taught him to read and write. For Frederick, nothing was more exciting. But then Frederick's master stopped his lessons. He did not think it was good for a slave to read and write. In fact, it was against the law to teach a slave such things. White Southerners did not want slaves to get any "dangerous ideas."

When his lessons stopped, Frederick knew

for the first time how truly evil slavery really was. He dreamed of freedom from that day on.

Resisting Slavery

When he was 16, Douglass had his darkest hours as a slave. His master hired him out to a very cruel man named Edward Covey. Covey was known as a slave breaker, because he knew how to break the spirit of any slave who did not obey him. Covey whipped Douglass without mercy many times. At last Douglass could take it no more. When Covey tried to whip him again, Douglass put up his fists. He and Covey fought for nearly two hours. Finally Covey quit. He never tried to give Douglass a whipping again. Douglass was lucky. Some slaves who fought back were severely punished—or even killed.

Frederick Douglass was 21 when he decided to escape to New York. At the time, he was working in a Baltimore shipyard. He borrowed the papers of a free black sailor and dressed himself in a seaman's outfit. Then he got on a train headed North. It was a dangerous trip. Slave catchers were always on the lookout for runaway blacks. But Douglass made it safely to New York. There he got in touch with people who belonged to the Underground Railroad. They sent him to New Bedford, Massachusetts.

Douglass wanted to live quietly. He did not want to do anything that would let slave catchers know where he was. Then one day he was asked to speak at an anti-slavery meeting in Nantucket. Despite the danger, he accepted. Soon other abolitionists wanted to hear him speak.

Douglass was a fine speaker. Large

Frederick Douglass was the son of a black slave mother and an unknown white father. He named himself Douglass after the hero of *The Lady of the Lake* by Sir Walter Scott.

crowds came to hear him wherever he went. Sometimes they were not very friendly. In a few towns, Douglass was beaten by angry mobs (wild crowds of people). But he did not give up speaking.

Escaping From Slave Catchers

Douglass wrote all about his life as a slave in his book, *The Narrative of the Life of Frederick Douglass*. He named his masters and gave his own real name. Soon slave catchers were sent to arrest him. Douglass went to England to escape them. Douglass made many friends in England. Some of Douglass's friends paid for his freedom.

In 1847, Douglass returned to the United States. He moved to Rochester,

New York, and started an anti-slavery newspaper. He called it *The North Star* after the star that guided runaway slaves at night. The newspaper did not bring in much money. Yet Douglass managed to keep it going over the next 15 years. It was the first abolitionist newspaper started by a black, and it gave a voice to other black writers. It was read by many abolitionists—both black and white.

During these years, Douglass kept up his attack on slavery. His **editorials** (statements of opinion in newspapers or magazines) tried to show why slavery was wrong. Douglass helped many runaway slaves, and gave them money he had earned making speeches. His home in Rochester, New York, was a station on the Underground Railroad.

Douglass also called for equal treatment of the free black people of the North. He protested "whites only" signs in public places. He quarreled with black barbers who would cut only white men's hair. Moreover, Douglass called for equal treatment of women. He attended the Woman's Rights Convention in Seneca Falls, New York, in 1848.

The fight against slavery and the fight for women's equality were linked. In this battle for human rights, Frederick Douglass was one of the greatest heroes.

One of the cruelest aspects of slavery that Frederick Douglass and other abolitionists campaigned against was the practice of selling human beings in markets like this one. Blacks born into slavery and free blacks kidnapped from the North were lined up and auctioned off to the highest bidders.

THE RESURRECTION OF HENRY BOX BROWN AT PHILADELPHIA.
Who escaped from Richmond Va. in a Box 3 feet long 2½ ft. deep and 2 ft wide

Slaves found many ways to escape to freedom. This cartoon, called "The Resurrection of Henry Box Brown at Philadelphia," shows how a slave made his way North curled up in a tiny wooden box.

CHAPTER CHECK

WORD MATCH
1. Seneca Falls, New York
2. slave breaker
3. editorials
4. Nantucket, Massachusetts
5. mobs

a. place where Douglass gave his first speech
b. crushed the spirit of slaves who didn't follow orders
c. site of first women's rights convention
d. wild crowds of people
e. statements of opinion in a newspaper or magazine

QUICK QUIZ
1. What happened to young Frederick Douglass that made him determined to be free?
2. Why did Douglass have to escape to England? What happened to him there?
3. What was *The North Star* and why was it important?

THINK ABOUT IT
1. Frederick Douglass could have spent his life in hiding. Instead, he chose to speak and write publicly against the evils of slavery. Why do you think he made this choice?
2. Douglass wanted freedom for black slaves, but he also called for the equal treatment of women. How do you think Douglass connected these issues?

17 BLEEDING KANSAS

This 1856 photograph shows a "Free-Soil Battery." These men were protecting Topeka, Kansas, home of the Free-Soilers, against attack by supporters of slavery.

In May 1856, a federal marshall named J. B. Donaldson led a mob of 800 angry men into Lawrence, Kansas, a stronghold of anti-slavery settlers. The men were armed and carried four brass cannons, which they placed at strategic points around the town.

Donaldson placed his men under the leadership of a local county sheriff who directed them to ransack the city. They rushed to the offices of two anti-slavery newspapers and destroyed everything in them. The men tried to blow up the town's hotel, and when that failed, they set it on fire.

No one was killed, but the nation was shocked by the incident. All of this violence had been done by a federal **posse** (group of citizens acting in the name of the law). It was the first time pro-slavery forces took such dramatic action against abolitionists. Although the Civil War would not begin for several more years, in 1856 it seemed like it had already broken out in the state of Kansas.

The Kansas–Nebraska Act

The trouble began in 1854, when Illinois Senator Stephen Douglas introduced a bill

AMERICAN ADVENTURES

in Congress to organize and settle the vast Nebraska Territory (present-day Nebraska and Kansas, and parts of Montana, North Dakota, South Dakota, Wyoming, and Colorado). Douglas, a powerful and popular man, was in favor of building a new railroad. He hoped it would start in his hometown of Chicago and run west through Nebraska Territory. The railroad could only be built in settled territory, which required approval by Congress.

Many Southerners opposed settlement in Nebraska Territory unless it was open to slavery. The North opposed slavery in this territory. The Nebraska Territory was located above the parallel which marked where slavery was permitted by the Missouri Compromise of 1820. Douglas offered a compromise. The territory could be divided into two parts—Kansas and Nebraska. The issue of whether slavery would be allowed would be settled by **popular sovereignty** (the right of the people to vote on an issue). In this case, the issue was whether to permit or outlaw slavery.

Reactions to the Act

After months of debate, Douglas gained the Southern support he needed in Congress and the Kansas–Nebraska Act passed. Southern states were happy because both new territories were north of the Missouri Compromise line. This meant that the South could expand slavery throughout the West. Northerners were outraged at the possibility of the territories accepting slavery. Abolitionists held meetings to protest the Kansas–Nebraska Act and demand its repeal.

Free-Soilers, who opposed the extension of slavery into the territories, also protested the Act. The abolitionists and the Free-Soilers joined together to form a new political party, the Republican party. One of the Republican party's central goals was to stop the spread of slavery into western territories. After the Kansas–Nebraska Act ruled that people in the territories should vote on slavery, both the North and the South sent settlers to these new lands. Most settlers headed to Kansas where the race for political control was fast and frantic.

Abolitionists in Massachusetts formed the New England Emigrant Aid Society. This group persuaded over 1200 New England farmers to move to Kansas. It sent them guns to fight their Southern neighbors. Henry Ward Beecher, a famous member of the New York clergy, made a speech declaring that sometimes armed violence was a necessary evil to fight slavery. Thereafter, rifles shipped from New England were called **Beecher's Bibles.**

Southerners too, rushed into Kansas. Wrote pro-slavery Senator David Atchison of Missouri: "Ten thousand families can take possession of and hold every acre of timber in the Territory of Kansas, and this secures the prairie. . . . We are playing for a mighty stake; if we win, we carry slavery to the Pacific Ocean."

Meanwhile, the Southerners who rushed into Kansas heard alarming rumors that the New England Emigrant Aid Society wanted to invade Kansas, kidnap all slaves, and take them to freedom. More than 1700 slave owners from Missouri crossed the border to Kansas in one day. They didn't plan on settling there, but they wanted to cast their votes for slavery. When the election finally took place in March 1855, pro-slavery forces won. Territorial lawmakers quickly met to make laws for the Kansas Territory.

The laws they enacted supported the Southerners. One law made slavery legal. Another said that any citizen who spoke against slavery could be put in jail. Some lawmakers opposed to slavery were driven out of the territorial legislature.

The Free-Soilers and abolitionists called the election of 1855 a fraud. The anti-slavery force held another election, but the pro-slavery group refused to take part in it. Now there were two separate governments in Kansas. The pro-slavery legislature met in Leavenworth. The anti-slavery, or free-state government met in Topeka. Each claimed to be Kansas Territory's legal government.

Bleeding Kansas

For almost a year, violence increased. Barns and farms were burned, horses were stolen, and Northern and Southern settlers shot each other. Then, a pro-slavery grand jury **indicted** (charged with a crime) members of the Topeka government for treason. A pro-slavery mob sacked Lawrence, a stronghold of the Northern settlers, on May 21, 1856. The North became outraged and the territory became known as Bleeding Kansas.

At the same time, Massachusetts Senator Charles Sumner delivered a speech in Congress that was highly critical of the South's role in Kansas. It was also personally insulting to Senator Andrew Butler of South Carolina. Three days later, Butler's nephew, Congressman Preston Brooks, approached Sumner in the Senate and beat him unconscious with a cane as horrified lawmakers looked on. Sumner never really

Kansas–Nebraska Act, 1854

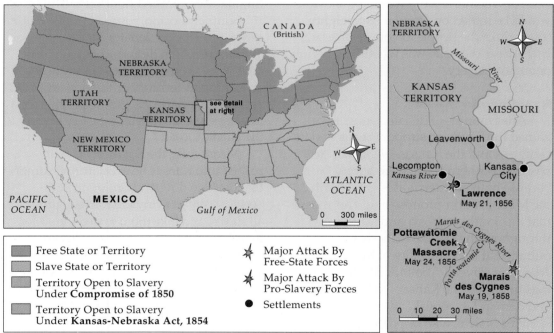

Free State or Territory
Slave State or Territory
Territory Open to Slavery Under **Compromise of 1850**
Territory Open to Slavery Under **Kansas-Nebraska Act, 1854**

Major Attack By Free-State Forces
Major Attack By Pro-Slavery Forces
Settlements

Compare this map to the map on page 285 which shows the Missouri Compromise of 1820. Were the Kansas and Nebraska territories north or south of the Missouri Compromise line?

recovered from the beating. Violence seemed to be everywhere. "Everybody here feels as if we are upon a volcano," said one South Carolinian in Washington.

To avenge the free staters of Lawrence, an abolitionist named John Brown staged a raid on the village of Pottawatomie (paht-uh-WAHT-uh-mee) Creek. With four of his sons and three other men, he attacked the settlement, shooting and killing five men and boys. None of the victims were slave owners, but they were known to have been supporters of slavery.

The next morning, people heard about the murders at Pottawatomie Creek. Angry farmers from Missouri crossed the Kansas border to form a Southern militia. Settlers in Kansas formed a Northern militia.

For months, the two forces threatened to attack each other. They never came to battle, but reprisals (acts of revenge) continued to take place all over Kansas. The free staters tilled their fields in groups for safety, and they always carried their rifles.

Abolitionists Harriet and Franklin Adams and their eight children were constant targets of pro-slavery forces. One of the Adams' children later recalled that men entered and searched their house for weapons and valuables. While Franklin was away, the children were "frightened . . . and amazed at mother when she [scolded] the men for rummaging thru her wardrobe and bureau and messing up the house."

In the "battle" of Osawatomie (OH-sa-WAHT-uh-mee), pro-slavery men attacked the home base of John Brown, killing 12 or more and wounding many others. More houses and barns were burned and a pro-slavery mob entered Leavenworth to threaten the lives of 50 free-state leaders if they didn't leave the territory. The atmosphere of violence and anger continued in Kansas until the Civil War began a few years later.

CHAPTER CHECK

WORD MATCH

1. posse
2. popular sovereignty
3. indicted
4. Beecher's Bibles
5. reprisals

a. charged with a crime
b. acts of revenge
c. group of citizens organized to carry out the law
d. the right of people to vote on an issue
e. rifles shipped from New England

QUICK QUIZ

1. What was the Kansas–Nebraska Act? What prompted the term Bleeding Kansas?
2. Why did two governments form in the new state of Kansas? What were their capitals?
3. What was the role of John Brown in the fight over Kansas? How did his enemies take revenge?

THINK ABOUT IT

1. Do you think the question of slavery could have been settled without violence? Why?
2. Reverend Henry Ward Beecher made a speech declaring that sometimes armed violence is necessary to oppose an evil like slavery. Would you favor the use of force against an evil law?

18 THE DRED SCOTT CASE

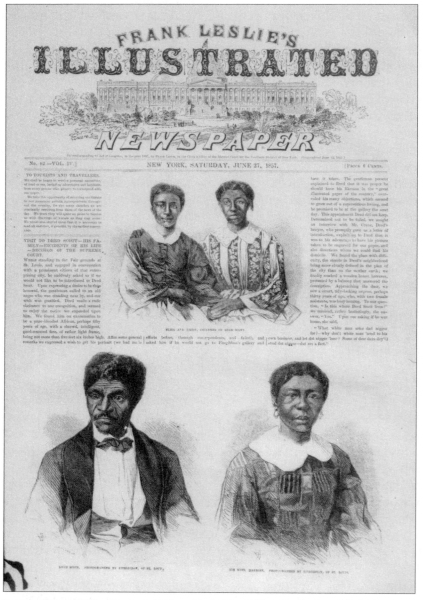

Dred and Harriet Scott were slaves who believed they had a legal right to freedom. Scott took his case all the way to the U.S. Supreme Court.

Were slaves human beings with rights—or were they just property? If they were taken into a state or territory that did not allow slavery, did they become free—or remain slaves? Could a slave become a citizen?

These questions deeply divided the nation in the 1850s. By this time, many Northerners had joined the abolitionist movement. The abolitionists wanted to abolish slavery altogether.

In the South, most whites believed that they had a right to own slaves. Some also believed that they had a right to take their slaves with them into any part of the country, even free states and free territories. These people believed that the abolitionists were nothing but troublemakers. Some Northerners agreed.

In 1857, it looked as if the United States Supreme Court would finally settle the question of slavery in the territories. It had decided to hear the case of a black couple named Dred and Harriet Scott. Years earlier, Scott and his wife, both slaves, had been taken by their master from the slave state of Missouri to the free state of Illinois. Later, Dred Scott had lived with his master in the free Wisconsin Territory. Then they had been brought back to Missouri.

A group of abolitionists decided to help the Scotts win their freedom. They argued that the Scotts became free people when they were taken to a free state and a free territory. They were no longer slaves when they returned to Missouri. This case was heard first in the state court and then in the federal court of Missouri. Finally, it came before the U.S. Supreme Court.

Roger Taney, the chief justice of the Supreme Court, had been appointed by Andrew Jackson in 1836. The Supreme Court was highly respected in the country. Taney had always avoided cases on issues—such as slavery—that he thought had more to do with politics than law. But Taney agreed to take on the Dred Scott case. He hoped to settle a question that was tearing the nation apart.

On March 6, 1857, the Supreme Court announced its decision. Five of the justices, including Taney, were Southerners. Seven were Democrats. Excitement was high. As the justices entered the courtroom, a hush fell over the crowd.

Separate Opinions

Each of the justices issued a separate **opinion** (formal statement) in the case. Taney and six other justices decided against Dred Scott.

Dred Scott was a slave who tried to win his freedom in court. The 1857 Dred Scott decision declared that no black, either free or slave, could claim the rights of U.S. citizenship.

Eastman Johnson's painting, *Negro Life in the South*, portrays black life in the South in the turbulent decade before the Civil War. The situation for Southern blacks had been quite bleak since the Dred Scott decision in 1857.

On the important issue of slavery in the territories, Taney and five other justices declared that Congress could not keep slavery out. Slaves were property, Taney argued, just like clothes or horses. The Fifth Amendment to the Constitution said that no person could have his property taken away without **due process of law** (an orderly set of rules for bringing a lawsuit, or a person accused of a crime, to trial). Congress could not pass laws that would take away a Northerner's right to own horses. Neither could it take away a Southerner's right to own slaves.

The Missouri Compromise of 1820 drew a line through the territory of the Louisiana Purchase along Missouri's southern border. Slavery was illegal north of this line, except in Missouri. Now the Court was saying that the Missouri Compromise went against the Constitution. The Missouri Compromise denied slaveholders their right to own property (meaning slaves).

Judicial Review

In the Dred Scott case, the Supreme Court overturned the Missouri Com-

They said Dred Scott was still a slave. Since slaves were not citizens, Scott could not bring **suit** (a legal case) in a federal court.

Taney went even further. He claimed that the writers of the Constitution did not intend for blacks to become citizens. Free blacks had gained the right to vote in certain states after 1787. But, said Taney, that did not make them U.S. citizens. Taney's argument was very weak. Only two justices agreed with him on this point. Free blacks had, in fact, been citizens of some states for many years. And the Constitution (Article IV, Section 2) gave the citizens of each state the rights of U.S. citizens.

promise of 1820. It was the first time since 1803 that the Court used its power of judicial review and declared an **act of Congress** (federal law) unconstitutional. And it was the first time the Court had ever thrown out a major act of Congress.

Many Southerners were pleased by the Court's decision. Slave owners felt that they had won a great victory. Most Northerners were angry. The abolitionists were very discouraged. Protest meetings were held in the North and the West. More and more people felt drawn to the abolitionist movement and the Republican party. The Republicans were against the spread of slavery into the territories.

The Republicans said that the Court had given an opinion in the Dred Scott case, not a decision. They charged that the Court had gone far beyond the legal question: Were Dred and Harriet Scott still slaves?

After their case was decided, both Harriet and Dred Scott were granted their freedom by their master. But the Dred Scott case did not end the dispute (argument) over slavery. Instead, it deepened the division between the North and the South. Many feared that these great differences could not be settled peacefully. Four years later, Americans were fighting each other in the Civil War.

CHAPTER CHECK

WORD MATCH
1. opinion
2. suit
3. due process of law
4. dispute
5. act of Congress

a. legal proceeding
b. argument
c. formal statement
d. law
e. the set of rules that must be followed to reach a legal trial

QUICK QUIZ
1. Why did Dred and Harriet Scott believe they were free?
2. Why did the Supreme Court say Scott could not bring his suit to federal court?
3. How did Chief Justice Taney use the Fifth Amendment to support his opinions?

THINK ABOUT IT
1. How do you think the Supreme Court's ruling in the Dred Scott case was influenced by the prejudices of the justices? Do you think justices today are influenced by personal prejudices?
2. Chief Justice Taney said that even though free blacks had voted since 1787, they were not citizens. What do you think of his decision?

CHAPTER 19 RAID ON HARPERS FERRY

This painting, *The Last Moments of John Brown,* shows the way some Northerners imagined Brown met his death—saluted as a hero by a black woman and her child.

"Old Brown," as he was often called, was a restless man. For most of his life, John Brown had floated from place to place and job to job. In the 1840s, he became interested in helping black slaves. Within the next few years, he became passionate about this cause.

In 1855, he followed five of his sons to Kansas Territory. There, he and his sons killed five pro-slavery Southern men in retaliation for the sacking of Lawrence. Brown thought God intended his victims to die. He was sure that God was against slavery. Brown was also sure that bloodshed was the only way to end slavery.

After the raid in Kansas, Brown set out on the great plan of his life. He hoped to raise a small army in the North and move South. He would set up a stronghold in the mountains of Virginia. From there, he would help to free Virginia's slaves. After this, he hoped that slaves all over the South would rise up and kill their masters. And this, Brown thought, would end slavery in the United States once and for all.

The plan was so daring that some people later called it insane. Yet Brown kept looking for ways to put his ideas into action. He raised money among abolitionists—first in upstate New York, then in Boston. He told his friends that he could not fail. "If God be for us," he quoted from the Bible, "who can be against us?"

Time of Testing

In July 1859, Brown rented a farm near the Virginia–Maryland border. The farm was about five miles from Harpers Ferry where federal arms were stored. Brown and his men—16 whites and 5 blacks—attacked Harpers Ferry on October 16. They captured the federal warehouse where guns were stored. Some of Brown's men rounded up slave owners and took them prisoner.

Brown's plans now called for a march to the Virginia mountains. From there he and his men would start a war against slavery in the South. But Brown stalled, waiting for local slaves to join him. The slaves didn't appear, perhaps because they feared federal troops nearby. Instead of fleeing, Brown took refuge with his men in

John Brown (1800–1859) fiercely believed slavery was evil. He once ran a "station" on the Underground Railroad, but later turned to violence.

the fire-engine house.

The next day, 1500 U.S. soldiers and marines surrounded the engine house. They were commanded by Colonel Robert E. Lee, the future military leader of the South. Brown and his men refused to surrender, even though their fight was hopeless. One by one, they were shot down.

The next morning, Brown was again asked to surrender. One of his sons was dead, and another dying. Brown himself was wounded. Yet he still refused to give up. Marines rushed the building and battered down the door. An officer entered and knocked Brown out with his sword.

Trial for Treason

A week after being captured, Brown was put on trial for treason. His lawyers told him to make a **plea** (excuse) of insanity, but Brown refused to do so. He said he knew what he was doing. He had come to free the slaves. What he had done, he said, "was not wrong, but right." He said that freeing slaves was "the greatest service man can render [give] to God."

During the trial and after it, Brown handled himself with great dignity. Virginia's Governor Wise was moved to call him "a man of clear head" and "courage." Even so, a jury found Brown guilty of treason. On December 2, 1859, he was hanged at Charles Town, Virginia (now in West Virginia).

Northern newspapers outdid themselves in praising Brown. Abolitionists spoke of him as if he were a saint. One famous writer, Louisa May Alcott, said the **gallows** (structure used for hanging) were "a stepping stone to Heaven" for Brown.

Some went even further. They used Brown's death to make a protest against the South and all of its slave owners. One abolitionist, Wendell Phillips, was especially outraged. "John Brown has twice as much right to hang Governor Wise," Phillips said, "as Governor Wise has to hang him." Phillips and others went on to call for slave uprisings.

Southerners did not take Northern protests lightly. Some of them may have admired Brown's actions, but they did not admire his goals. These Southerners were even more disturbed to learn that Brown had drawn support from some famous people in the North such as Senator Charles Sumner. Some Southerners feared that Northerners were about to promote terror all over the South.

"Is the Union really a Union at all?" some Southerners asked. By early 1860, this question became a vital one. Within a few months, Americans would elect a new president. It was becoming clear that the future of the Union would depend heavily on the president they chose.

This peaceful and pretty view of Harpers Ferry, Virginia (now West Virginia), gives no hint of the violence on October 16, 1859, when John Brown and 21 other rebels attacked the arsenal there.

To many Northerners, John Brown's rebellion was an act of great courage. To many Southerners, it seemed the act of a wicked and insane criminal. After being tried and convicted, Brown was hanged. This 1942 painting by Horace Pippin, a black American artist, shows Brown being taken to his execution in the winter of 1859.

CHAPTER CHECK

WORD MATCH

1. Robert E. Lee
2. plea
3. Louisa May Alcott
4. gallows
5. John Brown

a. excuse
b. future leader for the South during Civil War
c. leader of raid on Harpers Ferry
d. a structure used for carrying out the death sentence by hanging
e. a famous writer and abolitionist who praised John Brown as a saint

QUICK QUIZ

1. What did John Brown hope to accomplish by his raid on Harpers Ferry?
2. How did John Brown's lawyers want him to plead in court? Why did they advise that?
3. What was the reaction among abolitionists concerning Brown's sentence?

THINK ABOUT IT

1. Do you think John Brown was a great man for what he did? Why or why not?
2. Brown believed freeing the slaves was right, that it was God's work. He said nothing he did to achieve this—even murder—was wrong. What do you think?

20 THE UNION BREAKS UP

Abraham Lincoln (1809–1865) gained national attention in 1858 when he campaigned for an Illinois Senate seat. He lost the election, but people remembered his sharp mind and quick wit.

The Chicago convention hall was overflowing. Thousands of people jammed into the building, cheering, whistling, and stomping. The noise was so intense, one reporter said, that "a herd of buffalos or lions could not have made a more tremendous roaring."

What was all the noise about? The **Republican party**, in the third day of its national convention, was trying to pick its candidate for president. All day long, the excitement—and the noise level—grew as the delegates voted once, twice, three times. By the third ballot, they had picked their man. He was Abraham Lincoln, the tall, unpolished-looking but eloquent lawyer from Springfield, Illinois.

From Lincoln's early life, few people would have predicted this success. Lincoln was born in 1809 in a rough, one-room log cabin in Kentucky. His parents were poor, uneducated farmers who struggled to make a living from their land.

Neither young Abe nor his sister Sarah attended school very often. There was too much work to do on the farm.

But once in a while, they would walk together to the local "blab" school. There, students of all ages gathered in one room and said their lessons aloud—all at the same time.

Once Abe learned to read, there was no stopping him. He read whatever books or newspapers he could find, whenever he had a spare minute. A cousin later remembered, "I never saw Abe after he was twelve that he didn't have a book in his hand or in his pocket. It didn't seem natural to see a feller read like that."

Like his father Thomas, Abe loved to tell stories and make people laugh. But he also had a quiet, moody side.

Entering Politics

As a young man, Lincoln moved to New Salem, Illinois, and later to Springfield. He became interested in politics and the law, winning a seat in the Illinois State Legislature in 1834. In 1837, after studying law on his own for three years, he became an attorney. From 1847 to 1849, Lincoln served in the U.S. House of Representatives.

In the 1850s, Lincoln became drawn to the growing national debate over slavery. He was very upset by the passage in 1854 of the Kansas– Nebraska Act. This law allowed each territory to decide for itself whether it would allow slavery within its borders.

Although Lincoln believed slavery was

In 1860, Lincoln again ran against Stephen A. Douglas—and this time he won. This button was worn by one of Lincoln's supporters.

wrong, he was not an abolitionist. He did not propose trying to **ban** (an official order not allowing something) slavery in places where it already existed, partly because he didn't think it was possible. Lincoln opposed the spread of slavery. He felt the United States should not encourage the growth of a practice that contradicted so many of the ideals on which the nation was founded.

Lincoln believed that the framers of the Constitution had wanted and expected slavery to eventually die out of its own accord. He was willing to let that happen. But he was not willing to watch slavery expand into new areas. The result, he feared, would be that slavery would become legal all over the nation.

Running for the Senate

In 1858, Lincoln campaigned for the U.S. Senate as a member of the newly formed Republican party. He ran against U.S. Senator Stephen A. Douglas, a Democrat who was up for reelection. Douglas had pushed strongly for the Kansas– Nebraska Act. He believed in popular sovereignty.

During the Senate campaign, Lincoln and Douglas held a series of seven debates in small towns in Illinois. The debates were well-attended, with people coming from miles around to hear the two candidates. The crowd sometimes joined in the debates, shouting remarks of agreement or protest.

Lincoln lost the election for the Senate seat. But the debates made him famous all over the nation. People now knew him as a skillful and convincing orator.

A Leader for the North

In the next several months, Lincoln traveled through the North making passionate speeches against slavery. People in the North began to think of him as a leader. On May 18, 1860, in that frenzied Chicago convention hall, the Republican party chose him as its candidate for president.

From the start, it seemed that Lincoln had a good chance to win. The **Democratic party** was divided between Southerners and Northerners. Southern and Northern Democrats could not agree on a candidate, so they ran two. This weakened the Democrats' chances of winning.

The Northern Democrats picked Stephen A. Douglas. The Southerners chose John C. Breckinridge, a strong supporter of slavery. A third party, the Constitutional Union party, nominated John Bell of Tennessee.

In those days, presidential candidates usually did not campaign for themselves. Lincoln stayed in Springfield through the summer and fall of 1860. But his supporters campaigned hard for him all over the North. They emphasized his reputation for honesty and his youth spent on the frontier. Lincoln was a man of the people, they said. Lincoln's supporters also emphasized the threat of slavery spreading to all parts of the nation if a Democrat were to win.

Meanwhile, the South was in an uproar. Southern leaders were sure that Lincoln, if elected, would try to destroy their way of life. Some of them declared that their states would secede from the Union if Lincoln won. One Georgia newspaper wrote: "Let the consequences be what they may . . . the South will never submit to such humiliation and degradation as the election of Abraham Lincoln."

Some Northern leaders wanted Lincoln to make a statement that would reassure the South. But Lincoln kept silent. He had no intention of **tampering** (interfering in a bad way) with slavery in the states where it already existed, but he opposed extending slavery to new areas.

A New President

On November 6, 1860, Lincoln won the election. He defeated Douglas by about 500,000 votes. On December 20, South Carolina seceded, declaring that it was no longer part of the Union. By February 1, six other states had joined South Carolina.

Lincoln was to be sworn in on March 4, 1861. On February 11, he left Springfield for Washington. He traveled by train, taking a roundabout route through the North. He made many stops along the way to speak to the people that had gathered to see their new president.

In Lincoln's inaugural address, he said that no state had the right to secede from the Union. But he also made the promise to Southern states that "the government will not assail you, unless you first assail it." He offered the South peace. "We are not enemies, but friends," he said. "We must be friends."

It was too late. The South had made up its mind. Seven Southern states—South Carolina, Mississippi, Florida, Alabama, Georgia, Louisiana, and Texas —had seceded from the Union. They formed the Confederate States of America. In a few weeks, the first shots of the Civil War would ring out.

The shell blasts at Fort Sumter on April 12,1861, signaled the beginning of the Civil War. Though the drawing is exaggerated, it reflects the waves of shock people felt with a new war on the horizon.

CHAPTER CHECK

WORD MATCH
1. "blab" school
2. tampering
3. ban
4. Democratic party
5. Republican party

a. party of Lincoln
b. a place for learning where students recited lessons aloud
c. interfere with in a bad way
d. nominated two presidential candidates in 1860
e. an official order not to allow something

QUICK QUIZ
1. What was Abraham Lincoln's position on slavery?
2. Why did the South secede when Lincoln was elected president?
3. What message did Lincoln convey to the South in his inaugural address?

THINK ABOUT IT
1. What do you think Lincoln meant by saying "the government will not assail you, unless you first assail it."
2. Why do you think Lincoln passionately opposed slavery? In what ways do you think his early life may have affected his views on slavery?

21 FORT SUMTER

The first shots of the U.S. Civil War (1861–1865) were fired at Fort Sumter, South Carolina. After the South's victory there, Confederate troops raised their new national flag—the Stars and Bars.

The time: 4:30 in the morning.
The date: April 12, 1861.
The place: Charleston, South Carolina.
Suddenly, a cannon roars. A shell sails across Charleston harbor and bursts on Fort Sumter. It is the first shot fired in the Civil War.

Why were Americans firing on other Americans? Southerners feared that Abraham Lincoln would do away with slavery if he had the chance. After Lincoln was elected president, seven Southern states seceded from the Union and set up the Confederate States of America. They now claimed they were a new nation, separate from the United States. They even formed their own army, in case President Lincoln tried to force them back into the Union.

The soldiers of the Confederacy were often called Johnny Rebs, or Rebels, both by themselves and by Union troops. Union soldiers were usually called Yanks

THE UNION IS DISSOLVED!

This flyer headline printed by a Charleston newspaper announced the news that South Carolina had withdrawn from the Union. It was the first of 11 states to do so after word of Lincoln's election spread.

by the Confederates.

The Confederate Army began to take over the Union forts in the South. Some of the soldiers in the forts were Southerners. Many of them joined the Confederate Army. Others who said they were loyal to the United States were sent North.

"Surrender the Fort!"

One Union fort that held out was in Charleston, South Carolina. It was Fort Sumter, an old brick building on an island in the harbor. It was commanded by Major Robert Anderson. Anderson held the fort with 8 officers and 68 men. They expected trouble, but they were ready. "Sir," one of Anderson's men said, "we'll fight off those Johnny Rebs even if we have to use our fists."

From the shore, a Rebel soldier shouted, "Surrender, Yanks! Give up the fort or get blown to kingdom come!"

Fort Sumter was very low on food and ammunition. The Rebels would not allow any supplies from shore to reach the fort. So Major Anderson sent President Lincoln a message. He said that he had to have fresh supplies or he would be forced to surrender. Lincoln decided to send some supplies by ship to help the fort.

General Pierre Beauregard (BOH-ruh-gahrd) was the commander of the Rebel Army in Charleston. The Confederate government gave him these orders: If the fort did not surrender, he must take it by force. On April 11, Beauregard sent a message to Major Anderson. General Beauregard ordered him to give up the fort. Anderson refused. But he also said, "If you do not batter the fort to pieces, we shall be starved out in a few days."

There was no real need for the Rebels to fire on Fort Sumter. All they had to do was stop any supply ships from reaching the fort. But the South wanted to show that it was ready to fight for its independence.

The first Rebel shell screamed across the harbor at 4:30 A.M. Soon the sky was lit up by bursting shells. Fort Sumter's bricks began to crumble under the pounding. Fires broke out in the soldiers' bunk rooms. Major Anderson was short of ammunition. He couldn't waste any. So he waited till daylight before he ordered his men to return the Rebel fire.

For 37 hours the Rebel guns pounded the fort. In Charleston, men and women watched the shelling from the roofs of houses. Finally, on the afternoon of April 13, Major Anderson knew he had to **surrender** (give up). Fort Sumter was in ruins. His men were tired and starving. After the surrender on April 14, Anderson and his men were allowed to leave the fort safely on a Union ship.

News of the battle spread quickly throughout the nation. In the South, the news of the surrender made people cheer. In the North one man said, "Sumter is lost, but freedom is saved."

So began the Civil War. After actual fighting had broken out, eight other slave states chose sides. Four of them—Maryland, Delaware, Kentucky, and Missouri—stayed with the Union. Four

The South Secedes, 1860–1861

Which states seceded from the Union before the attack on Fort Sumter? Which states seceded after the attack on Fort Sumter?

AMERICAN ADVENTURES

others—Virginia, North Carolina, Tennessee, and Arkansas—joined the Confederacy. Now the Confederacy included 11 states to carry on the war.

This engraving by Currier and Ives shows the 1861 attack on Fort Sumter from the Confederate troops' point of view. These men are loading and firing their cannons at the Fort, whose flag can be seen in the distance beyond the smoke.

CHAPTER CHECK

WORD MATCH
1. General Pierre Beauregard
2. Rebels
3. Major Robert Anderson
4. Yanks
5. surrender

a. give up
b. commander of the Rebel Army in Charleston
c. commander at Fort Sumter in Charleston
d. nickname for Union soldiers
e. nickname for Confederate soldiers

QUICK QUIZ
1. Why was Fort Sumter attacked by Southern troops?
2. Without supplies, Fort Sumter would have been forced to surrender. Why did the South choose to attack the fort, rather than preventing supplies from reaching it?

THINK ABOUT IT
1. What do you think is meant by the remark, "Sumter is lost but freedom is saved"? Do you agree with it? Why or why not?
2. Colonel Anderson held out against the Rebel army as long as he could. Do you see any similarities between the defense and attack of Fort Sumter and the Battle of the Alamo?
3. Do you think it was important that the victorious Rebel troops let Major Anderson and his men leave safely on a Union ship? Do you agree with this decision? Why or why not?

THE ROAD TO WAR

History Detective

1. With my passage by Congress in 1850, Northerners were required to return runaway slaves. What am I?

2. I was a slave whose master had brought me into free territory. I believed I was entitled to my freedom. My case was finally brought to the Supreme Court. Who am I?

3. We were a group of Americans who were opposed to slavery in new areas like Kansas and Nebraska. Who are we?

4. I believed bloodshed was the only way to end slavery. I led two battles against pro-slavery groups before being hanged for treason. Who am I?

5. By the third ballot in a Chicago convention hall, we had picked Abraham Lincoln to represent us in the 1860 presidential election. Who are we?

Voices From the Past

Frederick Douglass was a former slave who went on to write and speak against slavery. In his *Life and Times*, America has one of its best records of slavery.

I suppose myself to have been born in February 1817. My first experience of life began in the family of my grandmother. The practice of separating mothers from their children and hiring them out at distances was a marked feature of the slave system. My only recollections of my mother are a few hasty visits made in the night on foot, after the day's tasks were over. Of my father, I knew nothing....

1. Why wouldn't a slave know when he or she had been born? What might someone feel if they did not know when they were born?

2. Why do you think mothers and fathers would be separated from their children? How would you describe family life in a community of slaves?

Hands–On History

Making a Legal Decision—The year is 1857 and you are a member of the U.S. Supreme Court. Before you stands Dred Scott. You will have to rule whether traveling into free territories is grounds to grant this man and his wife their freedom. Write an explanation of what your decision will be.

YESTERDAY'S NEWS

The American Adventures Newspaper

Little Giant and Long Abe in Last Debate

Alton, Ill. 1858—Senator Stephen Douglas and his challenger for office concluded their series of seven debates throughout the Illinois territory. The two men could not be more different. The five-foot-tall, pudgy Douglas travels in high style, riding from town to town in a private railroad car, sipping brandy, and smoking cigars. He is always surrounded by friends and advisors and accompanied by his beautiful wife. The six feet-four inch, thin Lincoln travels more modestly, as an ordinary passenger on the regular trains. His wife Mary, usually stays home with their two sons. She was reported to have attended this last debate in Alton. When on the speaking platform, Douglas is clad in an expensive, plantation style suit; Lincoln wears only the same wrinkled suit. On November 2, Illinois will decide which will be their next U.S. senator.

Abraham Lincoln has gained national attention as he challenges Stephen Douglas in the 1858 Senate race in Illinios.

1.

Lincoln and Douglas have made slavery the major issue in the election. "This government," says Lincoln, "was instituted to secure the blessings of freedom. Slavery is an unqualified evil to the Negro, to the white man, to the soil, and to the State." Douglas counters, "I am opposed to Negro equality. I believe this government was made by the white man for the white man to be administered by the white man."

Whether he wins the election or not, Lincoln made a name for himself in these debates. He dared to say things that politicians have been afraid to say.

People's reactions to Lincoln's words have been mixed. **2.**

You Be the Reporter

Match each question with its news item above.
1. What headline would you write for this story?
2. Using what you have learned about public feelings toward slavery during this period, finish this article. Tell how different parts of the country might feel about what Lincoln has said about slavery and America.

COMPARING A GRAPH AND A MAP

Intense conflicts over slavery made the 1860 election a stormy one. When the Democrats nominated Stephen Douglas as their candidate for president, pro-slavery Democrats from the South broke away from the party and nominated their own candidate—John C. Breckinridge. In the 1860 election, Douglas still came in second in popular votes, but he came in last in electoral votes! How was this possible?

Popular votes are those cast by individual voters in the population. Under the United States Constitution, however, these voters do not choose the president. They choose "electors" of their states; and it is these electors who actually choose the president in an electoral vote. To understand how this worked in 1860, first study the pie graph below.

The pie graph shows the results of the popular vote in 1860. Refer to the graph to answer these questions on a separate sheet of paper.

1. What was the total number of popular votes cast for **(a)** Lincoln? **(b)** Douglas? **(c)** Breckinridge? **(d)** Bell?

2. Compare the total votes cast for the four candidates. **(a)** By how many votes did Lincoln beat Douglas? **(b)** Would the combined popular vote of Douglas and Breckinridge have exceeded Lincoln's popular vote? Explain.

3. What percentage of the popular vote was cast for **(a)** Lincoln? **(b)** Bell? **(c)** Douglas and Breckinridge together?

When the electoral votes were counted in 1860, Douglas came in last. The map opposite shows why. The number of electors a state has always depends on how many senators and representatives it has in Congress. In 1860, for example, Ohio had 2 senators and 21 representatives, so

Popular Vote, 1860

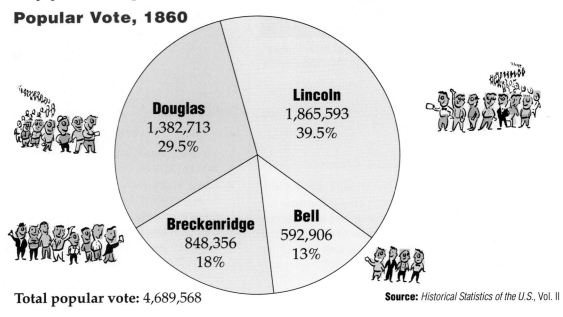

Douglas
1,382,713
29.5%

Lincoln
1,865,593
39.5%

Breckenridge
848,356
18%

Bell
592,906
13%

Total popular vote: 4,689,568

Source: *Historical Statistics of the U.S.*, Vol. II

it had 23 presidential electors. The map shows how many electors each state had in 1860.

Usually electors vote for the candidates who win the majority of popular votes in their states. So even though some of its popular vote went to Douglas in 1860, all 23 of Ohio's electoral votes were cast for the majority candidate—Lincoln.

Refer to the map and answer the following questions on a separate sheet of paper.

4. Study the map's key. How is each political party and candidate identified on this map?

5. Find the electoral votes for Douglas. **(a)** How many did he receive? **(b)** Which state cast all of its electoral votes for him? **(c)** What happened in New Jersey?

6. Which states cast their electoral votes for John Bell? How many votes did he get?

7. How many states cast all of their electoral votes for Breckinridge? How many votes was that?

8. How many states cast all of their electoral votes for Lincoln? How many electoral votes did he win all together?

9. How does the map reflect this statement: "The United States in 1860 was deeply divided between North and South?"

10. The following statement is false: "In 1860, the South had a larger population than the North." The map does not give population figures. How could you still use it to show that the statement is indeed false?

Electoral Vote, 1860

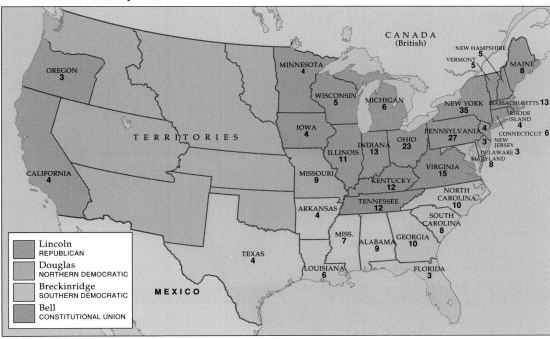

A TORN

LOOKING AHEAD

In 1858, Abraham Lincoln made a speech predicting the future. The conflict between the North and South "will not cease, until a crisis shall have been reached, and passed," said Lincoln. "A house divided against itself cannot stand. I believe this government cannot endure, permanently half slave and half free."

Two years later Lincoln was elected president, and the crisis over slavery he predicted came true. The issue tore the Union apart. The "house divided" between free states and slave states broke apart.

The Civil War (1861 to 1865) eventually settled this and other important questions. In the

After the South fired on Fort Sumter, the nation's conflict deepened into all-out war. Both sides felt great pride seeing their young men march off to war.

NATION 5

UNIT

1865

●

1865

Lee surrenders to Grant at Appomattox Court House.

Lincoln killed.

Union and Confederate Resources

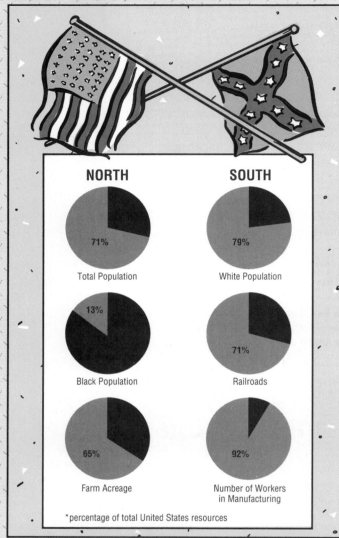

NORTH	SOUTH
71% Total Population	79% White Population
13% Black Population	71% Railroads
65% Farm Acreage	92% Number of Workers in Manufacturing

*percentage of total United States resources

What were the North's greatest economic advantages over the South? What were the South's strengths? How do you think differences between the North and the South affected the outcome of the Civil War?

war in U.S. history. In some families, one brother fought for the North, another for the South. The war caused much death and destruction and left many towns and cities in ruins. More Americans died in the Civil War than in all other wars combined in which Americans fought. More than 620,000 Americans—including some 29,000 blacks—lost their lives during the Civil War. Comparable losses today would equal the deaths of five million people.

North and South

When the war began, each side was confident that it could win. Each indeed had certain advantages. The North was better equipped to fight a long war than the South. The North had a much larger population. Perhaps the biggest advantage of the North was that it had factories which could produce as many rifles, bullets, and uniforms as its army needed.

The Confederacy also had some advantages, and some disadvantages. Most important to the South, the war was often fought on Southern soil. Defending their homes and families helped Southerners maintain a strong fighting spirit. But the South had few factories and could not produce many supplies. Soon after the war began, some Southern soldiers were marching barefoot. The greatest military disadvantage found the Southern army

end, slavery was abolished. Never again would a state try to secede from the Union. But Americans paid a very heavy price to settle these questions.

The Civil War was the most terrible

lacking decent guns, uniforms, and food.

At first, many people in the North were uncertain about how to respond to Southern secession. Lincoln had wisely let the South fire the first shot. So the news of Southerners firing on federal troops and the U.S. flag angered most Northerners. They wanted to punish the South for trying to destroy the Union.

Early Military Strategy

Winfield Scott, first commanding general of the Union Army, devised a careful strategy hoping to force the South's surrender. Scott wanted to bring the Southern states back into the Union while causing as little bloodshed and destruction as possible. He proposed that the navy blockade Southern ports so that essential supplies from Europe could not be delivered. If Southern waterways were closed off, Scott believed, the South would be forced to surrender. His strategy became known as the Anaconda Plan since, like the fierce snake, it sought to choke its victim.

Jefferson Davis, Confederate president during the war, also adopted a conservative plan. Believing that European nations would eventually help the South, he resisted attacking the North.

Newspaper editorials on both sides urged a quick and decisive attack. After a battle or two, it was thought the "cowardly Yankees" or the "slovenly Rebels" would give up.

War Continues

Despite early enthusiasm, the war gained little Northern support during the first months. Many of the early battles ended as a draw or a Southern victory. Many Southerners thought the North would give up soon. But finally, in 1862, the North won a key victory at the Battle of Antietam.

Following this victory, President Lincoln issued the **Emancipation Proclamation.** The Proclamation declared that all slaves living under Confederate rule would be free as of January 1, 1863. The Emancipation Proclamation changed the war. Northerners now wanted to do more than just save the Union. Now they also fought to end slavery. Both sides realized that the war would determine the future course of their country.

By the summer of 1863, the tide of the war shifted. In July, the Confederacy lost two important battles—Gettysburg, Pennsylvania, and Vicksburg, Mississippi. After these defeats, the South never successfully launched another major attack against the North.

In 1864, Northern armies marched through the South. Especially damaging was the army of General William Sherman. His troops destroyed everything in their path.

Blacks proudly joined the Union cause, but did not see action until late in the war. When in battle, blacks and whites rarely fought together.

By the spring of 1865, the Northern advantage in troop numbers and in equipment had the South worn out. In April, the Southern troops surrendered.

A Modern War

For the first time, new technology played a significant role in an American war. The Civil War was a war of technological "firsts." It was the first war to use large masses of American men. Railroads were used to move troops and supplies. It was also the first U.S. war to use **telegraph** (a system of communication that changes a coded message into electric impulses), armored ships, and balloons. When the Union troops marched through the South, they used these new forms of technology not only to defeat the Confederate Army, but also to try to destroy the spirit of the Southern people.

Northern and Southern civilians supported the war effort. Because most young men were away as soldiers, those people left behind bore heavy burdens. Women, children, and older people ran farms, businesses, and plantations. Women made supplies for the army and served as nurses. Some women, such as Mary Chesnut of South Carolina, kept diaries about the war's effects on their lives.

Lee and Grant

The dramatic times also brought forth great military leaders. Robert E. Lee, a strong, kind man from Virginia, had been a colonel in the U.S. Army when the war

The Union and the Confederacy, 1861

How many states were there in the Union? How many territories? How many states supported the Confederacy? How many territories?

AMERICAN ADVENTURES

broke out. He opposed the South's secession from the Union. But Lee also knew that he could not fight against his own state, so he left the U.S. Army and joined the Confederacy. Lee became one of the greatest military leaders in American history.

The Northern army did not have such able leadership. It took three years and six generals before Ulysses S. Grant took over control of the Union armies. Grant was a sloppy dresser and did not look much like a general. But he got the job done. Grant's strategy was to attack without letting up. Although some people opposed these tactics, Grant finally pounded the South into surrendering.

The nation's most brilliant leader was Abraham Lincoln. As president, Lincoln was a clever politician. Through his hard, patient work, Lincoln was able to guide the nation through its most difficult crisis.

Lincoln did not think of Southerners as enemies. He saw Confederate soldiers as human beings who were suffering as deeply as Union soldiers. Lincoln hated the bloodshed and death that the war caused. It hurt him to see fellow human beings treated as slaves. "If slavery isn't wrong," he once said, "then nothing is wrong."

In March 1865, when it seemed that the war was almost over, Lincoln made his last great speech to the American people. He asked that, after the war, people treat each other "with malice [ill will] toward none, with charity for all." Only a few weeks later, an **assassin** shot and killed President Lincoln. It was the saddest ending to a tragic war.

The Confederate troops' fighting spirit was fueled by their strong desire to preserve the traditions of the South—as well as slavery, this included its grand plantations, Southern belles, and gentlemen callers.

22 THE FIRST BULL RUN

At the First Battle of Bull Run, Confederate General Thomas Jackson stood his ground so firmly that he received the nickname Stonewall from General Barnard Bee. Jackson's determination helped the South win this battle, and made the North realize the war would not end quickly.

Young McHenry Howard was awakened in the summer night of 1861 by the roar of an arriving train. He quickly gathered his equipment and joined the other Confederate soldiers marching toward the train. Howard was on his way to his first battle. He rode part of the way on an outside platform, and part on the roof of a crowded rail car. Like the other soldiers, he went for hours without food or drink.

After much delay and confusion, the train pulled into the station at Manassas Junction, a railway town in northern Virginia. By afternoon, the sun was blazing. Black smoke rose in the distance and cannons roared.

Howard and the other Confederate soldiers marched toward a stream known as Bull Run. The young men were hungry and parched with thirst. They drank from puddles in the road, and desperately gobbled blackberries from bushes they passed.

Union soldiers approached from the North. They assembled by the thousands in Washington, D.C., and Alexandria, Virginia, and marched through thickly wooded countryside. These newly **enlisted** (having joined a branch of the armed forces) soldiers were also young and inexperienced. They too endured heat, exhaustion, and endless days. Sometimes clad in ragged uniforms like their Confederate brothers, most existed on rations of dried beef, crackers, and coffee.

Union troops left their homes and their families so that they could fight "to maintain the best government on earth." They believed slavery was "a moral and political evil."

On that morning of July 21, 1861, crowds of Northern spectators, many of them members of Congress, followed the Union troops by train from Washington, D.C. Many had packed picnic lunches. Some were confident that the first battle of the Civil War would end in victory for the Union.

The Battle of Bull Run

People spread out their lunches a few miles from Bull Run where the battle was expected to take place. The spectators could not see much of the fight, but they could hear the booming of the cannons and could see puffs of gunsmoke drift up into the summer sky.

Suddenly the fun stopped. Some 30,000 Union soldiers confronted 22,000 Confederate troops on the pastures and wooded hills that surrounded Bull Run. After the Northern army penetrated (made a way into or through) the first Confederate lines, General Thomas J. Jackson and his Rebel troops refused to yield further.

On the dusty terrain of Henry House Hill, a Confederate leader shouted, "There is Jackson standing like a stone wall! Rally behind the Virginians!" The General thus earned the nickname Stonewall. The young Northerners panicked and were driven off. Only 30 miles outside their nation's capital, Union troops met defeat. Wounded soldiers and shocked onlookers scampered back toward Washington, D.C. Disorganized and exhausted themselves, Confederate Rebels were unable to pursue the retreating enemy.

The Shock of Defeat

"Today will be known as BLACK MONDAY," a New Yorker wrote after he heard about the Union defeat. "We are utterly and disgracefully routed, beaten, whipped." Stunned Northerners realized

War Without Victory, 1861–1862

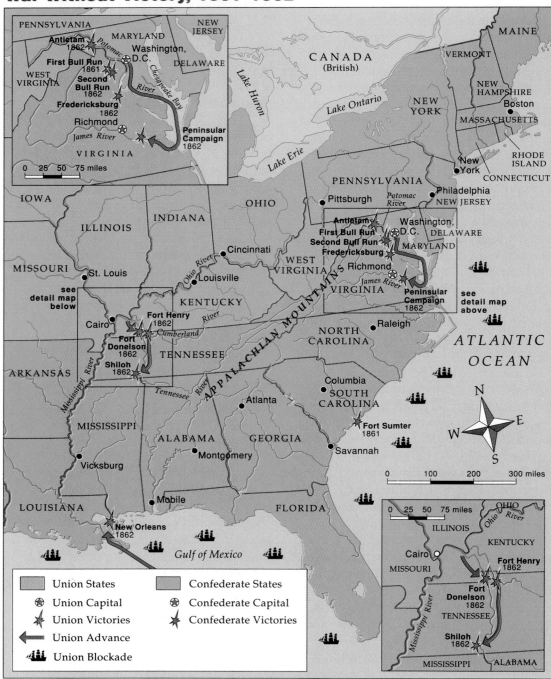

How many Union victories were there in the Union? How many Confederate victories? Refer to the key if you need help.

after the Battle of Bull Run (Southerners called it the Battle of Manassas), that the war would not be won so easily.

Southerners rejoiced as local newspapers predicted a swift victory in the war. One Southern political leader said that "this hard-fought battle [was] virtually the close of the war." But military advisors were more cautious. Recognizing that the Union would not give up easily, they pressed to prepare their troops and to stockpile supplies.

After the war was over, participants on both sides agreed that the Southern victory at Bull Run "proved the greatest misfortune that [could] have befallen the Confederacy." People now understood what the Civil War would be like. It would not be a picnic. It would not be fun. Instead, it would be a grim, life-and-death struggle.

Both North and South hurried to build up their arms supplies. These Union soldiers were dwarfed by their stockpile of weapons, soon to be carried into war.

CHAPTER CHECK

WORD MATCH
1. Thomas J. Jackson
2. enlisted
3. Jefferson Davis
4. penetrated
5. Winfield Scott

a. Confederate president during Civil War
b. made a way into, or through
c. having joined a branch of the armed forces
d. first commanding general of the Union Army
e. general nicknamed Stonewall because of his refusal to yield during battle

QUICK QUIZ
1. Why did some Northerners think it was urgent that a Union army should march into and occupy Richmond, Virginia?
2. What two reasons did most Union soldiers give for fighting in the Army?

THINK ABOUT IT
1. Describe the different reactions of Northerners and Southerners to the first Battle of Bull Run.
2. Why did some think that the Southern victory at the first Bull Run was actually a great misfortune for the South?

CHAPTER 23 ANTIETAM AND EMANCIPATION

In October 1862, President Lincoln [center] met with General McClellan [sixth from left]. The month before, McClellan had fought the Battle of Antietam-—and Lincoln had issued the Emancipation Proclamation.

"A truly sickening and horrible sight," wrote a young Union soldier. "No tongue can tell, no mind conceive, no pen portray the horrible sights I witnessed this morning." He described one of the Civil War's most horrible and important battles—Antietam in Maryland. Before the one-day battle was over, nearly 24,000 men were dead or wounded—more casualties than occurred in any other single day of the war. Although the battle seemed to end in a military stand-off, it later proved to be a major turning point in the war.

After his victory at the second Battle of Bull Run in August 1862, Confederate General Robert E. Lee wanted a truly great victory that would prove the might of the Confederacy. Such a victory would bring diplomatic recognition from Great Britain and France. This victory, he believed, could also force the North to give up trying to subdue the South. He decided to invade the North, giving the war-weary Southern farmers a chance to harvest their crops. On September 4, his 55,000 Confederate troops crossed the Potomac River, only 30 miles from Washington, D.C.

In Washington, a sense of panic grew.

136

AMERICAN ADVENTURES

General George B. McClellan, leader of the Union's Army of the Potomac, had lost track of Lee's position. Were the Rebels headed for Washington itself? By an amazing stroke of luck, a Union officer found a copy of Lee's battle plans wrapped around some cigars left in an abandoned camp. From these plans, McClellan learned that Lee had divided his army into four parts.

The Battle Begins

McClellan caught up with Lee at Antietam Creek, near Sharpsburg, Maryland, on September 17, 1862. With only 40,000 men, Lee was greatly outnumbered by 70,000 Union troops, but he decided to fight. The battle began at dawn and continued all day. It produced no clear victor, but casualties mounted quickly. Over 2000 Union soldiers fell in a few minutes.

When the battle ended that night, both armies had about the same territory. The night was filled with the groans and cries from the wounded and dying—almost 12,000 on each side.

The next day, Lee stood ready to defend his ground with weakened troops if attacked. But McClellan seemed satisfied with his position and chose to stay put. Lee **retreated** (withdrew troops from a position) back across the Potomac. His campaign to win a major victory, and perhaps end the war, failed. Britain, once considering an alliance with the Confederacy, now changed its mind because an independent Confederacy seemed less certain.

"You fought well and stood well," said one Union officer to a wounded Confederate soldier after the battle. "Yes," he replied, "and here we lie." For the South, Antietam was considered a **strategic** (well-planned or directed) defeat.

Lincoln Takes a Stand

The results of Antietam influenced President Lincoln's policies. During the early years of the war, President Lincoln faced conflict within his own Republican party. When elected, he had promised to save the Union and to stop the further spread of slavery. But Lincoln never said he would free all the slaves. After months of war many anti-slavery people in his own party, known as Radical Republicans, demanded that he free the slaves immediately. The Radical Republicans saw slavery as the cause of the war and wanted to see it abolished forever. Other Republicans argued that slave labor enabled the South to keep fighting. If Lincoln freed the slaves they might run away from the plantations and help the Union.

Criticism of Lincoln increased. Horace Greeley, a powerful newspaper publisher, strongly attacked Lincoln for not freeing

As news of Lincoln's Emancipation Proclamation spread throughout the Confederacy, slaves gathered to celebrate their freedom.

The Battle of Antietam, 1862

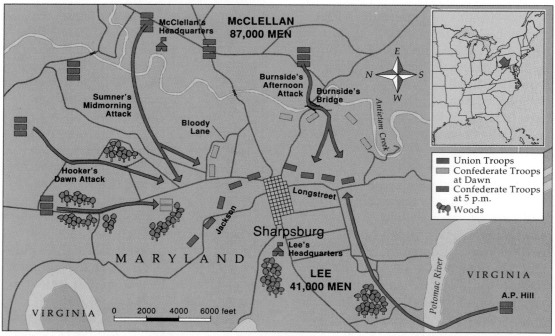

How many soldiers did each side have at the Battle of Antietam? How far did Lee's troops at Burnside's Bridge have to retreat before dawn and at 5PM?

all the slaves. To respond publicly to his critics, and to clarify his own position, Lincoln wrote the following to Greeley in August 1862:

> *My paramount object in this struggle is to save the Union, and is not either to save or destroy Slavery. If I could save the Union without freeing any slave, I would do it; and if I could save it by freeing all the slaves, I would do it; and if I could do it by freeing some and leaving others alone, I would also do that.*

Lincoln finally decided to free the slaves. He felt it would provide a moral reason for the North to fight on in a terrible war. It would also motivate free blacks to join the army and slaves to escape to the North.

The Emancipation Proclamation

Lincoln considered the Union check of Lee at Antietam a good time to announce his news. After all, Lee had retreated and the Confederates were forced from Union territory. On September 22, 1862, he issued the Emancipation Proclamation. In it, he told the Confederates that if they surrendered before January 1, 1863, they could keep their slaves. But if they did not, he would sign the Proclamation and all the slaves would become free. None of the Rebel states surrendered.

On January, 1, 1863, Lincoln was greeted by thousands of people at the White House. With an old steel pen, he signed the Proclamation. The slaves in the Confederacy were declared free.

"If my name ever goes down in history," Lincoln said, "it will be for this act. My whole soul is in it."

Many Southerners reacted bitterly. They believed the Emancipation Proclamation would encourage slaves to revolt. Confederate President Jefferson Davis said the act made reunion of the two countries "forever impossible."

In the North, opinion was divided. The Radical Republicans and abolitionists were thrilled. Some Northerners, particularly Northern Democrats, did not care about freedom for the slaves. They only wanted to fight to restore the Union. They felt freeing the slaves would only make the

Clara Barton is known today as one of the most famous and courageous nurses to serve during the Civil War.

South fight harder, since they now had more to lose by surrendering. They also did not want millions of freed blacks to move to Northern cities where they would compete with whites for jobs.

Black slaves were given new hope. An estimated half-million escaped into Union territory seeking freedom. By the end of the war, blacks made up nearly 10 percent of the entire Union Army. Lincoln's reasoning proved correct. The freeing of slaves helped the North win the war. But the significance of the Emancipation Proclamation went far beyond the war—it provided freedom for an entire group of people.

CHAPTER CHECK

WORD MATCH
1. George B. McClellan
2. retreated
3. diplomatic recognition
4. strategic
5. Horace Greeley

a. powerful newspaper publisher and abolitionist
b. withdrew troops from position as a result of enemy attack
c. general who was leader of Union's Army of the Potomac
d. well-planned or directed, relating to a military action
e. acknowledgement made by another nation

QUICK QUIZ
1. What made the Battle of Antietam so unusual?
2. What was General Lee's original plan? Why did he pick this strategy?
3. Did the Emancipation Proclamation encourage any slaves to escape to freedom?

THINK ABOUT IT
1. Why was the Battle of Antietam considered a turning point in the Civil War?
2. Describe President Lincoln's position on slavery. Did it change during the war? If so, describe how.

24 A SOUTHERN DIARIST

Even while sons of the South were falling on battlefields, many people in Confederate states tried to keep up old traditions. This family on a Virginia estate gathered for a well-mannered game of croquet.

Mary Boykin enjoyed her school days away from home in Charleston, South Carolina. At Madame Talvande's French School, she learned to speak and read French fluently. She read the works of Charles Dickens and other great English writers.

Mary's life was filled with elegant parties. At one, she received the special attentions of a young man, James Chesnut, who would later become her husband. But one day word came that Mary's father wanted her home. He had heard stories about her courtship with Chesnut. Mary's father did not want her strolling in the moonlight in Charleston. This was considered shocking behavior. Mary was taken to her father's new plantation on the Mississippi frontier.

Her journey, by carriage and horseback, lasted four weeks. What she saw when she arrived in the strange new land impressed her deeply. The terrain was rough and there were few houses. Some nights Mary heard wolves howling under the house. Her nearest neighbor was a great Indian chief from the Chocktaw tribe.

At her new home, Mary began to question the relationship between

Indians, slaves, and whites. "I received there my first ideas," she later wrote, "that Negroes were not a divine institution for our benefit—or we for theirs."

Plantation Life

When Mary returned to South Carolina, she married James Chesnut. The young couple settled at Mulberry, the Chesnut family plantation, located just outside Camden.

Mulberry, with its magnificent oak trees and rolling green lawns, had "everything that a hundred years or more of unlimited wealth could accumulate." James Chesnut's father was one of the wealthiest landowners in South Carolina.

Mary led a pampered life at Mulberry. But soon she felt bored and frustrated. She was unable to have children of her own and her husband's parents were strong and domineering.

Servants attended to Mary's every need. She found herself with plenty of free time. "The amenities [polite ways] and trifles of Mulberry bore me so," she wrote in her diary. As first the daughter of one man with political ambitions, then the wife of another, Mary's aspirations were often overlooked. She was like many white women who lived on plantations. Not only were they denied basic legal and civil rights, they could not find meaningful work.

"I think these times make all women feel their humiliation in the affairs of the world,"

Women left at home founds ways to express their patriotism. Sewing Confederate symbols into clothing, as on this child's dress, was popular.

she wrote in her diary in August 1861. "With men it is on to the field— 'glory, honour, praise, & . . . power.' Women can only stay at home."

Political Life

But unlike many Southern women, Mary did not stay at home. For a time she lived with her husband in Washington, D.C., where he served in the United States Senate. After the election of Abraham Lincoln, the Chesnuts returned to the South. James wanted to help the young Confederacy establish itself.

Early in 1861, the couple traveled to Montgomery, Alabama, where James attended the Confederate Provisional Congress. In Montgomery, Mary became friends with Varina Davis, wife of Jefferson Davis, the president of the Confederacy.

Mary accompanied her husband on several political journeys. And she visited the sick and wounded men after the first Battle of Bull Run. Her political ambitions for her husband were sometimes greater than his own. "Oh," she wrote in April 1861, "if I could put some of my reckless spirit into these discreet, cautious, lazy men."

"Made Glad the Hearts"

Several years after the summer of 1861, Mary wrote a moving account of one of her visits to the wounded at the Battle of Bull Run: "We went to the hospital with a carriageload of peaches and grapes. Made glad the hearts of some men thereby. . . .

A SOUTHERN DIARIST

Those eyes sunk in cavernous depths haunted me as they followed me from bed to bed."

Sometimes wounded men from both the North and South were taken to the same hospital. Mary later described the tensions between the two groups: "Occasionally [a wounded soldier] looked sulky, for were we not the hated Southerners? But I think as a general rule all that was forgotten in the hospital."

Mary also observed how black soldiers who fought for the Union were treated: "We saw among the wounded at the federal hospital a Negro soldier. He was with the others, on equal terms—and a sister was nursing him."

Mary Boykin Chesnut kept a lively eye on the events of the war. Her diaries give us a special view of that time.

"A Monstrous System"

Mary had begun to keep a diary in February 1861. She continued to record her thoughts and feelings as the "black cloud" of war darkened Southern life. Only her diaries from the years 1861 and 1865 survive.

Sometimes Mary simply scribbled down the names of visitors to her home, and snippets of conversation. She commented on the actions of Southern leaders, and wrote about her social activities.

Mary also expressed her views about slavery: "God forgive us," she wrote in March 1861, "but ours is a monstrous system & wrong & [evil.]" Although she believed firmly that slavery was "a curse to any land," she recognized that as a South Carolina slave holder, she participat-ed in a corrupt system. Mary sometimes equated the denigration (disrespect for character and reputation of someone) and suppression of women with the plight of the slaves. "Poor women! Poor slaves!" she wrote.

Escaping Sherman's Path

At the end of the war, Mary and James were left almost penniless. For several months in 1864, they had traveled across the South as refugees, escaping from General Sherman's army.

In May 1865, the couple returned to Camden, where there were "nothing but tall blackened chimneys to show that any man [had] ever trod this road before us." Mary bitterly described the devastation of the countryside: "This is Sherman's track," she wrote. "It is hard not to curse him."

Mary Chesnut's Civil War

For almost 20 years after the South's surrender, Mary wrote about the Civil War. She worked steadily despite serious illness and several tragedies in her family.

After experimenting with novels and an **autobiographical** tale of her girlhood, she wrote in the form of a diary. She based this diary on actual entries she had made during the war years.

When she died in 1886, her work, still in rough form, lacked a title. It was finally published in 1905, under the title *The Dixie Diaries*. The work gained the respect of critics and historians. "This diary," wrote

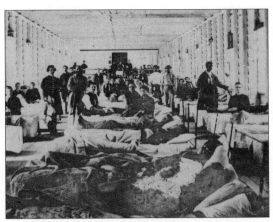

Famed Civil War photographer Matthew Brady captured this scene of a hospital camp near Alexandria, Virginia. Mary Chesnut visited such places during the war.

the critic Edmund Wilson, "is an extraordinary document . . . a masterpiece."

Editors of the book presented it as an actual diary, rather than a work of fiction. As a result, many historians were misled. In 1981, a scholar presented a new version of the work, *Mary Chesnut's Civil War*. And, in 1984, the original diaries were published for the first time.

But Chesnut's fiction—without "sentiment, moonshine, and special pleading"—best evokes the lives of those who were destroyed by the sin of slavery. Chesnut knew that the spirit of the South had been crushed by the war. "The weight that hangs upon our eyelids," she wrote, "is of lead."

CHAPTER CHECK

WORD MATCH
1. autobiographical
2. *The Dixie Diaries*
3. amenities
4. *Mary Chesnut's Civil War*
5. denigration

a. the 1905 original version of Mary Chesnut's book
b. showing disrespect
c. polite ways
d. about the story of one's own life
e. Mary Chesnut's re-edited book, known to be fiction

QUICK QUIZ
1. As a young married woman, what was Mary Chesnut's life like?
2. What did Mary Chesnut notice about the wounded black soldiers?
3. What was the "monstrous system" to which Mary Chesnut referred?

THINK ABOUT IT
1. Why do you think Mary Chesnut wrote: "Poor women! Poor blacks!"?
2. Mary Chesnut saw wounded Northern and Southern soldiers lie in hospital beds beside each other. What do you think she meant by writing that "all was forgotten in the hospital"?

25 GETTYSBURG AND VICKSBURG

Soldiers were not the only ones to suffer from the war's fierce clashes. Battles fought near farms and towns threatened families and destroyed livestock and crops.

The top two Civil War commanders, Ulysses S. Grant and Robert E. Lee, were playing for high stakes in June 1863. Lee was launching an invasion of the North that would take his Confederate army as far north as Gettysburg, Pennsylvania. Nine hundred miles away to the south, Grant was leading a Union army into a siege of Vicksburg, Mississippi.

Lee wanted peace, but he wanted peace terms to favor the South. At the same time, Grant developed an important military strategy to defeat the South. If the Union could gain control of Vicksburg, the last Confederate stronghold on the Mississippi River, the Union could win the war. This could happen because the North would win total control of the Mississippi River, and split the South in half.

The Battle of Gettysburg

Lee's army of 70,000 men reached Gettysburg on July 1, and was quickly confronted by a Union army of 90,000 men led by General George G. Meade. Fighting on the first two days led to no decision. Then, on July 3, Lee ordered 15,000 Confederate soldiers, under General George Pickett, to attack the center of the Union line, even though it was positioned on high ground. So began one of the most famous charges in American war history.

Confederate Lieutenant G.W. Finley described the Rebel advance:

"As we came in sight, the [Union] artillery [guns of large size, too heavy to carry] opened upon us all along our front.

Whenever it struck our ranks, it was fearfully destructive. One company, numbering 35 or 40 men, was almost swept from the line by a single shell." As the Confederate forces advanced, Union forces opened fire from behind a stone fence on a hill.

"Cannon and muskets were raining death upon us," recalled Finley. "When we were about 75 or 100 yards from that stone wall, some of the men holding it began to break for the rear. Without orders, our line poured a volley or two into them, and then rushed upon the fence. The Federals [Union troops] fired their last shots full in our faces, and so close I thought I felt distinctly the flames of the explosion.

"At that instant, suddenly a terrific fire burst upon us and, looking around, I saw close to us a fresh line of Federals attempting to drive us from the stone fence. But after exchanging a few rounds with us, they fell back behind the crest. . . ."

Many more Union soldiers were rushed to the scene of the Confederate breakthrough. Bloody hand-to-hand fighting took place. Charles Carleton Coffin, a Northern newspaper reporter, described the scene:

"There are bayonet thrusts, [sword] strokes, pistol shots. There are oaths, yells, curses, hurrahs. Men are going down on their hands and knees, spinning around like tops, throwing out their arms, gulping up blood, falling—legless, armless, headless. There are ghastly heaps of dead men. Seconds are centuries, minutes are ages.

"The Rebel column has lost its power. The lines waver. The soldiers of the front rank look around for their supports. They are gone—fleeing over the field, broken, shattered, thrown into confusion by the remorseless fire. The ground is thick with dead, and the wounded are like withered leaves of autumn."

Lieutenant Jesse Bowman Young described the reaction of the Union soldiers to their victory:

"Cheer after cheer rose from the triumphant boys in blue, resounding in the vale below, and making the very heavens throb."

The next day, July 4, Lee's battered army began its retreat to Virginia. Gettysburg was a turning point in the war. Lee had lost more than 20,000 men—dead, wounded, and prisoners. Never again would he have troops strong enough to launch a major **offensive** (attack by armed forces) into the North. After Gettysburg, the war would be fought—and finished—in the South.

This painting shows Union troops on McPherson's Ridge being overrun by Confederates during the battle at Gettysburg. But the Union eventually won the battle, which was an important turning point in the war.

GETTYSBURG AND VICKSBURG

The Siege of Vicksburg

By the middle of May 1863, Union forces had surrounded the town of Vicksburg, Mississippi. Heavily fortified, Vicksburg repelled attacks. Finally Grant decided to blockade the town until shortages of food and other supplies forced it to surrender. Meanwhile, Union artillery shelled the town, making life unsafe for **civilians** (people not active members of the armed forces) and soldiers alike. Many civilians began living in caves, which were dug into the sides of hills.

Mary Loughborough, the mother of a

The Battles of Gettysburg and Vicksburg, 1863

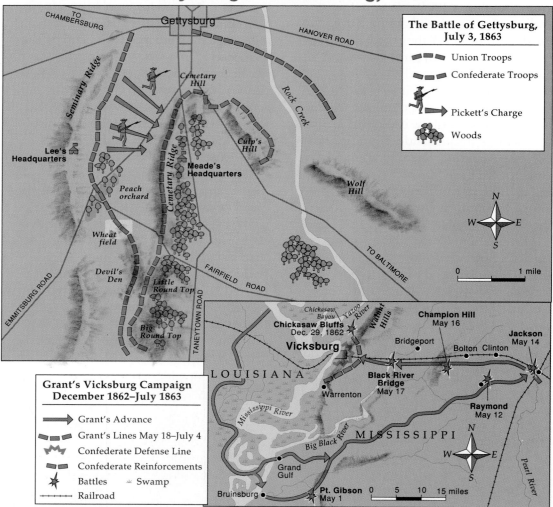

Locate the positions of the Union and Confederate forces at the Battle of Gettysburg. Suppose Pickett's charge had succeeded. What effect would it have had on the Union forces? Now study the map of the Seige of Vicksburg. What natural features protected the city from the attack? How many miles did Grant's troops march from Bruinsburg to Vicksburg? Why do you think Grant chose such a roundabout route to Vicksburg?

AMERICAN ADVENTURES

two-year-old girl, described cave life during the siege:

"Our dining, breakfasting, and supper hours were quite irregular. When the shells were falling fast, the [slaves] who were preparing our meals outside came in for safety. Some families had light bread made in large quantities, and subsisted on it with milk, provided their cows were not killed from one milking to another. Most of us lived on corn bread and bacon. . . .

"And so I went regularly to work, keeping house underground. We were safe at least from fragments of shell—and they were flying in all directions."

Soon after, Loughborough discovered that her cave was not as safe as it seemed.

"I was reading in safety, I imagined, when the unmistakable whirring of shells told us that the battery we so much feared had opened fire. I ran to the entrance to call the [slaves] in."

Suddenly a shell whirled into the center of the cave. "And thus we remained for a moment, with our eyes fixed in terror on the missile of death," recalled Loughborough. "George, the [slave], rushed forward, seized the shell, and threw it into the street.

"Fortunately, the fuse had nearly died out, and the shell fell harmless. It remained near the mouth of the cave as a trophy of the fearlessness of our [slave] and our remarkable escape."

On July 4, the same day that Lee began his retreat from Gettysburg, Vicksburg surrendered. There, about 30,000 Confederate soldiers became prisoners of war. The North now controlled the Mississippi River, and the Confederacy was split in two. The supply line over which men, munitions, and meat came from Texas was closed. The defeat of the Confederacy now appeared to be only a matter of time. Yet the war dragged on for two more years, and many more men would die before it ended.

CHAPTER CHECK

WORD MATCH

1. artillery
2. offensive
3. Vicksburg
4. Gettysburg
5. civilians

a. any persons not active members of the armed forces
b. battle where Northern troops split Confederacy in half
c. battle that was the turning point of the Civil War
d. guns of large size, too heavy to carry
e. an attack by armed forces

QUICK QUIZ

1. Which side had the largest number of troops at the Battle of Gettysburg?
2. Why did Grant want to gain control of Vicksburg?

THINK ABOUT IT

1. Why do think reading the stories of people who actually saw and experienced battles makes a strong impression on you, the reader?
2. Mary Loughborough described mealtime in a cave by writing: "the only luxury of the meal consisting of its warmth". What do you think she meant?

SHERMAN'S MARCH TO THE SEA

General Sherman's men burned much of the once-proud city of Atlanta [above] to the ground. As his army marched from Atlanta to the sea, it left devastated lands—and bitter Southerners—in its wake.

Atlanta, Georgia was in flames. During the night of November 15, 1864, General William "Tecumseh" Sherman had ordered Union soldiers to torch the city. An aide to General Sherman described the scene in these words:

"First, bursts of smoke. Then tongues of flame. Then huge waves of fire roll up into the sky. Soon the skeletons of great warehouses stand out against sheets of roaring, blazing, furious fires. . . . It is dreadful to look upon."

By dawn, Atlanta was a heap of ashes. Only a few hundred homes and

some churches were spared.

Why did Sherman order the destruction of the city that his army had captured six weeks earlier? Sherman believed total ruin was necessary to defeat the South. It was not enough, he said, to defeat Confederate armies on the battlefield. The factories, machine shops, and railroads that supplied them with the weapons of war had to be destroyed. He believed the plantations and farms of the South had to be destroyed so that the civilians who supported the Rebel armies would be made to suffer. He wanted "to make war so terrible" that the South's will to resist would be broken. This, he said, was the quickest way to end the conflict and to bring peace.

Sherman's Plan

Sherman's plan was to march his army from Atlanta to Savannah, which is on the Atlantic Coast of Georgia, a distance of 285 miles. Along the way they would destroy everything of value to the Confederate armies. In a telegram to his commander, General U.S. Grant, Sherman said, "I can make the march and make Georgia howl!"

Sherman's army of 62,000 veteran troops began leaving Atlanta on the night of the fire. Most of the soldiers were boys —many were under 18. "My little devils," Sherman called them. They called him "Uncle Billy." More than 25,000 horses and mules pulled 25-mile-long wagon trains. These trains, however, could not carry enough food to feed such a large army. Sherman ordered his troops to "forage liberally" for food. This meant stripping the country-side of all the food it needed.

Many of Sherman's soldiers took this order as a license to **loot** (steal or take goods by force) farms and plantations. Groups of foragers, whom Southerners labeled **bummers,** helped themselves to anything they could carry away. A Union officer described a group returning to camp from a raid on a plantation:

"At the head of the procession was an ancient family carriage drawn by a goat, a cow with a bell, and a jackass. Tied behind were a sheep and a calf. The vehicle was loaded down with pumpkins, chickens, cabbages, carrots, turkeys, squashes, sweet potatoes, honey and every other imaginable thing a lot of fool soldiers could take it into their heads to bring away."

Sometimes small groups of foragers were attacked by Confederates and executed. Their bodies were placed along a road for all the Union troops to see. Often on the bodies signs were pinned saying, "Death to all foragers." Yet many Southerners complained bitterly that their own soldiers also engaged in foraging.

During the first days of the march, Sherman's army burned many homes. Sometimes one brave person saved a home. In one town, for example, a woman was ordered to leave her house and take her children and black slaves with her. "We're gonna burn it down," the soldiers told her. The woman replied calmly, "If you burn our house, you'll burn us too. We will not leave." The soldiers felt ashamed and turned away.

Pathway of Destruction

While soldiers spared some homes, anything else that could be of use to the Confederate armies was burned. Factories, thousands of bales of cotton, cotton gins, and sawmills were set afire. The greatest destruction was to railroads. During the march, Sherman's army wrecked more than 300 miles of tracks. The men

After his sweep through Georgia, Sherman led an even more destructive march through South Carolina. His goal was to break the South's fighting spirit.

developed a special way of doing this work. A **regiment** (large military unit) would line up along one side of a railroad track. Then they would raise an entire section and flip it over. This would jar the rails loose from the wooden ties. The soldiers would then gather the ties together and burn them. The rails were thrown on top of the fires until they became red hot in the middle. Then the rails were picked up with big wrenches and twisted around trees until they were useless. The men called them Sherman's neckties.

Confederate resistance to Sherman's advance was very weak. Almost every man able to fight was serving in Confederate regiments outside the state. Only about 13,000 untrained troops faced Sherman's battle-hardened soldiers. At Griswoldville, a militia force bravely charged a portion of Sherman's army. As the Confederate line moved forward, men were killed by heavy cannon and rifle fire. Soon the field was littered with 600 Confederate bodies. After the battle, a Union officer described the scene:

"Old, gray-haired men, and boys not over 15 years old, lay dead or twisting in pain. 'Water,' one boy said, 'can you get me some water?' His chest was torn open . . . . I did pity those boys."

To Savannah

Sherman's troops entered Milledgeville, Georgia's capital at the time, on November 23. They were cheered by blacks who lined the sidewalks. An old black woman shouted, "God bless you Yanks! You've come at last!"

In this scene from the movie *Gone with the Wind*, Scarlett O'Hara [left] is surrounded by hundreds of the Confederate soldiers wounded in the battle against Sherman's men in Atlanta.

On Thanksgiving, the Union troops feasted and celebrated noisily. The celebration was cut short, however, by the arrival of some Union soldiers who had escaped from the terrible Confederate prison camp at Andersonville, Georgia. These men had been starved almost to death. They wept when they saw so much food around the Union camp fires.

Union troops looted the capitol building at Milledgeville, and chopped up the pews of churches for firewood. A newspaper editor wrote: "If an army of Devils were to invade the country, they would not be much worse than Sherman's army."

As Sherman's army neared Savannah, it was slowed more by swamps than by enemy resistance. Sometimes the men had to wade through icy waters up to their armpits. When they lit fires to warm up, Rebel guns opened up on them. The fires had to be stamped out. One soldier wrote: "The rest of the night we were compelled to dance around in our wet clothes to keep ourselves from freezing to death."

The Confederate troops guarding Savannnah retreated on December 22, to avoid being trapped inside the city. Sherman's army marched in to this city-by-the-sea the next day. Sherman sent President Lincoln a telegram announcing his victory. It said: "I beg to present to you, as a Christmas gift, the city of Savannah. . . ."

In the North, Sherman became a great hero overnight. In the South, he was denounced as a fiend who made war on helpless civilians. But his march proved to everyone the overwhelming power of the Union armies, and helped bring an end to the war. Sherman readily admitted that his march through Georgia was "a hard [kind] of warfare."

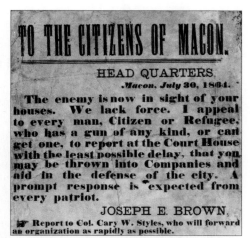

As Sherman's men neared, Georgia's governor issued this warning to the city of Macon. Old men, young boys, and already-wounded soldiers were the only ones left to defend the city.

CHAPTER CHECK

WORD MATCH
1. Sherman's neckties   **a.** steal or take goods by force
2. forage   **b.** Sherman's soldiers who stole goods
3. bummers   **c.** to get or take food from
4. regiments   **d.** destroyed railroad track
5. loot   **e.** large military units

QUICK QUIZ
1. What was the purpose of Sherman's march through Georgia?
2. What was so unusual about the Confederate militia who fought at Griswoldville?
3. Why was there so little Confederate resistance to Sherman's destructive march?

THINK ABOUT IT
1. Describe Sherman's idea of total ruin in warfare. Do you agree with this strategy? Why or why not?
2. Do you think Sherman was a hero or a villian?
3. How do you think destroying non-military targets and harming or killing civilians breaks peoples' will to fight a war?

27 THE SOUTH SURRENDERS

With General Lee's surrender, the Confederacy was no more. These war-weary soldiers weep as they fold up the Confederate flag for the last time and prepare to march—this time, for home.

In the tiny village of Appomatox (ap-uh-MAT-ucks) Court House, Virginia, a tired-looking soldier sat in a farmhouse parlor. He wore a spotless uniform with a red sash. A sword hung by his side. This soldier was Confederate General Robert E. Lee.

On April 9, 1865, General Lee knew his side was beaten. His troops were battered and starving. A few days before, they had given up Richmond, Virginia, the Confederate capital. Now surrounded and outnumbered by Union soldiers, they were cut off from a retreat.

He knew the foolishness of continuing to fight. Hours earlier one of his officers advised him to break up his army and to let them go on fighting in the hills. Lee rejected the advice. To let the fighting continue, he believed, would further destroy an already ravaged (violently destroyed) countryside and people. The longer the struggle went on, the longer it would take the South—and the entire nation—to recover.

Lee and Grant

Lee waited for General Ulysses S. Grant to arrive. Grant was Lee's counterpart—the commander of the Union forces. Earlier, Lee had said, "There is nothing left for me to do but go and see General Grant, and I would rather die a thousand deaths."

Wearing a wrinkled private's coat, General Grant entered the farmhouse followed by half a dozen officers. Grant's boots and trousers were spotted with mud. Only the gold stars on his shoulders showed his rank.

This was not the first time the two generals met. Almost 20 years earlier, both had fought in the Mexican War. Even at that time, there was a great contrast in the two men's manner and appearance. In fact, Lee, then a colonel in the U.S. Army, once told the young Lieutenant Grant that he was not dressed properly.

At the start of the Civil War, Lee opposed slavery and had set his own slaves free. He did not like the idea of the south seceding from the Union. But he could not bring himself to fight against his home state of Virginia. Like most Southerners, Lee believed that his state and its rights were more important than the sovereignty of the Union.

Lee served the Confederacy well. He had a great ability to measure an enemy's strength and location. Perhaps as important, he inspired passionate loyalty among his soldiers. Historians

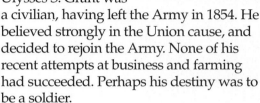

In this 1864 photo, Lee wears the formal sash and sword he later wore for his surrender to Grant.

The ever-rumpled Grant matched Lee in military brilliance, if not in personal style.

have judged him one of the greatest military leaders in U.S. history.

Rejoining the Army

When the Civil War broke out, Ulysses S. Grant was a civilian, having left the Army in 1854. He believed strongly in the Union cause, and decided to rejoin the Army. None of his recent attempts at business and farming had succeeded. Perhaps his destiny was to be a soldier.

Grant became a colonel and then, in August 1861, a **brigadier general.** He won fame for demanding unconditional surrender from Southern commanders. In fact, people in the North began saying that Grant's initials, U.S., stood for "unconditional surrender."

Grant Takes Command

In March 1864, Lincoln made Grant commander of the Union armies. During the following months, Grant attacked without letup. During the spring of 1864, Grant lost more than 60,000 men. But Confederate losses were also high. Because Grant's armies suffered so many casualties, people started calling him the butcher. This hurt him, but he knew only one way to win—to attack over and over again.

In the end, Grant's tactics were successful. Lee finally had no choice. He asked to meet Grant to discuss surrender. As the mud-splattered General Grant entered the

The Union Turns the Tide, 1863–1865

How many Union victories were there between 1863 and 1865? How many Confederate victories?

AMERICAN ADVENTURES

farmhouse, General Lee bowed and the two men shook hands. Then the two got down to ending the war.

Kindness From the Victor

Grant, "the butcher," showed himself to be a compassionate man after all. He took no Confederate prisoners. Lee's men were allowed to go home. As a gesture of respect, Grant allowed Confederate officers to keep their swords, and their horses or mules. "Let all the men who claim to own a horse or mule take the animals home with them to work their little farms," said Grant.

"General Sheridan," Grant asked a nearby officer, "how much food do you have?" When Sheridan replied, Grant ordered, "Give General Lee food for 25,000 men."

Lee shook hands with Grant and bowed to the other Union officers. Lee walked out of the farmhouse. Grant and his officers raise their hats in respect. Lee raised his, and without another word, rode off.

Later, Lee's men clustered about him as he rode slowly toward his tent. Cheers turned to sobs as the men said farewell to their beloved commander. When Lee reached his tent, he turned to face them. "Men," he whispered, "we have fought through the war together; I have done my best for you; my heart is too full to say more."

Meanwhile, Grant rode toward his camp, stopping along the way to write a telegram to President Lincoln. He heard guns firing in celebration within the Union lines. "Stop the firing," he said. "The Rebels are our countrymen again."

CHAPTER CHECK

WORD MATCH

1. ravaged
2. Appomatox Court House, Virginia
3. Richmond, Virginia
4. unconditional surrender
5. brigadier general

a. where Lee surrendered to Grant, ending the war
b. violently destroyed
c. capital of the Confederacy
d. military officer in rank above a colonel
e. Northerners said Grant's initials stood for this phrase

QUICK QUIZ

1. What situation did Lee face when he decided to surrender?
2. As a soldier, what did Grant believe was the one way to wage and win a war?
3. What did Grant do after Lee surrendered that showed he was a compassionate man who respected Southerners?

THINK ABOUT IT

1. Why do you think historians judge Robert E. Lee as one of the greatest leaders in U.S. military history?
2. Do you see any importance in Grant's gesture of allowing Confederate officers to keep their swords?
3. Why do you think Grant let any Confederate soldier who owned a horse or mule keep it? Why do think Grant ordered food to be given to Lee's troops?

28 THE ASSASSINATION OF LINCOLN

The Civil War took its toll on the nation—and on Abraham Lincoln. At left, a youthful-looking Lincoln in June 1860, before becoming president. At right, a weary man, just five days before he was killed.

The time: 10:15 P.M.
The date: April 14, 1865.
The place: Ford's Theatre in Washington, D.C.

In a box above the stage, President Lincoln and his wife Mary, watched a play called *Our American Cousin*. An engaged couple, Clara Harris and Major Henry R. Rathbone, was with them. In the darkness, a young man wearing a black suit slipped quietly into the box. In his right hand he held a small, single-shot pistol. In his left hand he held a dagger. Quickly he raised the pistol behind the President's left ear

and fired. The President's head fell onto his chest. He would never speak again. By 7:22 A.M. the next day, he would be dead.

How did it happen? Who was the man in the black suit who had done such a terrible thing?

John Wilkes Booth

John Wilkes Booth, the man who killed Lincoln, was a well-known actor who had a strong wish to win lasting fame. Booth also had wanted the South to win the Civil War. He hated Lincoln for trying to hold the Union together. In 1864, Booth decided he must do something to help the South win the war. His idea was to kidnap President Lincoln and take him to Richmond, Virginia, the Confederate capital. This would make Booth's name famous, and it would also hurt the man he hated.

Booth found five Confederate supporters to help. First they planned to kidnap Lincoln from Ford's Theater on January 18, 1865. But the plan did not work because President Lincoln did not go to the theater that night as expected. On March 20, the six men again tried to kidnap Lincoln. They learned that on that day Lincoln would visit the Soldiers' Home outside Washington, D. C. On a lonely road, they waited on horseback for his carriage to pass by. But Lincoln decided not to go to the Soldiers' Home that day. So this plan also failed.

Then, on April 13, Booth heard that President Lincoln would be at Ford's Theater the following night. By this time he had given up his kidnapping plan. Lee's army had surrendered four days before, so the point of his original idea was lost. Instead, Booth decided to kill the President for revenge.

The next morning,

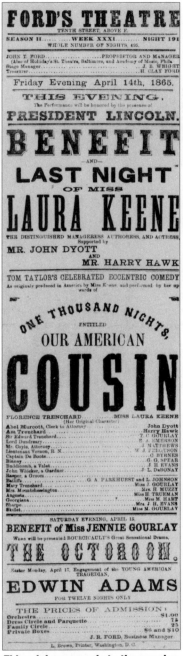

This ad drew crowds to the popular production, *Our American Cousin*, at Ford's Theatre. President Lincoln was shot while attending the show.

Booth went to Ford's Theater and made his plans. He decided he could easily make the jump from the President's box to the stage. Outside the rear door, a horse would be waiting for him. Booth decided that 10:15 P.M. would be the right time to make his move. At that time, there would be only one actor on the stage.

Shortly after 10:00 P.M. that evening, Booth arrived at the theater. He went up to the President's box. No one was guarding the door. The man who was supposed to be on guard was not at his post. Booth opened the door. In a moment the pistol was behind Lincoln's head and Booth fired.

Booth shouted, "Sic semper tyrannis!" (Thus always to tyrants!) Then he jumped to the stage, breaking his left leg in the fall. But before anyone could stop him, he was out the back door. He escaped on horseback.

The President is Dead!

Four soldiers carried Lincoln through the horrified crowd to a house across the street. The doctors knew he would die. They sent for Lincoln's son, Robert, and members of the Cabinet. The end came at 7:22 the next morning. At Lincoln's bed-

As this train carried Abraham Lincoln home to Springfield for the last time, a nation turned out to honor him. He had preserved the Union, but at the tremendous cost of many lives—including his own.

side, Secretary of War Edwin Stanton said, "Now he belongs to the ages."

On April 21, the President's coffin was put aboard a special funeral train.

John Wilkes Booth [above] yearned for fame—and revenge against Lincoln. He got both when he killed the President.

This train would take Lincoln's body home to Springfield, Illinois. Four years before, Lincoln had traveled by train from Springfield to Washington to become president. Now the train slowly traveled back over almost the same route.

Millions of people came out to watch the funeral train as it passed by. Day and night, in town after town, mourning people waited, stared, and threw flowers. Flags flew at half staff, bands played funeral marches, guns fired salutes. Church bells rang across the country. Abraham Lincoln was buried on May 4, 1865. About 75,000 people crowded into the cemetery to watch the burial.

What happened to John Wilkes Booth? On April 26, twelve days after he shot Lincoln, he was cornered in a barn in Virginia. The soldiers set the barn on fire. One soldier disobeyed orders to capture him and shot him to death.

CHAPTER CHECK

WORD MATCH

1. mourning
2. Edwin Stanton
3. John Wilkes Booth
4. Ford's Theatre
5. Springfield, Illinois

a. well-known actor who killed Lincoln
b. Secretary of War during Lincoln's presidency
c. expressing grief at someone's death
d. Lincoln's home, and city where he was buried
e. where Booth shot Lincoln

QUICK QUIZ

1. What did John Wilkes Booth say after he shot President Lincoln?
2. What was John Wilkes Booth's original plan?

THINK ABOUT IT

1. Why do you think Booth called Lincoln a tyrant?
2. Why did Booth decide against his original plan, and instead decide to kill Lincoln?
3. Describe the circumstances which allowed Booth to murder Lincoln at point-blank range?

A TORN NATION

History Detective

1. Many from Washington, D.C. brought their picnic lunches here to watch the first battle between the North and the South. However, it was not the pleasant experience that many had expected. Where am I?

2. Lincoln wrote me to free the slaves. These words provided a moral reason for the North to fight on in a terrible war, and to motivate free blacks to enlist in the Union army. What am I?

3. In me, she recorded her thoughts and observations during and after the Civil War. What am I? To whom did I belong?

4. I was just a small Pennsylvania town. But in a major battle, Union soldiers defeated the South here in what many people call the turning point of the Civil War. Where am I?

5. I led my soldiers through the South with one intention: to destroy the South so that it could never rise up again. Who am I?

Voices From the Past

On November 19, 1863, Abraham Lincoln dedicated the Gettysburg National Cemetery. The words that Lincoln spoke are forever marked in one of America's most important speeches. Here is what he said:

Fourscore and seven years ago our fathers brought forth upon this continent a new nation . . . dedicated to the idea that all men are created equal. Now we are in a great civil war. We are here on a great battle-field of that war. We have come to dedicate a portion of this field as a final resting-place for those who here gave their lives that this nation might live.

We here highly resolve that these dead shall not have died in vain; that this nation, under God, shall have a new birth of freedom, and that the Government of the people, by the people, and for the people shall not perish from the earth.

1. What ideas and feelings does Lincoln seem to be trying to instill in the American people listening to his speech?

Hands–On History

1. *Writing a diary entry*—Imagine that you are young and excited about joining the Union (or Confederate) army. Write an entry in a diary that shows your feelings. Write another diary entry showing your feelings two years later.

2. *Drawing an historical map*—Use library resources to locate the path that Sherman took as he destroyed the South. Draw and label a map showing his route.

YESTERDAY'S NEWS

The American Adventures Newspaper

LINCOLN SALUTES WOMEN

Washington, D.C., March 16, 1864—Rarely have cheers been heard as loud as those at the close of Lincoln's address today for the benefit of the sick and wounded soldiers of the army. He took this occasion to celebrate the women of the War. Most Americans believe that man is the only one suffering in the War, but Lincoln says this is not true. In fact, if not for women, the suffering would be much worse.

"In this extraordinary war," said Lincoln, ". . . nothing has been more remarkable than the relief of suffering of our soldiers and their families. And the chief agents for this are the women of America. If all that has been said by poets since the creation of the world in praise of women were applied to the women of America, it would not do them justice for their conduct during this war. God bless the women of America!"

Clara Barton, remembered as the "Angel of the Battlefield," administered first aid on the frontlines of many Civil War battles. She later became the founder of the American Red Cross.

1.

Before the War, there were no plans for who was to care for the sick and injured men. On both sides of the Civil War, it was women who took the initiative in organizing the medical supply and the nursing. It began out of two major organizations: the

Woman's Central Association, made up of 3,000 New York women and led by Dr. Elizabeth Blackwell; and the U.S. Sanitary Commission, led by Dorothea Dix. In all, 3,200 women on both sides have given their nursing services to the U.S. These organizations have sent women out to staff the many hospitals of the Union and the Confederacy. Most often, the women are not paid for their work and sacrifice.

Without these women sacrificing their time,

2.

You Be the Reporter

Match each question with its news item above.
1. What would be a good headline for this article?
2. How do you think the Civil War would have been different without the women nurses and volunteers? Complete the sentence and finish this article with your own thoughts.

YEAR	TITLE	AUTHOR
1776	Common Sense	Paine
1852	Uncle Tom's Cabin	Stowe
1906	The Jungle	Sinclair
1939	Grapes of Wrath	Steinbeck
1962	Silent Sping	Carson

TABLE SKILLS

DRAWING CONCLUSIONS FROM DATA

Why has the U.S. Civil War been called a "War without Victory?" The war lasted for four years and both the North and South suffered terrible losses. The table on the next page presents factual information or **data** about the major battles of the war. Take careful note of the kind of information provided in this table. How are the battles organized? What categories or column headings are used to organize important facts?

Historians record and use such facts to get an in-depth picture of what took place in the past. Government officials also refer to facts like these in making policy decisions. By comparing or combining data from the table opposite, you can draw some conclusions of your own about the Civil War.

Study the column headings at the top of the table. Then note the answers to these questions on a separate sheet of paper.

1. Find the first major battle of the war. **(a)** What battle was it? **(b)** In what state did it take place? **(c)** How many Confederate soldiers died or were wounded in the battle? How many Union soldiers?

2. Find the first and second Battles of Bull Run. **(a)** How many months passed between the two battles? **(b)** Who won each battle?

3. Judging from the information in the table, which state saw **(a)** the greatest amount of fighting? **(b)** the second greatest?

4. Study the results of the battles. **(a)** In which five battles did a northern offensive lead to a definite victory? **(b)** For which of these did the North pay the highest price?

5. In which of the major battles did a southern offensive lead to a decisive victory? at what cost to the South?

6. How many attacks were launched **(a)** by the North? by the South? **(b)** Did the efforts of attacking armies usually succeed or fail? Explain.

7. The Civil War battles killed or wounded many Americans on both sides. **(a)** What was the total number of losses suffered by both North and South in the Vicksburg campaign of 1863? **(b)** Which three battles or campaigns had the highest number of losses on both sides?

8. The turning point of the war occurred in July, 1863, when General Lee failed to take Gettysburg. **(a)** What other major battle occurred at that time? **(b)** After that time, in how many more major battles did the South win a clear-cut victory?

9. Find the last major campaign of the war. **(a)** Which campaign was it? **(b)** How long did it last? **(c)** What was the result?

10. In a number of major battles, the victor actually suffered more losses than the loser. **(a)** In which battles did this happen? **(b)** What conclusions can you draw about the Civil War from this information?

For Extra Credit: Create your own timeline of major civil war battles by using the data from the table. First, draw a five-year timeline and label each year from 1860 through 1865. Then show the battles of the Civil War in the order that they happened, with their correct dates.

Major Battles of the Civil War

	When Battle Occurred	Where Battle Occurred	Southern Losses [1]	Northern Losses [1]	Result of Battle
Antietam	Sept. 17, 1862	Maryland	12,000	12,000	Draw, ending in Southern retreat
Atlanta (campaign)	May 7-Sept. 2, 1864	Georgia	25,000	27,000	Northern advance successful
Bull Run (First)	July 21, 1861	Virginia	2,000	1,000	Northern attack defeated
Bull Run (Second)	Aug. 29-30, 1862	Virginia	9,000	10,000	Northern attack defeated
Chancellorsville	May 1-4, 1863	Virginia	11,000	11,000	Northern attack defeated
Chattanooga (battles near)	Nov. 23-25, 1863	Tennessee	3,000	5,000	Northern attack successful
Chickamauga	Sept. 19-20, 1863	Georgia	17,000	12,000	Southern attack successful
Cold Harbor	June 3, 1864	Virginia	2,000	6,000	Northern attack defeated
Fredericksburg	Dec. 13, 1862	Virginia	5,000	12,000	Northern attack defeated
Gettysburg	July 1-3, 1863	Pennsylvania	23,000	18,000	Southern attack defeated
Petersburg (campaign)	June 14, 1864-April 2, 1865	Virginia	13,000	17,000	Northern attack finally successful after long seige
Seven Days' Battles	June 26-July 1, 1862	Virginia	20,000	16,000	Southern counter-attack successful
Shiloh	April 6-7, 1862	Tennessee	11,000	13,000	Southern attack defeated
Spotsylvania	May 10-12, 1864	Virginia	9,000	11,000	Northern attack partly successful
Stones River	Dec. 31, 1862 Jan. 2, 1863	Tennessee	9,000	9,000	Southern attack partly successful
Vicksburg (seige of)	May 22-July 4, 1863	Mississippi	10,000	9,000	Northern attack successful
Wilderness	May 5-6, 1864	Virginia	10,000	18,000	Draw, but Northern attack defeated
Winchester	Sept. 19, 1864	Virginia	4,000	5,000	Northern attack successful

[1] Killed and wounded to the nearest 1,000. Most figures are unofficial estimates.

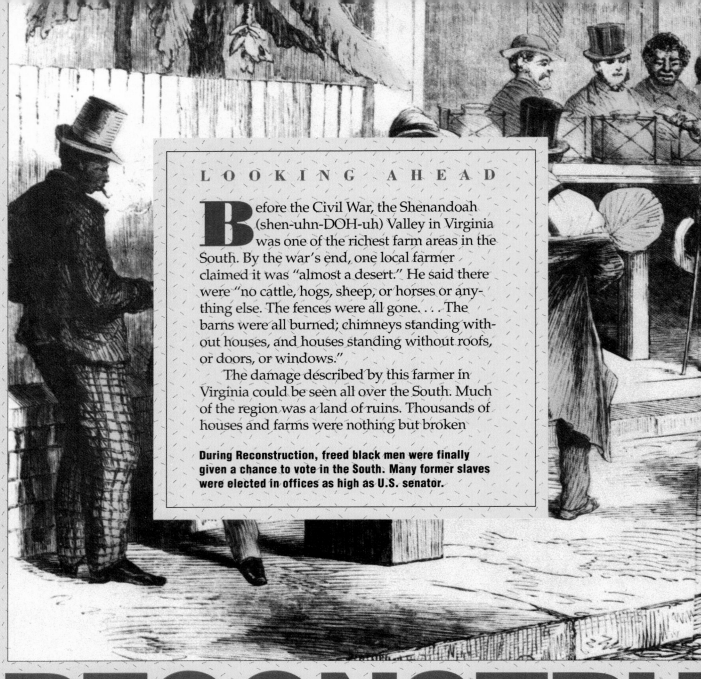

LOOKING AHEAD

Before the Civil War, the Shenandoah (shen-uhn-DOH-uh) Valley in Virginia was one of the richest farm areas in the South. By the war's end, one local farmer claimed it was "almost a desert." He said there were "no cattle, hogs, sheep, or horses or anything else. The fences were all gone. . . . The barns were all burned; chimneys standing without houses, and houses standing without roofs, or doors, or windows."

The damage described by this farmer in Virginia could be seen all over the South. Much of the region was a land of ruins. Thousands of houses and farms were nothing but broken

During Reconstruction, freed black men were finally given a chance to vote in the South. Many former slaves were elected in offices as high as U.S. senator.

RECONSTRU

1864	1866	1868	1870	1872

1865
Andrew Johnson succeeds Lincoln as president.

1866
Freedmen's Bureau establishes schools for poor blacks and whites.

1866
Civil Rights Acts protect blacks from unfair legislation.

1867
Reconstruction Act puts South under military rule.

1869
Ulysses S. Grant becomes president.

1870
All Confederate states readmitted to the Union.

CTION

6

1874　　　　1876

● **1875**
Blanche K. Bruce,
second black elected
to Senate.

● **1876**
Rutherford B. Hayes
elected president in
contested election.

UNIT

walls and empty fields. Many towns and cities had been burned to the ground. There was hardly a family in the South that had not lost someone in the war.

People all over the South felt confused. They knew that the Old South—of slaves and King Cotton—was gone. What would freedom mean for the four million black people in the South?

Many Northerners decided to live in the South after the Civil War. They became known as carpetbaggers because of the small fabric bags they hurriedly packed before heading South.

Rebuilding the South

As soon as the war ended, Americans began to argue about how to rebuild the South and reunite the nation. The 12 years between 1865 and 1877—the **Reconstruction** era—was a time of experimentation. It was also a time of struggle over the meaning of freedom and equality in America.

In Congress, the Radical Republicans had a ready answer for one Reconstruction problem. What was to become of the freed slaves? These Republicans answered, "Let Negroes vote, go to school, own land, and hold office. Let them live as equals with the whites."

In 1866, Congress passed the Thirteenth Amendment to the Constitution. This amendment prohibited slavery in any state of the nation. African Americans welcomed their freedom. But

they needed jobs and land to become economically, as well as politically, free citizens.

One former slave said, "When freedom came, folks went out singing, shouting, yelling, and knocking down everything." According to another man, "I felt like a bird out of a cage." Many blacks moved to cities to find work. Others looked for lost relatives. But soon it became apparent they faced hard times. Many lacked the education to get a job or money to buy a farm.

Congress established the Freedmen's Bureau to help the former slaves. The Freedmen's Bureau set up schools for both blacks and poor whites. It also provided food and legal help.

The idea of treating the former slaves as equals angered many white Southerners. These people hated the Republicans in Congress. They also resented Northerners who had come South to help black people or to go into business. They called these newcomers **carpetbaggers** because their suitcases were often made of carpet material. These bags reflected the hasty, last-minute decisions some Northerners made to move South.

Soon the Southern states began passing **Black Codes** which tried to take away many of the rights of African Americans. These Black Codes ruled that jobless blacks could be arrested and forced to work for a white boss. Blacks could not serve on juries or go to school with whites. They could be arrested if they walked in the streets after dark.

Black Southerners felt angry and frustrated by laws such as these. The new Thirteenth Amendment to the Constitution did away with slavery. Now it looked as if the Black Codes were setting up a new kind of slavery. The codes angered many Northerners. They thought the Black Codes showed that the South had not learned any lessons from the war.

They believed that Southerners did not really want to change their society.

Radical Republicans

Many powerful Republicans in Congress also felt this way. They were called **Radicals.** One of their most important leaders was Thaddeus Stevens of Pennsylvania. Stevens and the Radicals said that it was up to the U.S. government to force the South to change. They believed that no Southern states should be let back into the Union until certain conditions had been met by them.

The Radicals' tough Reconstruction plan divided the South into districts. Each

The Course of Reconstruction, 1865–1877

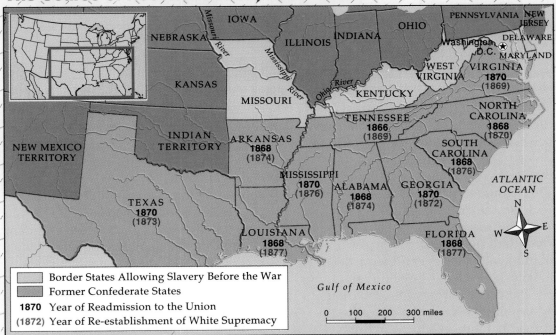

Border States Allowing Slavery Before the War
Former Confederate States
1870 Year of Readmission to the Union
(1872) Year of Re-establishment of White Supremacy

Which former Confederate state was the first to be readmitted to the Union? Which three states were the first to restore all-white governments? Why were freed slaves in Kentucky never protected by Reconstruction laws?

Much of Baton Rouge, Louisiana was burned to the ground when the Union and Confederate forces fought on August 5, 1862.

district would be governed by an Army general with U.S. troops to back up his orders. The Southern states would be required to set up new state governments. They would also have to accept the Fourteenth Amendment giving all African Americans the rights of U.S. citizens. Radical Reconstruction also required all states to give blacks the right to vote.

President Andrew Johnson did not agree with the Radical plan for Reconstruction. Johnson had been vice-president under Lincoln. After Lincoln's death, he decided to follow a plan like the one he thought Lincoln had wanted.

This plan made it easy for the Southern states to get back in the Union. They just had to repeal their secession laws, cancel their war debts, and ratify the Thirteenth Amendment.

The 1866 Congressional elections turned into a bitter fight between President Johnson and the Radical Republicans. Voters had to decide whose program for Reconstruction should be followed.

Johnson fought hard for his plan. He even went on a speaking tour of the North. But Northern voters were so angered by the Southern Black Codes that the Radicals easily won the election. The Radicals thought that Johnson had acted improperly. They tried to remove him from office, but failed by one Senate vote. Congress controlled Reconstruction from that time on.

Black Legislators

After the 1866 elections, the Radical Republicans put their plan for Reconstruction into operation. The rights of blacks in the South were backed up by new laws and by U.S. troops. For the first time, blacks began to vote and seek office. Running as Republicans, many African Americans were elected to state and local offices. Black leaders were also elected to Congress for the first time.

Members of the Ku Klux Klan, hiding behind their white hoods, made many secret terrorist attacks against Southern blacks during Reconstruction.

Two from Mississippi served in the U.S. Senate.

Black and white Republicans passed many laws to help all people in the South. These laws set up public schools for blacks and whites respectively. They allowed streets, roads, and bridges to be built. They gave relief to the poor. They made taxes fairer.

Many white Southerners resented Republicans' efforts to provide a more equal society for everyone. These white Southerners believed they could get rid of the Republicans by preventing black men from voting. There were many ways of doing this. The most effective was through secret terrorist groups such as the Ku Klux Klan. The KKK rode around at night, beating black people in their homes. Many blacks were murdered in cold blood.

Meanwhile, the Radicals were losing their hold on Congress. Some of their leaders had died. General Ulysses S. Grant, who was elected president in 1868, believed he could not keep U.S. troops in every Southern state where blacks and Republicans needed support. He began to pull troops out. As the troops left, white Democrats took over the Southern state governments. When this happened, African Americans in those states lost their rights.

A corrupt presidential election in 1877 resulted in the removal of the last U.S. troops. Republican rule in the South was finished. And so was Reconstruction. The South had been restored and the North and South reunited. But the benefits of freedom for African Americans would have to wait.

29 FREEDOM!

Schools like the Hampton Institute in Beaufort, South Carolina, educated freed blacks of all ages during Reconstruction. Here they are studying American history.

Matilda Dunbar was in the kitchen getting breakfast when the word came—all blacks were free. "I never finished that breakfast," recalled Dunbar. "I ran 'round and 'round the kitchen, clapping my hands and crying, 'Freedom has come! Rejoice!' Oh, how we sang and shouted that day!"

Another ex-slave found similar happiness in freedom, but couldn't find work. "No place to stay and nothin' to eat," said Jack Goodridge.

Matilda Dunbar's and Jack Goodridge's stories became familiar ones after the war. Now that slavery was over, thousands upon thousands of black people were overjoyed. Their dream had come true and there were many celebrations. But after the celebrations were over, many black people began to face new problems.

Now that they were free, how would they get work? Where would they find homes? How would they get food? They were free, but very few of them had money, land, or jobs. Most of them had only the clothes on their backs. Without land and economic independence, blacks wondered what freedom would mean.

Staying On

Some blacks stayed on the plantations and were employed by their old masters. Mary Lindsay, an ex-slave who found work with her former master, was disappointed. "I stayed on, 'cause I didn't have no place to go, and I carded and spinned the cotton and wool, and she make me just one dress. . . . So one night I just put that new dress in a bundle and set foot right down the big road a-walking west!"

But most white Southerners had little money to pay wages. They had lost everything in the war. Many white people survived these years because of the help given them by their former slaves. Some white Southerners felt kindly toward the freed slaves. Others did not. Those who didn't felt, "The Yankees freed you. Now let the Yankees feed you."

Many white Southerners feared newly-freed men and women. They worried that blacks would not work unless forced to. Many blacks resented the low wages and severe restrictions placed on them by former owners. They wanted their own land so they could be independent as well as free.

Freed blacks crowded into towns and cities. Parents searched for children sold during slavery. They lived in the ruins of buildings smashed in the war. Thousands died of hunger and sickness. Some white Southerners and Northern church groups, such as the Quakers, gave blacks food and medicine.

The Freedmen's Bureau

Many blacks got a great deal of help from the **Freedmen's Bureau,** an organization that was run by the Army. An act of Congress created the Freedmen's Bureau at the end of the war. The bureau gave out food and medicine to poor black and white people. It found jobs for blacks, negotiated labor contracts, and represented black citizens in court.

The Freedmen's Bureau's most important contribution was in education. It built more than 4000 schools for hundreds of thousands of black students, thus creating the first free public school system in the South.

In a few years, the numbers of Southern blacks who were **literate** (able to read and write) rose from about 3 percent to a remarkable 25 percent. "I never before saw children so eager to

Hampton Institute was one of many schools for blacks set up by Northern missionaries and teachers who followed the troops southward.

Freed blacks were encouraged by governmental authorities to farm their own land. In this way, more crops could be farmed and other blacks would be encouraged to work for themselves.

learn," wrote Charlotte Forten, a black teacher who went South to teach the ex-slaves. "Coming to school is a constant delight to them."

The Freedmen's Bureau also gave abandoned land to the freed slaves. Often the original landowners were in jail or prisoner-of-war camps. But this policy of giving away land was highly unpopular with Southern whites, and many people in the North as well. In the end, most of the land that had been given away was returned to its original owners.

The Black Codes

Southern whites felt that they had to control the ex-slaves. One by one, legislatures in Southern states began passing Black Codes. Under many of these codes, blacks could be arrested for almost any reason. They could not own guns or own property. They could not testify against whites in court. Many codes allowed blacks to be jailed if they held no labor contract. Some codes didn't allow them to live in cities.

Although the codes varied in different states, the purpose was to force blacks to continue working as a bound labor force. Blacks who were found guilty of breaking any laws would be made to work off their sentences and fines by labor. It was a new form of slavery.

The black man will clang the bell when a child pulls this mid-19th century toy. He has a lot to celebrate with the announcement of the Emancipation Proclamation and the passage of the Fifteenth Amendment.

CHAPTER CHECK

WORD MATCH

1. Mary Lindsay
2. Charlotte Forten
3. Freedmen's Bureau
4. Black Codes
5. literate

a. ex-slave who worked for her former master

b. able to read and write

c. black teacher who went South to teach ex-slaves

d. created to limit the freedom and rights of former slaves

e. organization to help ex-slaves with jobs, legal needs, and education

QUICK QUIZ

1. Why didn't white plantation owners let former slaves work for them as employees?
2. What were the purposes of the Black Codes?
3. Why did the South need rebuilding?

THINK ABOUT IT

1. The Freedmen's Bureau built more than 4000 schools for black students. Do you think this emphasis on education was important? Why or why not?
2. What, if any, connection do you see between Black Codes and slavery?

30 STEVENS AND JOHNSON

A stern Thaddeus Stevens sits [front row, second from left] with six other representatives. They faced the serious and unpleasant task of impeaching a president, Andrew Johnson.

In 1859, a hard-faced, crippled man stood up in the House of Representatives. As he prepared to speak, there was a brief moment of silence, then the room grew very noisy. It echoed with as many cries of praise and encouragement as with hoots of disapproval. The noise was so great that the clerk furiously pounded his gavel until it broke. Whenever Congressman Thaddeus Stevens spoke, emotions ran high.

Stevens had been born in Vermont in 1792, the crippled son of a poor farming family. But now, he was one of the most admired and most hated men in the nation—a leader of the Radical Republicans. He had worked all his life on behalf of rights for blacks. He would eventually become a great enemy of another controversial politician—Andrew Johnson.

The Runaway's Lawyer

Although Stevens didn't come from a rich family with a lot of advantages, he was a hard-working and good student. He studied at Dartmouth College in New Hampshire and began practicing law in Pennsylvania in 1816. From the beginning, he took on difficult cases that no other lawyers would touch. In one, he defended an accused murderer who was thought to be insane.

In the 1830s, Stevens began to defend the rights of blacks. Northern blacks, while not slaves, faced racial discrimination. They had to live in the worst parts of town and take the worst jobs. But most troubling were the slave catchers, who came across the border from Maryland looking for runaway slaves in Pennsylvania. If the slave catchers could not find the runaways, they would trap free blacks and force them into slavery. Stevens was outraged by the this. He began to defend so many runaways and other blacks in court that he became known as "the runaway's lawyer."

A Career in Congress

Stevens decided the best way to bring about abolition was to enter national politics. In 1848, he was elected to Congress on the Whig party ticket. In his very first speech, Stevens created an uproar in the House of Representatives when he strongly condemned slavery. Angry proslavery members of Congress surrounded his desk and shook their fists in his face.

Stevens' opposition to the Fugitive Slave law led some to accuse him of being an anti-slavery fanatic. "There can be no

Thomas Nast was a famous 19th-century cartoonist who played a strong role in exposing corrupt political and business leaders. Here he ridicules President Andrew Johnson by portraying him as "King Andy."

fanatics in the cause of genuine liberty," he replied. Stevens played an important part in the formation of the anti-slavery Republican party in Pennsylvania in 1855. Three years later, he was elected to Congress on the Republican ticket.

During the Civil War, Stevens played a key role in Congress. As chairman of the Ways and Means Committee, it was his responsibility to find money to finance the war. He continued to speak out against slavery. Stevens believed the Civil War was not being fought just to bring the Confederacy back into the Union—it was a war against slavery.

Forty Acres and a Mule

After the Emancipation Proclamation freed slaves in the Confederacy, Stevens pushed for more rights for blacks. He urged laws that would free all slaves in the United States. Stevens also wanted to protect the rights of freed blacks, including their right to vote.

Stevens realized that blacks needed economic security to be really free. He proposed giving all freed slaves "forty acres and a mule." Free land would permit former slaves to earn a living as farmers. The land could be taken from large Southern plantations.

"They have earned this," said Stevens. "They have worked upon the land for ages and they are entitled to it." But the plan was too unpopular in Congress and never became a reality. By the end of the war, Stevens was old and sick and could hardly walk. But he had one more enemy to fight before he died—President Andrew Johnson.

Conflicting Views

Johnson was an unusual figure in American politics. He was a Southerner who defended the right to own slaves, but he also hated rich slave owners. The interests of the Union and the Constitution were his first priority.

Like Stevens, Johnson was a stubborn, strong-willed, self-made man. He had been born in poverty in North Carolina and had become a tailor in Tennessee before entering state politics. A quick thinker and a good speaker, he rose to be governor of Tennessee and then senator. When the Civil War broke out, Johnson was the only Southern senator to support the Union. In the election of 1864, Lincoln selected him to run for vice-president. Lincoln's death in 1865 brought the nation a president with strong sympathy for the defeated South.

Johnson thought the nation should be lenient toward the South. He wanted to re-admit any state that agreed to abolish slavery and take back its declaration to secede. He pardoned practically all ex-Confederates. He allowed the South's old pro-slavery leaders to return to power. He let these leaders create the Black Codes in the South.

Johnson's policies infuriated Stevens and the Radical Republicans. They felt Johnson was undoing everything that had

French artist Edward Degas' painting, *Cotton Exchange*, is an example of his best work done while living in New Orleans.

been won by the war. In fact, Stevens and the Radicals wanted to completely change Southern society before the seceding states were admitted back into the Union. They planned to do this through military rule.

From Conflict to Crisis

Under the leadership of Stevens and the Radical Republicans, Congress passed laws expanding rights for blacks in 1867. These laws included the Civil Rights Act and the **Fourteenth Amendment,** which made all black males full citizens, with rights to equal protection under the law.

But Johnson would not sign these laws, so Congress voted again to pass them. The President spoke out bluntly and harshly against any measures that would strengthen black rights. He argued that this was a matter for the individual states to decide, not the federal government.

The Republicans saw Johnson as their worst enemy. The final straw came for Johnson when Congress passed the **Tenure of Office Act.** This law required that the president get the Senate's approval before firing any members of his cabinet. Johnson felt this unfairly limited his powers as president.

When Johnson fired Secretary of War Edwin Stanton, Congress moved to **impeach** (remove from office) the president. In the House of Representatives, Thaddeus Stevens, now too ill to walk, made the final speech calling for impeachment. Johnson, he declared bitterly, had failed to carry out the will of the people.

Impeachment

No U.S. president had ever stood trial in the Senate for misconduct. Stevens, along with six other representatives, led the attack against Johnson. Tickets for the trial sold out. The Senate gallery was packed with spectators. Rumors spread that Johnson was crazy, and had been involved in Lincoln's murder. None of this was true. Johnson did not attend the trial. He was defended by four lawyers.

In fact, it seemed that the Radicals didn't have a very strong case for removing the president from office. Conviction required a two-thirds majority and many Republicans were uncertain how to vote.

One of the undecided Republicans, Senator William Pitt Fessenden of Maine, was threatened with his life if he did not vote to **convict** (to prove a person guilty) the president. But he and six other Republicans would not convict Johnson.

In the end, Andrew Johnson was **acquitted** (declared not guilty) by one vote. He completed his term of presidency, but his power was broken. Thaddeus Stevens and Radical Republicans began their version of Reconstruction.

CHAPTER CHECK

WORD MATCH
1. impeach
2. Tenure of Office Act
3. acquitted
4. convict
5. Fourteenth Amendment

a. prove a person guilty
b. gave black adult males full citizenship
c. to remove from office
d. declared not guilty
e. required the president to get Senate's approval before firing any members of his cabinet

QUICK QUIZ
1. What was Thaddeus Stevens' early reputation as a lawyer?
2. Why did President Lincoln pick Andrew Jackson for his vice-president?

THINK ABOUT IT
1. Stevens felt freed blacks could earn economic security if they were given "40 acres and a mule," and that land could be taken from Southern plantations. Do you think that was a good idea? Explain.
2. Johnson thought the nation should treat the South with leniency. Stevens believed the South should be treated as a conquered country and put under military law. What do you think about these two different ideas?

31 BLACK LEGISLATORS

Seven prominent ex-slaves, including Frederick Douglass [center], and U.S. Senators Hiram R. Revels and Blanche K. Bruce, are honored in this poster.

The crowded visitors' gallery in the U. S. Senate buzzed with excitement. On February 25, 1870, an audience came to witness a historic event. At exactly 4:40 in the afternoon, Hiram R. Revels, a Republican from Mississippi, was sworn in as a senator. Revels was a black man, the first ever to become a member of the U.S. Senate.

During Reconstruction (1865 to 1877), blacks in the South voted in great numbers. They helped to elect 14 black Republicans to the U.S. House of Representatives. Besides Hiram Revels, another black Republican, Blanche K. Bruce, was elected to the Senate. A great many black men were elected as Republicans to state legislatures, and held other high offices also. Black legislators were strongest in South Carolina, where a majority of the people were black. In the first South Carolina legislature elected during Reconstruction, there were 87 blacks and 40 whites. In no other Southern state, however, did blacks reach a **majority.**

Hiram K. Revels

What kind of men were the black legislators elected during Reconstruction? Their education was equal to that of most other politicians of their day. Many of them were born free before the Civil War, worked in skilled trades or professions, and owned property.

Revels, for example, was born free in Fayetteville, North Carolina. Like many other free Southern blacks, he attended schools in the North. He studied for the ministry and graduated from Knox College in Illinois. During the Civil War, he helped organize a regiment of black soldiers and served as an Army **chaplain** (a minister, priest, or rabbi providing religious services in the armed forces). After the Union victory, he settled in Natchez, Mississippi, where he became minister of a black church. An eloquent speaker, he soon began his rise to fame and power in Mississippi politics. He was 42 when the state legislature elected him to the Senate.

A political cartoon shows one man's envy of Hiram Revels' election to the U.S. Senate.

Blanche K. Bruce

The period after the Civil War was marked by widespread corruption in politics. However, few black politicians of this time became involved in the scandals that were then sweeping the nation. James G. Blaine, the Republican party leader said, "They were, as a rule, studious, earnest, ambitious men whose public conduct would be honorable to any race."

Blanche Bruce was the nation's most famous black politician during Reconstruction. He was elected to a full term in the Senate for Mississippi in 1875. Bruce was born a slave in Prince Edward County, Virginia, in 1841. However, he escaped the harsh treatment most slaves endured. As a boy, he played with his master's only son, William, and was treated with special consideration. He was taught to read and write with William, and was a good student.

But after the Civil War began, Bruce ran away to Lawrence, Kansas, to become a free man. There he started a school for former slaves. Later, in Hannibal, Missouri, he started the first school for black children in that state. Wanting more education for himself, he attended Oberlin College in Ohio for one year before his money ran out. Then, in 1869, Bruce went to Mississippi, where Reconstruction policies had already started taking effect.

Bruce soon went into politics. He impressed voters, both black and white, with his handsome appearance and dignified manner. They elected him to a number of offices. In 1871, he ran for sheriff of Bolivar County. Bruce, a Republican, ran against a white Democrat. In a debate, the Democrat said, "Bruce is a decent man for his color, but he was a slave who did nothing but wait on his master. I tell you that a house servant ain't fit to be sheriff of this county."

"It is true that I was a house slave, but I freed myself, educated myself, and raised myself up in this world," answered Bruce. "If my opponent had started out where I did, he would still be there." His opponent never debated Bruce again.

Bruce won that election, and soon after was appointed superintendent of schools for Bolivar County. By 1872, the county had 21 schools with more than 1000 students. The schools were segregated, as they were almost everywhere in the South. But black parents were grateful to Bruce for giving their children a chance to get an education.

Bruce Goes to Washington

Bruce prospered in politics. He was able to buy 1000 acres of fertile land which he developed into a plantation. With black laborers, he raised cotton and became a wealthy man.

In 1873, there was talk of electing a black as governor of Mississippi. Many whites supported Bruce for the job because he was educated and dignified. But Bruce turned down the opportunity. Instead, he wanted to run for the U.S. Senate. The Mississippi legislature was dominated by whites, but it elected him to the U.S. Senate easily. In March 1875, Bruce began to serve in the Senate. He was then only 34 years old.

Unlike Revels, Bruce refused to use the word "colored" to describe his race. "I am a Negro, and proud of my race," he often said. When he arrived in Washington to be sworn in, there were already some who disliked him. It was the custom for a new senator to be escorted to the swearing-in ceremony by the other senator from his state. But when Bruce's name was called, the other senator from Mississippi, James A. Alcorn, pretended he did not see him. Alcorn was a white Republican who was now trying to win the favor of Mississippi Democrats.

Bruce understood. He walked down the aisle of the Senate, his head held high. Halfway toward the front, Bruce was met by Roscoe Conkling, a white Republican from New York.

"Excuse me, Mr. Bruce," he said. "I did not see that you were alone until this moment. Permit me to walk with you."

The two men walked forward arm in arm, and Bruce was sworn in as senator. He was the second black to sit in the Senate. He was also the last black senator until 1966. (That year, Edward Brooke, also a Republican, was elected to the Senate from Massachusetts.)

This lithograph, published by Currier and Ives in 1872, shows *The First Colored Senator and Representatives in the 41st and 42nd Congress of the United States.* Senator H.R. Revels of Mississippi is seated [left].

Fighting Discrimination

As a senator, Bruce fought hard for the rights of black Americans. He spoke out in protest of violence against blacks in Mississippi. Whites, he said, were using terror "not to protect their rights, but to destroy the rights of blacks." Bruce fought not only for blacks. He tried to help people of other races as well. Bruce defended the Indians who, he said, had been cheated out of their lands. He demanded that the United States "save and not destroy these people." Bruce also spoke against a bill to keep Chinese out of the United States. He said he was against all discrimination.

Bruce's term as senator ended in 1881. By that time, white Democrats had taken control of the Mississippi legislature. There was no hope that Bruce could run for re-election. But three Republican presidents were to give him important jobs in the federal government in Washington, D. C.

Bruce was 57 when he died on March 17, 1898. His funeral was attended by leading politicians—both black and white. *The New York Times* said that, next to Frederick Douglass, "he was the most important man of his race."

CHAPTER CHECK

WORD MATCH

1. majority
2. Hiram R. Revels
3. chaplain
4. Blanche K. Bruce
5. James A. Alcorn

a. black Republican senator from Missouri
b. white Republican senator from Mississippi
c. the group, party, or faction with the largest number of votes
d. minister, rabbi, or priest in armed forces
e. Republican and first black man to be elected to U.S. Senate

QUICK QUIZ

1. During Reconstruction, blacks voted in large numbers. In which Southern state were black voters strongest? Why?
2. How different were the black legislators elected during Reconstruction from the white politicians?

THINK ABOUT IT

1. An opponent tried to ridicule Blanche K. Bruce by saying a servant wasn't fit to be a sheriff. Bruce acknowledged his background but said he was proud of his achievements. Then Bruce asked his opponent, if he were born with Bruce's disadvantages would he have been able to change his situation? What do you think of Bruce's response? How do you think white voters reacted to it?
2. As a senator, Bruce fought for the rights of blacks, but he also saw Native Americans and Chinese being treated unjustly. What were Bruce's views? Why do you think he felt that way?

32 THE 1876 ELECTION

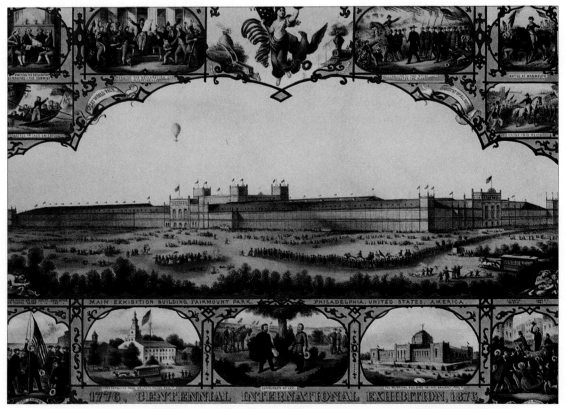

When the United States celebrated its centennial in 1876, a World's Fair was held in Philadelphia. Exhibits came from as close as Ohio and Kentucky and as far away as Germany and India.

The 1876 election was probably the most disgraceful in U.S. history. Certainly it was one of the most bitter. Both Democrats and Republicans lied, cheated, and even murdered to win.

Southern Democrats were determined to get the entire South back under white Democratic control. In 1876, Republicans remained in control in only three Southern states—South Carolina, Louisiana, and Florida. Everywhere else in the South, U.S. troops had been withdrawn. When federal troops left a state, white Democrats in that state replaced Republicans—both whites and blacks— in office. Democrats in Southern states used intimidation and violence to keep blacks from voting, and stuffed boxes with fake Democratic **ballots** (tickets by which a vote is registered). Not only Democrats, but Republicans as well, were cheating.

Voting officials in the three Republican-controlled states tried to rig the election in their party's favor. They threw out the votes of whole counties—honest votes as well as false ones.

Reformer Candidates

Far removed from this corrupt election struggle were the two presidential candidates. Both were respected as reformers. Samuel J. Tilden, New York's "millionaire bachelor" governor, was the Democratic candidate for president. An anti-crime crusader, he had exposed "Boss" Tweed, New York City's corrupt and powerful politician. Tilden was a brilliant but aloof lawyer who represented the wealthiest railroad owners.

Republican Rutherford B. Hayes was a family man. A graduate of Harvard Law School, he had been a general in the Union Army. As three-time governor of Ohio, Hayes helped reform the state prison system and mental hospitals. He also was a critic of railroad corruption.

On election night, Hayes went to bed certain that he had lost. Indeed, it seemed that Tilden had won the election. He had received many more popular

Democrats Samuel J. Tilden and Thomas A. Hendricks lost the 1876 election to Republican Rutherford B. Hayes. Tilden and Hendricks received more popular votes, but they were one electoral vote shy of winning.

votes than Hayes. Still, he did not yet hold a majority of electoral votes. He had 184 votes and he needed 185. In four states—South Carolina, Louisiana, Florida, and Oregon—the results were in doubt.

Because of the corruption, it was impossible to know who had won the election in the three Southern states. Each side claimed victory—and the states' electoral votes. There seemed to be no fair way to decide who had won the election.

One-Vote Difference

Finally Congress set up a committee of 15 Supreme Court judges and members of Congress to decide the matter. Seven members of the committee were Republicans. Seven were Democrats.

The 15th member of the committee, a judge, was supposed to be neutral. Yet at the last moment, when it was discovered he had a **political bias,** he resigned. A Republican judge took his place. In February 1877, the committee said that the Republicans— and Hayes—had won all four states. In each case, the committee vote was 8 to 7 in favor of the Republicans. Hayes would be the nation's next president.

Southern Democrats were outraged. "We have been cheated, shamefully cheated," declared one Tilden supporter. Angry Democrats formed militia units. "Tilden or blood!" they shouted.

People everywhere panicked. Northern newspapers called for "peace at any price." The North was already turning against Reconstruction. Many complained that violence and confusion in the Reconstruction states made it hard to do business with the South.

In Congress and in secret meetings, Republican and Democratic leaders worked out a compromise. Democrats agreed to accept the election of Hayes as president. In return, the Republicans agreed to abandon Reconstruction. This meant that the last U.S. troops would be removed from Louisiana and South Carolina. Southern Democrats would be allowed to take over state and local governments. Republicans also promised to support generous spending to rebuild the South.

On March 2, 1877,

Hayes was awarded 185 electoral votes and the presidency. Within one month, the last federal troops were withdrawn from the South. All of the South was now in the control of white Democrats. Blacks and white Republicans would have little or no power in the South for the next 90 years. The reforms were over, and Reconstruction was dead.

There were many tributes to George Washington during the United States centennial. An example would be this copy of a bookmark printed during the 1876 celebration.

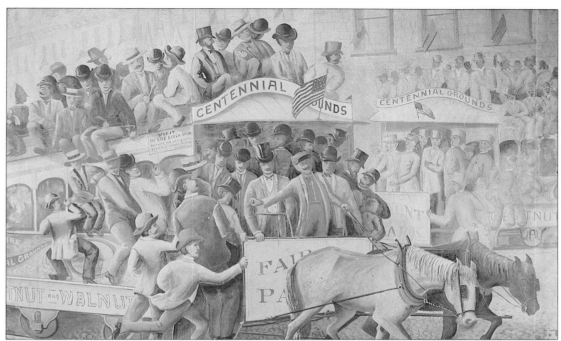

The 1876 World's Fair in Philadelphia attracted many crowds from all over the country. When it closed in November 1876, over 10 million people had come to the fair.

CHAPTER CHECK

WORD MATCH
1. Samuel J. Tilden   **a.** attitude in favor of or against a political issue, party, or person
2. ballots   **b.** Democratic presidential candidate and governor of New York
3. Rutherford B. Hayes   **c.** corrupt and powerful New York City politician
4. political bias   **d.** tickets by which a vote is registered
5. "Boss" Tweed   **e.** Republican presidential candidate and governor of Ohio

QUICK QUIZ
1. What was most memorable about the election of 1876? How was the winner selected?
2. Under what conditions was the election settled?

THINK ABOUT IT
1. Why did the Republicans agree to abandon Reconstruction?
2. After the last Federal troops were pulled out of the South in 1877, what became of the political situation? Who controlled the South?
3. Think about the word "Reconstruction." What did it mean to Northerners? To Southerners?

RECONSTRUCTION

History Detective

1. I tried to carry on like my predecessor, President Lincoln, would have. However, a group of Radical Republicans nearly had me impeached. Who am I?

2. I was a government organization that found jobs for blacks, organized schools, and gave abandoned land to freed slaves. What am I?

3. After the Union left the South, many southern states created me to allow them to arrest blacks for any reason, and to continue slavery in certain ways. What am I?

4. My proposal of "forty acres and a mule" to help former slaves was defeated. I should be remembered, however, as a friend to blacks. Who am I?

5. After having great success in my Mississippi community, I began serving as U.S. Senator in 1875, and would be the only Black to serve in that position until 1966. Who am I?

Voices From the Past

Many plantation owners offered their slaves jobs for pay after the Civil War. Many blacks accepted the jobs, but many refused. Here is a letter from Jourdan Anderson to his former master, Colonel P.H. Anderson:

I got your letter and was glad to find you had not forgotten [me], and that you wanted me to come back and live with you again, promising to do better for me than anybody else can. Mandy says she would be afraid to go back without some proof that you are disposed to treat us justly and kindly—and we have concluded to test your sincerity by asking you to send us our wages for the time we served you. At $25 a month for me, and $2 a week for Mandy, our earnings would amount to $1,680...We trust the good Maker has opened your eyes to the wrongs which you and your father have done in making us toil for you for generations without payment.

1. How do you think Jourdan's former master would react to this letter?

2. Do you think Jourdan is really considering going back to work for his former master? Why did he write the letter?

Hands–On History

Writing a letter—Your father has kept slaves on your family's plantation in South Carolina all your life. He talks of having to sell the plantation if he can't keep slaves. Write your father a letter giving him advice about this situation.

YESTERDAY'S NEWS

The American Adventures Newspaper

Washington, D.C., Feb. 11, 1866—Congress passed the first Civil Rights Act today. It is the first piece of legislation designed to help the treatment of freed blacks in Southern states. This is the latest attempt by the government to aid the slaves freed after the Civil War.

Up till now, blacks in the South have been greatly aided by only the Freedmen's Bureau. Perhaps one black in 20 among the newly freed could read and write. The Bureau has set up 4,000 schools, with 9,000 teachers and almost 250,000 students. By 1869 the Bureau estimates this will help teach two in ten freed blacks to read and write. Encouraged by the Bureau and sponsored by Protestant churches, thousands of Northern white teachers came South. The Northern black churches also sent teachers and money. Some freed blacks have stayed on to work in the South as sharecroppers. This allows them to farm land freely, as if it was their own. The new Civil Rights Act is considered to be the law that is needed to back up these positive changes in the South.

Hooded nightriders of the Ku Klux Klan travel the countryside terrorizing black people.

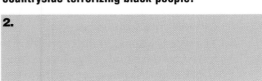

authorities often use these "Black Codes" to arrest any black they wish. But most alarming of all developments in the South is the formation of the Ku Klux Klan in Tennessee. This group was organized to block the federal government's efforts on behalf of Southern blacks. Hooded nightriders travel the countryside terrorizing black people. Arson, beatings, and murder are their weapons. As blacks are given more rights by the government in the North, their life in the South becomes more and more dangerous. As one black citizen has said,

3.

Columbia, S.C., May 8, 1867—In spite of these changes, much of the South refuses to let go of its past. Many southerners refuse to treat blacks as equals. There have been laws made by state legislatures in the South that make it possible to arrest blacks for any number of offenses. Local

You Be the Reporter

Match each question with its news item above.

1. Give this article a title.

2. What would be a good headline for this article?

3. Complete the sentence with a quotation that tells the seriousness of the situation.

INTERPRETING POLITICAL CARTOONS

Cartoons use drawings to tell a story or convey a message. In a similar way, a **political cartoo**n also expresses a message—usually the opinion of the cartoonist about a political event, issue, or person in political life. If you look at the **editorial page** (where opinions are written) in your local newspaper, you will probably see at least one political cartoon.

Political cartoons became a regular feature of weekly magazines in the United States in the 1850s. The cartoons of Thomas Nast, in particular, became very famous. Nast's cartoons about the Civil War and Reconstruction were read by hundreds of thousands of people and influenced public opinion in the North. Two Nast cartoons that appeared during Reconstruction and its aftermath are shown in this lesson.

This cartoon was printed in Harper's Weekly in 1877, after Rutherford B. Hayes was declared the winner of the 1876 presidential election. Use the cartoon to answer the questions below.

"ANOTHER SUCH VICTORY AND I AM UNDONE."—PYRRHUS

1. In 1876, the Republican party was the largest political party in the United States. Thomas Nast was the first cartoonist to show the party as an elephant. Why do you think he represented it this way?

2. This cartoon is about the final outcome of the 1876 presidential election. Based on your reading of Chapter 68, why were the results of that election in doubt? What political compromise resolved its outcome?

3. Describe the condition of the elephant in this cartoon. What was Nast saying about the condition of the Republican party?

4. Political cartoonists often use **irony**—that is, they say the opposite of what they mean. How does the caption under this cartoon express irony?

5. The words quoted in the caption are followed by the name of Pyrrhus, an ancient Greek king. Pyrrhus supposedly used the same words after defeating the Romans in a battle in which most of his soldiers were killed. Why do you think Nast used these words for this cartoon? What was he saying about the Republican victory?

The cartoon below appeared in Harper's Weekly in 1879. It expressed what Nast and many Northerners believed would happen in the South after Reconstruction. Use the cartoon to answer the follwing questions.

6. Letters, like pictures, can be symbols that stand for other things. "U.S.A.", for example, stands for United States of America. What is meant by "C.S.A." and "K.K.K." in the cartoon?

7. The cartoon contains written clues about the democratic principles that are supposed to govern the voting process. What are these clues?

8. Which army is giving up its power to control Southern **polls** (voting)? To whom is the power being transferred?

9. Read the three-line caption. How does the third line express irony? What clue is given in the drawing?

10. What opinion was Nast expressing in this cartoon? Based on your reading in Unit 6, do you think the cartoon gave an accurate picture of what happened in the South after the withdrawal of federal troops? Explain.

For Extra Credit: Cartoonists use a variety of images or symbols to stand for people, places, and ideas. What symbols are often used to stand for the Democratic Party? the United States? peace? See how many symbols you can identify from political cartoons in your local newspaper.

Relieving ("Bayonet") Guard
U.S.A. "Keep the Peace at the Polls."
C.S.A. "We'll KEEP it!"

Physical Map of North America

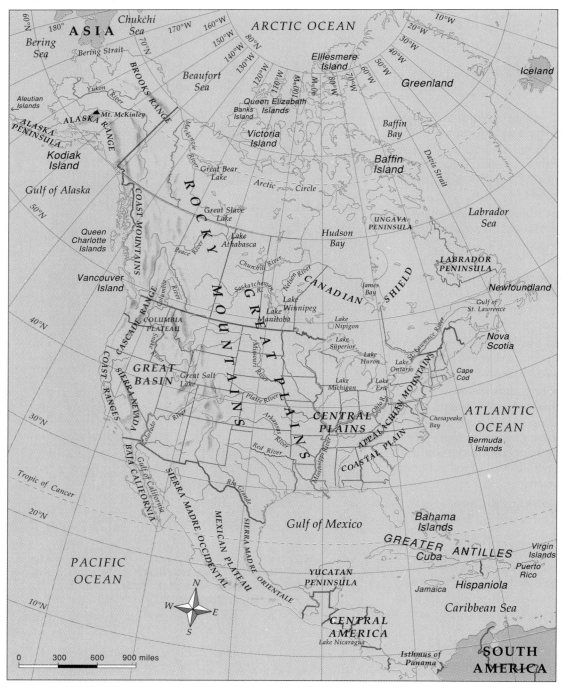

U.S. Territorial Growth Map

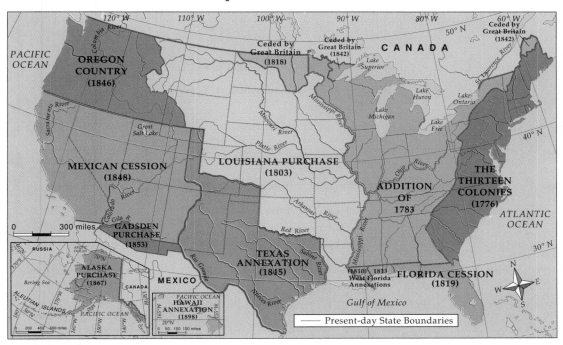

Top 10 Sources of Immigrants to the United States, 1965–1985

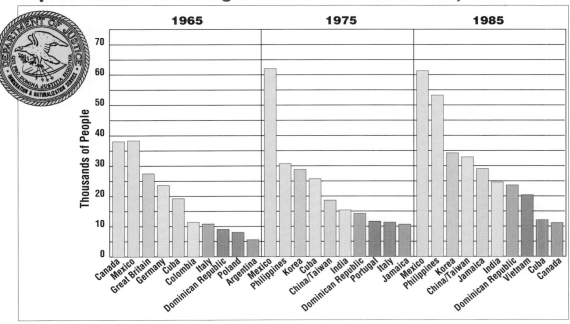

PRESIDENTIAL FACTS

President Term	Party	Vice-President	Birthplace/Born-Died	Facts
George Washington 1789–1797	None	John Adams	Westmoreland Co., Va./1732–1799	First president to appear on a U.S. postage stamp.
John Adams 1797–1801	Fed.	Thomas Jefferson	Braintree, Mass./1735–1826	Only president to be the father of another president—John Quincy Adams.
Thomas Jefferson 1801–1809	Rep.	Aaron Burr	Albemarle Co., Va./1743–1826	First president to be inaugurated in Washington, D.C.
James Madison 1809–1817	Rep.	George Clinton	Port Conway, Va./1751–1836	Was the only president to lead troops while in office—Battle of Bladensburg, Aug. 24, 1814.
James Monroe 1817–1825	Rep.	Daniel D. Tompkins	Westmoreland Co., Va./1758–1831	Was the first president to have been a senator.
John Quincy Adams 1825–1829	Rep.	John C. Calhoun	Braintree, Mass./1767–1848	Was the first and only son of a president to become president.
Andrew Jackson 1829–1837	Dem.	John C. Calhoun	Waxhaw Settlement, S.C./1767–1845	Was the only president to pay off the national debt.
Martin Van Buren 1837–1841	Dem.	Richard M. Johnson	Kinderhook, N.Y./1782–1862	Was both the eighth president and the eighth vice-president.
William Henry Harrison 1841	Whig	John Tyler	Berkeley, Va./1773–1841	Had 106 great-grandchildren, the most of any president.
John Tyler 1841–1845	Whig	——	Greenway, Va./1790–1862	Was the first president to have no vice-president during his entire term.
James K. Polk 1845–1849	Dem.	George M. Dallas	near Pineville, N.C./1795–1849	Was the first president to voluntarily retire after one term.
Zachary Taylor 1849–1850	Whig	Millard Filmore	Orange County, Va./1784–1850	Was the first president to have held no previous political office.
Millard Filmore 1850–1853	Whig	——	Locke, N.Y/1800–1874	Was the first president to have been an indentured servant.
Franklin Pierce 1853–1857	Dem.	William R. King	Hillsboro, N.H./1804–1869	Always insisted that grace be said before every meal.
James Buchanan 1857–1861	Dem.	John C. Breckinridge	near Mercersburg, Penn./1791–1868	Was the first and only president to never marry.
Abraham Lincoln 1861–1865	Rep.	Hannibal Hamlin	near Hogdenville, Ken./1809–1865	First president to be photographed at his inauguration
Andrew Johnson 1865–1869	Rep.	——	Raleigh, N.C./1808–1875	Was the only unschooled man to become president.
Ulysses S. Grant 1869–1877	Rep.	Schuyler Colfax	Point Pleasant, Ohio/1822–1885	His favorite breakfast was cucumbers soaked in vinegar.
Rutherford B. Hayes 1877–1881	Rep.	William A. Wheeler	Delaware, Ohio/1822–1893	Was the first president to visit the West Coast while in office.
James A. Garfield 1881	Rep.	Chester A. Arthur	Orange, Ohio/1831–1881	Liked to juggle Indian clubs to build his muscles.
Chester A. Arthur 1881–1885	Rep.	——	Fairfield, Vt./1830–1886	Had a French chef in the White House where dinners often lasted two to three hours.

PRESIDENTIAL FACTS

President Term	Party	Vice-President	Birthplace/Born-Died	Facts
Grover Cleveland 1885–1889	Dem.	Thomas A. Hendricks	Caldwell, N.J./1837–1908	Was the first and only president to be married in the White House.
Benjamin Harrison 1889–1893	Rep.	Levi P. Morton	North Bend, Ohio/1833–1901	In 1891, was the first president to have electricity in the White House.
Grover Cleveland 1893–1897	Dem.	Adlai E. Stevenson	Caldwell, N.J./1837–1908	First president to be elected to two non-consecutive terms.
William McKinley 1897–1901	Rep.	Garret A. Hobart Theodore Roosevelt	Niles, Ohio/1843–1901	Always wore a red carnation in his lapel for good luck.
Theodore Roosevelt 1901–1909	Rep.	Charles W. Fairbanks	New York, N.Y./1858–1919	Was the first president to win the Nobel Peace Prize.
William H. Taft 1909–1913	Rep.	James S. Sherman	Cincinnati, Ohio/1857–1930	First president to serve in the Supreme Court.
Woodrow Wilson 1913–1921	Dem.	Thomas R. Marshall	Staunton, Va./1856–1924	Was the first president to cross the Atlantic during his term in office.
Warren G. Harding 1921–1923	Rep.	Calvin Coolidge	Blooming Grove, Ohio/1865–1923	Was the first president to visit Alaska.
Calvin Coolidge 1923–1929	Rep.	Charles G. Dawes	Plymouth Notch, Vt./1872–1933	Had a reputation of never wasting a penny or a word.
Herbert C. Hoover 1929–1933	Rep.	Charles Curtis	West Branch, Iowa/1874–1964	Was the first president to visit China.
Franklin D. Roosevelt 1933–1945	Dem.	John N. Garner Henry A. Wallace Harry S. Truman	Hyde Park, N.Y/1882–1945	Was the only president to be elected to four terms.
Harry S. Truman 1945–1953	Dem.	Alben W. Barkley	Lamar, Missouri/1884–1972	Was the first president to televise a speech from the White House.
Dwight D. Eisenhower 1953–1961	Rep.	Richard M. Nixon	Denison, Texas/1890–1969	Was the first president to appear on color television.
John F. Kennedy 1961–1963	Dem.	Lyndon B. Johnson	Brookline, Mass./1917–1963	Was the first Boy Scout to become president.
Lyndon B. Johnson 1963–1969	Dem.	Hubert Humphrey	near Stonewall, Texas/1908–1973	First president to be sworn in by a woman—Sarah Hughes, a Federal District Judge.
Richard M. Nixon 1969–1974	Rep.	Spiro T. Agnew Gerald R. Ford	Yorba Linda, Calif./1913–	Was the first president to resign from office.
Gerald R. Ford 1974–1977	Rep.	Nelson Rockefeller	Omaha, Nebraska/1913–	Was the first to become president without being elected.
Jimmy Carter 1977–1981	Dem.	Walter F. Mondale	Plains, Georgia/1924–	Was the first president to be born in a hospital—the Wise Clinic in Plains, Georgia.
Ronald Reagan 1981–1989	Rep.	George Bush	Tampico, Ill./1911–	Believed in knocking on wood for good luck.
George Bush 1989–	Rep.	J. Danforth Quayle	Milton, Mass./1924–	Played first-base for his Yale University baseball team.

State	Admitted into the Union	Capital	Area in Square Miles	Population 1980	Population 1988	Electoral Votes
Alabama (Ala.)	1819	Montgomery	51,609	3,890,061	4,102,000	9
Alaska	1959	Juneau	586,412	400,481	524,000	3
Arizona (Ariz.)	1912	Phoenix	113,909	2,717,866	3,489,000	7
Arkansas (Ark.)	1836	Little Rock	53,104	2,285,513	2,395,000	6
California (Calif.)	1850	Sacramento	158,693	23,668,562	28,314,000	47
Colorado (Colo.)	1876	Denver	104,247	2,888,834	3,301,000	8
Connecticut (Conn.)	1788	Hartford	5009	3,107,576	3,233,000	8
Delaware (Del.)	1787	Dover	2057	595,225	660,000	3
Florida (Fla.)	1845	Tallahassee	58,560	9,739,992	12,335,000	21
Georgia (Ga.)	1788	Atlanta	58,876	5,464,265	6,342,000	12
Hawaii	1959	Honolulu	6450	965,000	1,098,000	4
Idaho (Ida.)	1890	Boise	83,557	943,935	1,003,000	4
Illinois (Ill.)	1818	Springfield	56,400	11,418,461	11,614,000	24
Indiana (Ind.)	1816	Indianapolis	36,291	5,490,179	5,556,000	2
Iowa (Ia.)	1846	Des Moines	56,290	2,913,387	2,834,000	8
Kansas (Kans.)	1861	Topeka	82,264	2,363,208	2,495,000	7
Kentucky (Ken.)	1792	Frankfort	40,395	3,661,433	3,727,000	9
Louisiana (La.)	1812	Baton Rouge	48,523	4,203,972	4,408,000	10
Maine (Me.)	1820	Augusta	33,215	1,124,660	1,205,000	4
Maryland (Md.)	1788	Annapolis	10,577	4,216,446	4,622,000	10
Massachusetts (Mass.)	1788	Boston	8257	5,737,037	5,889,000	13
Michigan (Mich.)	1837	Lansing	58,216	9,258,344	9,240,000	20
Minnesota (Minn.)	1858	St. Paul	84,068	4,077,148	4,307,000	10
Mississippi (Miss.)	1817	Jackson	47,716	2,520,638	2,620,000	7
Missouri (Mo.)	1821	Jefferson City	69,686	4,917,444	5,141,000	11
Montana (Mont.)	1889	Helena	147,138	786,690	805,000	4

State	Admitted into the Union	Capital	Area in Square Miles	Population 1980	1988	Electoral Votes
Nebraska (Neb.)	1867	Lincoln	77,227	1,570,006	1,602,000	5
Nevada (Nev.)	1864	Carson City	110,540	799,184	1,054,000	4
New Hampshire (N.H.)	1788	Concord	9404	920,610	1,085,000	4
New Jersey (N.J.)	1787	Trenton	7836	7,364,158	7,721,000	16
New Mexico (N.Mex.)	1912	Santa Fe	121,666	1,299,968	1,507,000	5
New York (N.Y.)	1788	Albany	49,576	17,557,288	17,909,000	36
North Carolina (N.C.)	1789	Raleigh	52,58	5,874,429	6,489,000	13
North Dakota (N.Dak.)	1889	Bismarck	70,665	652,695	667,000	3
Ohio	1803	Columbus	41,222	10,797,419	10,855,000	23
Oklahoma (Okla.)	1907	Oklahoma City	69,919	3,025,266	3,242,000	8
Oregon (Ore.)	1859	Salem	96,981	2,632,663	2,767,000	7
Pennsylvania (Penn.)	1787	Harrisburg	45,333	11,866,728	12,001,000	25
Rhode Island (R.I.)	1790	Providence	1214	947,154	993,000	4
South Carolina (S.C.)	1788	Columbia	31,055	3,119,208	3,470,000	8
South Dakota (S.Dak.)	1889	Pierre	77,047	690,178	713,000	3
Tennessee (Tenn.)	1796	Nashville	42,244	4,590,750	4,895,000	11
Texas (Tex.)	1845	Austin	267,339	14,228,383	16,841,000	29
Utah (Ut.)	1896	Salt Lake City	84,916	1,461,037	1,690,000	5
Vermont (Vt.)	1791	Montpelier	9609	511,456	557,000	3
Virginia (Va.)	1788	Richmond	40,817	5,346,279	6,015,000	12
Washington (Wash.)	1889	Olympia	68,192	4,130,163	4,648,000	10
West Virginia (W.Va.)	1863	Charleston	24,181	1,949,644	1,876,000	6
Wisconsin (Wis.)	1848	Madison	56,154	4,705,335	4,855,000	11
Wyoming (Wyo.)	1890	Cheyenne	97,914	470,816	479,000	3
District of Columbia		Washington	67	637,651	617,000	3

THE DECLARATION OF INDEPENDENCE

1. This is the preamble, or introduction, to the Declaration of Independence. Thomas Jefferson was the main author of the Declaration. Jefferson and the other American colonists believed that the time had come for them to break away from England and form their own nation. In the preamble, Jefferson writes that the colonists have a duty to state the reasons for their actions. He believes the colonists must explain to the world why they are declaring their independence from Britain.

2. In this section, Jefferson describes what he believes are the basic principles of democracy. This is perhaps the most meaningful part of the document. It is certainly the most well known. Jefferson believes that all people are born equal. That means they all have the same basic rights. The most important are "life, liberty, and the pursuit of happiness." People set up governments to protect these rights. Jefferson thought that governments should get their power by agreement of the people. This is different from previous types of government which got their authority from monarchs. Jefferson argues that when a government no longer protects the basic rights of the people, the people have a right to overthrow that government and set up a new one.

3. Jefferson adds that people do not change governments for minor reasons. In fact, they often put up with many abuses rather than change to something new and untried. But when a government grows too harsh and unjust, it becomes the people's duty to overthrow that government. The colonists believe that King George III has a long history of abusing his power. That is the reason why they are establishing a new government.

4. In the long section that follows, Jefferson lists 27 injustices committed by George III. Jefferson tries to blame the king for all the actions Britain has

1 | When in the Course of human events, it becomes necessary for one people to dissolve the political bands which have connected them with another, and to assume among the Powers of the earth the separate and equal station to which the Laws of Nature and of Nature's God entitle them, a decent respect to the opinions of mankind requires that they should declare the causes which impel them to the separation.

2 | We hold these truths to be self-evident, that all men are created equal, that they are endowed by their Creator with certain unalienable Rights, that among these are Life, Liberty and the pursuit of Happiness. That to secure these rights, Governments are instituted among Men, deriving their just powers from the consent of the governed. That whenever any Form of Government becomes destructive of these ends, it is the Right of the People to alter or to abolish it, and to institute new Government, laying its foundation on such principles and organizing its powers in such form, as to them shall seem most likely to effect their Safety and Happiness. Prudence, indeed, will dictate that Governments long established should not be changed

3 | for light and transient causes; and accordingly all experience hath shown, that mankind are more disposed to suffer, while evils are sufferable, than to right themselves by abolishing the forms to which they are accustomed. But when a long train of abuses and usurpations pursuing invariably the same Object evinces a design to reduce them under absolute Despotism, it is their right, it is their duty, to throw off such Government, and to provide new Guards for their future security. —Such has been the patient sufferance of these Colonies: and such is now the necessity which constrains them to alter their former Systems of

4 | Government. The history of the present King of Great Britain is a history of repeated injuries and usurpations, all having in direct object the establishment of an absolute Tyranny over these States. To prove this, let Facts be submitted to a candid world.

5 | He has refused his Assent to Laws, the most wholesome and necessary for the public good.

He has forbidden his Governors to pass Laws of immediate and pressing importance, unless suspended in their operation till his Assent should be obtained: and when so suspended, he has utterly neglected to attend to them.

He has refused to pass other Laws for the accommodation of large districts of people, unless those people would relinquish the right of Representation in the Legislature, a right inestimable to them and formidable to tyrants only.

He has called together legislative bodies at places unusual, uncomfortable, and distant from the depository of their Public Records, for the sole purpose of fatiguing them into compliance with his measures.

He has dissolved Representative Houses repeatedly, for opposing with manly firmness his invasions on the rights of the people.

He has refused for a long time, after such dissolutions, to cause others to be elected: whereby the Legislative Powers, incapable of Annihilation, have returned to the People at large for their exercise: the State remaining in the mean time exposed to all the dangers of invasion from without, and convulsions within.

He has endeavoured to prevent the population of these States: for that purpose obstructing the Laws for Naturalization of Foreigners: refusing to pass others to encourage their migration hither, and raising the conditions of new Appropriations of Lands.

He has obstructed the Administration of Justice, by refusing his Assent to Laws for establishing Judiciary Powers.

He has made Judges dependent on his Will alone, for the tenure of their offices, and the amount and payment of their salaries.

He has erected a multitude of New Offices, and sent hither swarms of Officers to harass our People, and eat out their substance.

He has kept among us, in times of peace, Standing Armies without the Consent of our legislatures.

He has affected to render the Military independent of and superior to the Civil Power.

5 taken against its American colonies. George III is accused of deliberately trying to destroy the colonists' rights and government.

5. Jefferson begins by describing how George III has unjustly used his power. Jefferson blames the king for trying to control the colonial legislatures. George III is accused of not approving necessary laws passed by the colonists. He has dismissed assemblies that disobeyed royal governors. He has forced the colonial legislatures to meet in unusual and distant places. And he has not called for elections to replace the colonial assemblies which he has dismissed.

6. Here Jefferson accuses the king of prohibiting the American colonists from moving west and settling the new land. Also, George III has prevented justice from being done. He has insisted that judges serve only as long as he was pleased with them. Finally, he has annoyed the colonists by keeping British troops in America after the end of the French and Indian War. **6** And he has sent large numbers of customs officials to harass them.

THE DECLARATION OF INDEPENDENCE

7. Jefferson then describes how the king has joined with others, meaning Parliament, to control the colonies. The colonists always argued that Parliament had no right to make laws for them because they were not represented in it. This argument was challenged by passage of the Declaratory Act in 1766. This act stated that the king and Parliament had total authority over the colonists. Still, many colonists continued to argue that Parliament had no right to tax them. Among the later actions of Parliament which angered the colonists was the Quebec Act, which kept French civil law in Quebec. Other unjust acts included the Quartering Act and the blockade of colonial ports.

8. In this section, Jefferson describes the warlike actions of the king. Instead of helping the colonists and protecting them, he has waged war on them. He has restricted their trade with other nations. He has hired foreign troops and sent them to America to fight against the colonists. He has encouraged the slaves in America to revolt against their masters. And he has persuaded Native Americans to attack settlers on the frontier.

7 He has combined with others to subject us to a jurisdiction foreign to our constitution, and unacknowledged by our laws: giving his Assent to their acts of pretended legislation:

For quartering large bodies of armed troops among us:

For protecting them, by mock Trial, from Punishment for any Murders which they should commit on the Inhabitants of these States:

For cutting off our Trade with all parts of the world:

For imposing taxes on us without our Consent:

For depriving us, in many cases, of the benefits of Trial by Jury:

For transporting us beyond Seas to be tried for pretended offences:

For abolishing the free System of English Laws in a neighbouring Province, establishing therein an Arbitrary government and enlarging its Boundaries so as to render it at once an example and fit instrument for introducing the same absolute rule into these Colonies:

For taking away our Charters, abolishing our most valuable Laws, and altering fundamentally the Forms of our Governments:

For suspending our own Legislatures, and declaring themselves invested with Power to legislate for us in all cases whatsoever.

8 He has abdicated Government here, by declaring us out of his Protection and waging War against us.

He has plundered our seas, ravaged our Coasts, burnt our towns, and destroyed the lives of our people.

He is at this time transporting large Armies of foreign Mercenaries to compleat the works of death, desolation and tyranny, already begun with circumstances of Cruelty & perfidy scarcely paralleled in the most barbarous ages, and totally unworthy the Head of a civilized nation.

He has constrained our fellow Citizens taken Captive on the high Seas to bear Arms against their Country, to become the executioners of their friends and Brethren, or to fall themselves by their Hands.

He has excited domestic insurrections amongst us, and has endeavoured to bring on the inhabitants of our

frontiers, the merciless Indian Savages whose known |8
rule of warfare, is an undistinguished destruction of all
ages, sexes and conditions.

In every stage of these Oppressions We have |9
Petitioned for Redress in the most humble terms: Our
repeated Petitions have been answered only by repeated injury. A Prince, whose character is thus marked by
every act which may define a Tyrant, is unfit to be the
ruler of a free People.

Nor have We been wanting in attentions to our
British brethren. We have warned them from time to
time of attempts by their legislature to extend an
unwarrantable jurisdiction over us. We have reminded
them of the circumstances of our emigration and settlement here. We have appealed to their native justice
and magnanimity, and we have conjured them by the
ties of our common kindred to disavow these usurpations, which would inevitably interrupt our connections
and correspondence. They too have been deaf to the
voice of justice and of consanguinity. We must, therefore, acquiesce in the necessity, which denounces our
Separation, and hold them, as we hold the rest of
mankind, Enemies in War, in Peace Friends.

We, therefore, the Representatives of the United
States of America, in General Congress, Assembled, |10
appealing to the Supreme Judge of the world for the
rectitude of our intentions, do, in the Name, and by
Authority of the good People of these Colonies,
solemnly publish and declare, That these United
Colonies are, and of Right ought to be, Free and
Independent States; that they are Absolved from all
Allegiance to the British Crown, and that all political
connection between them and the State of Great
Britain, is and ought to be totally dissolved; and that as
Free and Independent States, they have full Power to
levy War, conclude Peace, contract Alliances, establish
Commerce, and to do all other Acts and Things which
Independent States may of right do. And for the sup-
port of this Declaration, with a firm reliance on the
Protection of Divine Providence, we mutually pledge
to each other our Lives, our Fortunes and our sacred
Honor.

9. During this time, the colonists have peacefully tried to resolve the conflict. They have repeated-ly asked for relief only to receive further suffering. They even asked the British people for help, but to no avail. Therefore, the colonists now believe that they have no choice but to sepa-rate and form their own nation.

10. In this final section, the colonists formally declare their independence from Britain. The signers of this document are rep-resentatives of the people of the United States and are acting with their consent. They declare that the colonies no longer have any connection to Great Britain and are totally independent states. These states can now make war and sign treaties. And the signers promise their lives, money, and honor to defend their independence.

THE CONSTITUTION OF THE UNITED STATES OF AMERICA

1. The Preamble is the opening of the Constitution. It states the purpose of the Constitution and describes the type of government to be set up. It also explains the goals to be achieved.

2. Congress has the power to make all federal laws. It is divided into a Senate and a House of Representatives.

3. Members of the House of Representatives are elected every two years. Representatives must be at least 25 years old. They also have to live in the state which they represent.

4. The number of Representatives each state receives is based on its population. Therefore a census is taken every ten years to determine each state's population. At first, each state received a Representative for every 30,000 people. Since 1929, the total number of Representatives in the House has been fixed at 435. Each state is entitled to at least one Representative. The 16th Amendment changed the collection of direct taxes. The 3/5 reference to slaves was canceled by the 13th and 14th Amendments.

5. When a House member dies or resigns, that state's governor must call a special election to fill the vacant seat. The House has the right to elect its own officers, including a Speaker, or spokesperson. The House has the power to impeach, or formally accuse, a federal official of wrongdoing.

6. Each state shall have two Senators who serve for six-year terms. The 17th Amendment changed the way that Senators are chosen. Now they are elected by the people of the state.

7. One third of the Senate is elected every two years. The 17th Amendment changed the way vacancies are filled. Today the governor of the state may choose a replacement until an election can take place. All Senators must be at least 30 years old and residents of the states they represent.

1 | **Preamble.** We, the people of the United States, in order to form a more perfect Union, establish justice, insure domestic tranquility, provide for the common defense, promote the general welfare, and secure the blessings of liberty to ourselves and our posterity, do ordain and establish this Constitution for the United States of America.

2 | **Article I.** Section 1. All legislative powers herein granted shall be vested in a Congress of the United States, which shall consist of a Senate and a House of Representatives.

3 | **Section 2.** The House of Representatives shall be composed of members chosen every second year by the people of the several states; and the electors in each state shall have the qualifications requisite for electors of the most numerous branch of the state legislature.

No person shall be a Representative who shall not have attained the age of twenty-five years, and been seven years a citizen of the United States, and who shall not, when elected, be an inhabitant of that state in which he shall be chosen.

4 | Representatives ~~and direct taxes~~ shall be apportioned among the several states which may be included within this Union, according to their respective numbers, ~~which shall be determined by adding to the whole number of free persons, including those bound to service for a term of years, and excluding Indians not taxed, three fifths of all other persons.~~ The actual enumeration shall be made within three years after the first meeting of the Congress of the United States, and within every subsequent term of ten years, in such manner as they shall by law direct. The number of Representatives shall not exceed one for every 30,000, but each State shall have at least one Representative, ~~and until such enumeration shall be made, the State of New Hampshire shall be entitled to choose three, Massachusetts eight, Rhode Island and Providence Plantations one, Connecticut five, New York six, New Jersey four, Pennsylvania eight, Delaware one, Maryland six, Virginia ten, North Carolina five, South Carolina five, and Georgia three.~~

5 | When vacancies happen in the representation from any state, the executive authority thereof shall issue writs of election to fill such vacancies.

The House of Representatives shall choose their Speaker and other officers; and shall have the sole power of impeachment.

6 | **Section 3.** The Senate of the United States shall be composed of two Senators from each State, chosen ~~by the legislature thereof,~~ for six years; and each Senator shall have one vote.

7 | ~~Immediately after they shall be assembled, in consequence of the first election,~~ they shall be divided as equally as may be into three classes. ~~The seats of the Senators of the first class shall be vacated at the expiration of the second year, of the second class at the expiration of the fourth year, and of the third class at the expiration of the sixth, year,~~ so that one third may be chosen every second year; ~~and if vacancies happen by resignation, or otherwise, during the recess of the legislature of any State, the Executive thereof may make temporary appointments until the next meeting of the legislature, which shall then fill such vacancies.~~

No person shall be a Senator who shall not have attained the age of 30 years, and been nine years a citizen of the United States, and who shall not, when elected, be an inhabitant of that state for which he shall be chosen.

8 | The Vice-President of the United States shall be President of the Senate, but shall have no vote, unless they be equally divided.

[1] Those parts of the U.S. Constitution which are no longer applicable or have been changed by ammendments are marked through.

The Senate shall choose their other officers, and also a President *Pro Tempore,* in the absence of the Vice-President, or when he shall exercise the office of President of the United States.

The Senate shall have the sole power to try all impeachments. When sitting for that purpose, they shall be on oath or affirmation. When the President of the United States is tried, the Chief Justice shall preside: and no person shall be convicted without the concurrence of two thirds of the members present.

Judgment in cases of impeachment shall not extend further than to removal from office, and disqualification to hold and enjoy any office of honor, trust, or profit, under the United States; but the party convicted shall nevertheless be liable and subject to indictment, trial, judgment, and punishment according to law.

Section 4. The times, places and manner of holding elections for Senators and Representatives, shall be prescribed in each state by the legislature thereof; but the Congress may at any time by law make or alter such regulations, except as to the places of choosing Senators.

The Congress shall assemble at least once in every year, ~~and such meeting shall be on the first Monday in December,~~ unless they shall by law appoint a different day.

Section 5. Each House shall be the judge of the elections, returns, and qualifications of its own members, and a majority of each shall constitute a quorum to do business; but a smaller number may adjourn from day to day, and may be authorized to compel the attendance of absent members, in such manner, and under such penalties, as each House may provide.

Each House may determine the rules of its proceedings, punish its members for disorderly behavior, and, with the concurrence of two thirds, expel a member.

Each House shall keep a journal of its proceedings, and from time to time publish the same, excepting such parts as may, in their judgment, require secrecy; and the yeas and nays of the members of either House on any question, shall, at the desire of one fifth of those present, be entered on the journal.

Neither House, during the session of Congress, shall, without the consent of the other, adjourn for more than three days, nor to any other place than that in which the two Houses shall be sitting.

Section 6. The Senators and Representatives shall receive a compensation for their services, to be ascertained by law, and paid out of the Treasury of the United States. They shall, in all cases, except treason, felony, and breach of the peace, be privileged from arrest during their attendance at the session of their respective Houses, and in going to, and returning from, the same; and for any speech or debate in either House, they shall not be questioned in any other place.

No Senator or Representative shall, during the time for which he was elected, be appointed to any civil office under the authority of the United States, which shall have been created, or the emoluments whereof shall have been increased during such time; and no person holding any office under the United States, shall be a member of either House during his continuance in office.

Section 7. All bills for raising revenue shall originate in the House of Representatives; but the Senate may propose or concur with amendments as on other bills.

Every bill which shall have passed the House of Representatives and the Senate, shall, before it becomes a law, be presented to the President of the United States; if he approves he shall sign it, but if not he shall return

8 | **8. The Vice-President of the United States serves as President, or chairperson, of the Senate. However, he or she can only vote to break a tie. The Senate chooses all its other officers.**

9 | **9. The Senate has the power to try federal officials after the House has accused them. The person on trial has the same legal rights as any person on trial. Two-thirds of the Senate must find the person guilty for conviction. Punishment is limited to removal from office. But the convicted person can then be tried in a normal court of law.**

10 | **10. Each state can make its own rules about elections for Congress. But Congress has the right to change these state election laws. Congress must meet at least once each year. The 20th Amendment moved the opening date of Congress to January 3.**

11 | **11. Both the House of Representatives and Senate can refuse to seat members. Neither house can conduct business unless half its members are present. Each house can make rules for the conduct of its members. Each house must keep a written record of its business. Neither house can recess for more than three days without the consent of the other.**

12 | **12. Each member of Congress is paid a salary by the U.S. Treasury. Members set their own pay. No member of Congress can be arrested while serving in Congress. And no member of Congress can hold another office in the U.S. government while serving in Congress.**

13 | **13. All bills, or proposed laws, for raising money through taxes must be introduced in the House of Representatives. Any bill that passes both houses of Congress is sent to the President. If the President signs the**

bill, it becomes law. If the President does not like the bill, the President can veto, or refuse to sign, the bill. The bill is then sent back to Congress. Congress can either drop the bill or try to pass it over the President's veto. To override the President's veto, two-thirds of both houses of Congress need to approve the bill.

13

it, with his objections, to that House in which it shall have originated, who shall enter the objections at large on their journal, and proceed to reconsider it. If after such reconsideration two thirds of that House shall agree to pass the bill, it shall be sent, together with the objections, to the other House, by which it shall likewise be reconsidered, and if approved by two thirds of that House, it shall become a law. But in all such cases the votes of both Houses shall be determined by yeas and nays, and the names of the persons voting for and against the bill shall be entered on the journal of each House respectively. If any bill shall not be returned by the President within 10 days (Sundays excepted) after it shall have been presented to him, the same shall be a law in like manner as if he had signed it, unless the Congress by their adjournment prevent its return, in which case it shall not be a law.

Every order, resolution, or vote, to which the concurrence of the Senate and House of Representatives may be necessary (except on a question of adjournment), shall be presented to the President of the United States; and before the same shall take effect, shall be approved by him, or being disapproved by him, shall be repassed by two thirds of the Senate and House of Representatives, according to the rules and limitations prescribed in the case of a bill.

14. This section states the powers granted to Congress. Congress may collect taxes to pay the nation's debt and provide for the security and welfare of the country. All federal taxes must be the same throughout the nation. Congress can borrow money. It has the right to control trade, transportation, and communication between the various states and with foreign nations. Congress can decide how immigrants become citizens. It has the power to coin money and set its value, and determine how people who make fake money shall be punished. Congress may also establish post offices, patent and copyright laws, and national courts.

14

Section 8. The Congress shall have power

To lay and collect taxes, duties, imposts and excises, to pay the debts, and provide for the common defense and general welfare of the United States; but all duties, imposts, and excises shall be uniform throughout the United States;

To borrow money on the credit of the United States;

To regulate commerce with foreign nations, and among the several states, and with the Indian tribes;

To establish an uniform rule of naturalization, and uniform laws on the subject of bankruptcies throughout the United States;

To coin money, regulate the value thereof, and of foreign coin, and fix the standard of weights and measures;

To provide for the punishment of counterfeiting the securities and current coin of the United States;

To establish post-offices and post-roads;

To promote the progress of science and useful arts, by securing, for limited times, to authors and inventors, the exclusive right to their respective writings and discoveries;

To constitute tribunals inferior to the Supreme Court;

15. Congress can define the punishment for people who commit crimes against ships at sea. Only Congress has the right to declare war. It has the power to determine the size of the armed forces and how much money is spent on maintaining them. Congress may call up the state militias for federal service. Today the militias are called the National Guard.

15

To define and punish piracies and felonies committed on the high seas, and offences against the law of nations;

To declare war, grant letters of marque and reprisal, and make rules concerning captures on land and water;

To raise and support armies: but no appropriation of money to that use shall be for a longer term than two years;

To provide and maintain a navy;

To make rules for the government and regulation of the land and naval forces;

To provide for calling forth the militia to execute the laws of the Union, suppress insurrections and repel invasions;

To provide for organizing, arming, and disciplining the militia, and for governing such part of them as may be employed in the service of the United States, reserving to the states respectively, the appointment of the officers, and the authority of training the militia according to the discipline prescribed by Congress;

To exercise exclusive legislation, in all cases whatsoever, over such district (not exceeding ten miles square) as may, by cession of particular states, and the acceptance of Congress, become the seat of the government of the United States, and to exercise like authority over all places purchased by the consent of the legislature of the State in which the same shall be, for the erection of forts, magazines, arsenals, dock-yards, and other needful buildings. And,

To make all laws which shall be necessary and proper for carrying into execution the foregoing powers, and all other powers vested by this Constitution in the government of the United States, or in any department or officer thereof.

Section 9. ~~The migration or importation of such persons as any of the States now existing shall think proper to admit, shall not be prohibited by the Congress prior to the year one thousand eight hundred and eight; but a tax or duty may be imposed on such importation, not exceeding ten dollars for each person.~~

The privilege of the writ of *habeas corpus* shall not be suspended, unless when in cases of rebellion or invasion the public safety may require it.

No bill of attainder or *ex post facto* law shall be passed.

~~No capitation, or other direct tax, shall be laid, unless in proportion to the census or enumeration herein before directed to be taken.~~

No tax or duty shall be laid on articles exported from any state.

No preference shall be given by any regulation of commerce or revenue to the ports of one state over those of another; nor shall vessels bound to, or from, one state be obliged to enter, clear, or pay duties in another.

No money shall be drawn from the treasury, but in consequence of appropriations made by law; and a regular statement and account of the receipts and expenditures of all public money shall be published from time to time.

No title of nobility shall be granted by the United States; and no person holding any office of profit or trust under them, shall, without the consent of the Congress, accept of any present, emolument, office, or title of any kind whatever, from any king, prince, or foreign state.

Section 10. No state shall enter into any treaty, alliance, or confederation; grant letters of marque and reprisal; coin money; emit bills of credit; make any thing but gold and silver coin a tender in payment of debts; pass any bill of attainder, *ex post facto* law, or law impairing the obligation of contracts, or grant any title of nobility.

No state shall, without the consent of the Congress, lay any imposts or duties on imports or exports, except what may be absolutely necessary for executing its inspection laws; and the net produce of all duties and imposts, laid by any state on imports or exports, shall be for the use of the treasury of the United States; and all such laws shall be subject to the revision and control of the Congress. No state shall, without the consent of Congress, lay any duty of tonnage, keep troops, or ships of war, in time of peace, enter into any agreement or compact with another state, or with a foreign power, or engage in war, unless actually invaded, or in such imminent danger as will not admit of delay.

Article II. Section 1. The executive power shall be vested in a President of the United States of America. He shall hold his office during the term of four years, and together with the Vice-President, chosen for the same term, be elected as follows:

Each state shall appoint, in such manner as the legislature thereof may direct, a number of electors equal to the whole number of Senators and

16 16. Congress controls the District of Columbia, which includes the national capital. Congress also has the right to make all laws necessary to carry out the other powers granted to the national government by the Constitution. This clause was included to insure that Congress could adapt to the changing needs of the nation.

17 17. This section includes all the powers denied to Congress. This paragraph states that Congress could not outlaw the slave trade before 1808. It was abolished in that year.

18

18. All prisoners must be told why they are being held, and no one shall be imprisoned unlawfully. No person can be punished for committing an act before that act became unlawful. The clause about direct taxes was changed by the 16th Amendment. No taxes can be placed on goods exported from any state. And no law can be passed favoring one state over another in trade. The federal government can only spend money if Congress approves it. No titles of nobility can be granted.

19 19. This section includes all the powers denied to the states. No state can enter into a treaty with a foreign government or coin its own money. Like the federal government, no state can unlawfully imprison a person. States cannot tax imports or exports without the consent of Congress. No state can keep an army or navy without the consent of Congress or make war unless invaded.

20 20. The President is responsible for carrying out the laws passed by Congress. The President and Vice-President are elected every four years.

21

21. The President and Vice-President are chosen by special electors from each state. The number of Presidential electors each state receives is equal to the number of Senators and Representatives that state has in Congress. Each state may decide how to select its electors. No federal official or member of Congress can serve as an elector. The 12th Amendment changed the way that the President and Vice-President are selected. Now each elector votes for one candidate for President and another for Vice-President. Congress has set the first Tuesday after the first Monday of November as the day each state chooses it Presidential electors.

21 Representatives to which the state may be entitled in the Congress; but no Senator or Representative, or person holding an office of trust or profit under the United States, shall be appointed an elector.

~~The electors shall meet in their respective States, and vote by ballot for two persons, of whom one at least shall not be an inhabitant of the same State with themselves. And they shall make a list of all the persons voted for, and of the number of votes for each; which list they shall sign and certify, and transmit sealed to the seat of the government of the United States, directed to the President of the Senate. The President of the Senate shall, in the presence of the Senate and House of Representatives, open all the certificates, and the votes shall then be counted. The person having the greatest number of votes shall be the President, if such number be a majority of the whole number of electors appointed; and if there be more than one who have such majority, and have an equal number of votes, then the House of Representatives shall immediately choose by ballot one of them for President; and if no person have a majority, then from the five highest on the list the said House shall in like manner choose the President. But in choosing the President, the votes shall be taken by States, the representation from each State having one vote; a quorum for this purpose shall consist of a member or members from two thirds of the States, and a majority of all the States shall be necessary to a choice. In every case, after the choice of the President, the person having the greatest number of votes of the electors shall be the Vice-President. But if there should remain two or more who have equal votes, the Senate shall choose from them by ballot the Vice-President.~~

22 The Congress may determine the time of choosing the electors, and the day on which they shall give their votes; which day shall be the same throughout the United States.

No person except a natural-born citizen, ~~or a citizen of the United States, at the time of the adoption of this Constitution,~~ shall be eligible to the office of President; neither shall any person be eligible to that office who shall not have attained the age of thirty-five years, and been fourteen years a resident within the United States.

22. The President must be a citizen of the U.S. by birth and at least 35 years old. If for some reason the Presidency becomes vacant, the Vice-President becomes President. The 25th Amendment deals with a President's inability to perform his or her duties. Presidents are paid a fixed salary for their entire term. Before taking office, the President must promise to defend the Constitution.

In case of the removal of the President from office, or of his death, resignation, or inability to discharge the powers and duties of the said office, the same shall devolve on the Vice-President, and the Congress may by law provide for the case of removal, death, resignation, or inability, both of the President and Vice-President, declaring what officer shall then act as President, and such officer shall act accordingly until the disability be removed, or a President shall be elected.

The President shall, at stated times, receive for his services, a compensation, which shall neither be increased nor diminished during the period for which he shall have been elected, and he shall not receive within that period any other emolument from the United States or any of them.

Before he enter on the execution of his office, he shall take the following oath or affirmation:

"I do solemnly swear (or affirm) that I will faithfully execute the office of President of the United States, and will, to the best of my ability, preserve, protect, and defend the Constitution of the United States."

23. This section deals with the powers of the President. The President is the Commander in Chief of the Armed Forces. The President may order written reports from Cabinet officers and pardon persons convicted

23 **Section 2.** The President shall be Commander-in-Chief of the Army and Navy of the United States, and of the militia of the several states, when called into the actual service of the United States; he may require the opinion, in writing, of the principal officer in each of the executive departments, upon any subject relating to the duties of their respective offices, and he shall have power to grant reprieves and pardons for offenses against the United States, except in cases of impeachment.

He shall have power, by and with the advice and consent of the Senate, to make treaties, provided two-thirds of the Senators present concur; and he shall nominate, and by and with the advice and consent of the Senate, shall appoint ambassadors, other public ministers and consuls, judges of the Supreme Court, and all other officers of the United States, whose appointments are not herein otherwise provided for, and which shall be established by law. But the Congress may by law vest the appointment of such inferior officers, as they think proper, in the President alone, in the courts of law, or in the heads of departments.

The President shall have power to fill up all vacancies that may happen during the recess of the Senate, by granting commissions which shall expire at the end of their next session.

Section 3. He shall, from time to time, give to the Congress information of the state of the Union, and recommend to their consideration such measures as he shall judge necessary and expedient. He may, on extraordinary occasions, convene both Houses, or either of them; and in case of disagreement between them, with respect to the time of adjournment, he may adjourn them to such time as he shall think proper. He shall receive ambassadors and other public ministers. He shall take care that the laws be faithfully executed; and shall commission all the officers of the United States.

Section 4. The President, Vice-President, and all civil officers of the United States, shall be removed from office on impeachment for, and conviction of, treason, bribery, or other high crimes and misdemeanors.

Article III. Section 1. The judicial power of the United States shall be vested in one Supreme Court, and in such inferior courts as the Congress may, from time to time, ordain and establish. The judges, both of the Supreme and inferior courts, shall hold their offices during good behavior; and shall, at stated times, receive for their services, a compensation, which shall not be diminished during their continuance in office.

Section 2. The judicial power shall extend to all cases, in law and equity, arising under this Constitution, the laws of the United States, and treaties made, or which shall be made, under their authority; to all cases affecting ambassadors, other public ministers, and consuls; to all cases of admiralty and maritime jurisdiction; to controversies to which the United States shall be a party; to controversies between two or more states, ~~between a state and citizens of another state,~~ between citizens of different states, between citizens of the same state claiming lands under grants of different states, and between a state, or the citizens thereof, and foreign states, citizens, or subjects.

In all cases affecting ambassadors, other public ministers and consuls, and those in which a state shall be party, the Supreme Court shall have original jurisdiction. In all the other cases before mentioned, the Supreme Court shall have appellate jurisdiction, both as to law and fact, with such exceptions, and under such regulations, as the Congress shall make.

The trial of all crimes, except in cases of impeachment, shall be by jury; and such trial shall be held in the State where the said crimes shall have been committed; but when not committed within any state, the trial shall be at such place or places as the Congress may by law have directed.

Section 3. Treason against the United States, shall consist only in levying war against them, or in adhering to their enemies, giving them aid and comfort. No person shall be convicted of treason unless on the testimony of two witnesses to the same overt act, or on confession in open court.

23 of federal crimes. The President can make treaties with foreign governments, but they must be approved by two-thirds of the Senate. The President chooses judges for the Supreme Court and other high officials. They must also be approved by the Senate. The President can make temporary appointments to federal offices when the Senate is not in session.

24 **24.** Every year, the President must give to Congress a report on the state of the nation. The President can call a special session of Congress if necessary. The President, or any other high government official, can be removed from office for any major wrongdoing.

25 **25.** The Supreme Court is the final authority in matters of law. Congress can also set up other lesser national courts. Federal judges hold their office for life unless proven guilty of any wrongdoing. Their pay cannot be lowered during their term in office.

26 **26.** The federal courts settle disputes concerning the Constitution and conflicts between the U.S. and other nations. They also settle legal questions of U.S. law and problems between citizens of various states. The 11th Amendment prohibited residents of one state from suing another state. Most of the cases appearing before the Supreme Court begin in the lower courts. All trials must be tried in the state where the crime originally occurred. The Supreme Court determines if those cases were tried correctly.

27 **27.** A person can only be convicted of treason for actions committed against the United States. A person cannot be convicted of treason for thinking treasonous thoughts.

Congress has the right to set the punishment for traitors. The family of convicted traitors cannot be punished.

28. Each state must recognize the legal actions and official records of every other state. Persons who move to another state must be treated the same way as the citizens of that state. A person charged with a crime, who flees to another state, must be returned to the state where the crime was committed. The clause referring to the return of fugitive slaves was canceled by the 13th Amendment.

29. Congress has the power to control all land belonging to the United States. It has the right to govern the Western territories and create new states. No new state can be made from part of an existing state without that state's consent. New states will be equal to the existing states. Every state will be guaranteed a republican form of government and protection from foreign invasion.

30. The Constitution can be changed, if necessary, by adding amendments. Three-fourths of all the states need to approve a proposed amendment. No amendment can deprive a state of its equal representation in the Senate.

31. The United States promises to pay all debts incurred by any previous government. The Constitution and all federal laws and treaties are the supreme law of the land. They have priority over any state laws that conflict with them. All federal and state officials must promise to support the Constitution. The Constitution became the supreme law of the land after nine of the original thirteen states approved it.

27 The Congress shall have power to declare the punishment of treason, but no attainder of treason shall work corruption of blood, or forfeiture, except during the life of the person attainted.

28 **Article IV. Section 1.** Full faith and credit shall be given in each state to the public acts, records, and judicial proceedings of every other state. And the Congress may by general laws prescribe the manner in which such acts, records, and proceedings shall be proved, and the effect thereof.

Section 2. The citizens of each state shall be entitled to all privileges and immunities of citizens in the several states.

A person charged in any state with treason, felony, or other crime, who shall flee from justice, and be found in another state, shall, on demand of the executive authority of the state from which he fled, be delivered up to be removed to the state having jurisdiction of the crime.

No person held to service or labor in one state, under the laws thereof, escaping into another, shall, in consequence of any laws or regulation therein, be discharged from such service or labour, but shall be delivered up on claim of the party to whom such service or labour may be due.

29 **Section 3.** New states may be admitted by the Congress into this Union; but no new state shall be formed or erected within the jurisdiction of any other state; nor any state be formed by the junction of two or more states, or parts of states, without the consent of the legislatures of the states concerned, as well as of the Congress.

The Congress shall have power to dispose of and make all needful rules and regulations respecting the territory or other property belonging to the United States; and nothing in this Constitution shall be so construed as to prejudice any claims of the United States, or of any particular state.

Section 4. The United States shall guarantee to every state in this Union a republican form of government, and shall protect each of them against invasion; and on application of the legislature, or of the executive (when the legislature cannot be convened), against domestic violence.

30 **Article V.** The Congress, whenever two thirds of both Houses shall deem it necessary, shall propose amendments to this Constitution, or, on the application of the legislatures of two thirds of the several states, shall call a convention for proposing amendments, which, in either case, shall be valid to all intents and purposes, as part of this Constitution, when ratified by the legislatures of three fourths of the several states, or by conventions in three fourths thereof, as the one or the other mode of ratification may be proposed by the Congress; provided that no amendment, which may be made prior to the year one thousand eight hundred and eight, shall in any manner affect the first and fourth clauses in the ninth section of the first article; and that no state, without its consent, shall be deprived of its equal suffrage in the Senate.

31 **Article VI.** All debts contracted, and engagements entered into, before the adoption of this Constitution, shall be as valid against the United States, under this Constitution, as under the confederation.

This Constitution and the laws of the United States which shall be made in pursuance thereof, and all treaties made, or which shall be made, under the authority of the United States, shall be the supreme law of the land; and the judges, in every state, shall be bound thereby, any thing in the constitution or laws of any state to the contrary notwithstanding.

The Senators and Representatives before mentioned, and the members of the several state legislatures, and all executive and judicial officers, both of the United States and of the several states, shall be bound, by oath or affirmation, to support this Constitution; but no religious test shall ever be required as a qualification to any office or public trust under the United States.

Article VII. ~~The ratification of the conventions of nine States, shall be sufficient for the establishment of this Constitution between the States so ratifying the same.~~

TEN ORIGINAL AMENDMENTS: **THE BILL OF RIGHTS**
(These first 10 amendments were adopted in 1791.)

Article I. Congress shall make no law respecting an establishment of religion, or prohibiting the free exercise thereof; or abridging the freedom of speech, or of the press; or the right of the people peaceably to assemble, and to petition the government for a redress of grievances.

Article II. A well regulated militia being necessary to the security of a free state, the right of the people to keep and bear arms shall not be infringed.

Article III. No soldier shall, in time of peace, be quartered in any house without the consent of the owner; nor in time of war, but in a manner to be prescribed by law.

Article IV. The right of the people to be secure in their persons, houses, papers, and effects, against unreasonable searches and seizures, shall not be violated; and no warrants shall issue, but upon probable cause, supported by oath or affirmation, and particularly describing the place to be searched, and the persons or things to be seized.

Article V. No person shall be held to answer for a capital or otherwise infamous crime, unless on a presentment or indictment of a grand jury, except in cases arising in the land or naval forces, or in the militia, when in actual service, in time of war or public danger; nor shall any person be subject for the same offenses to be twice put in jeopardy of life or limb; nor shall be compelled, in any criminal case, to be witness against himself; nor be deprived of life, liberty, or property, without due process of law; nor shall private property be taken for public use without just compensation.

Article VI. In all criminal prosecutions the accused shall enjoy the right to a speedy and public trial, by an impartial jury of the state and district wherein the crime shall have been committed, which district shall have been previously ascertained by law, and to be informed of the nature and cause of the accusation; to be confronted with the witnesses against him; to have compulsory process for obtaining witnesses in his favor; and to have the assistance of counsel for his defense.

Article VII. In suits at common law, where the value of controversy shall exceed twenty dollars, the right of trial by jury shall be preserved; and no fact tried by a jury shall be otherwise re-examined in any court of the United States than according to the rules of the common law.

Article VIII. Excessive bail shall not be required, nor excessive fines imposed, nor cruel and unusual punishments inflicted.

Article IX. The enumeration in the Constitution of certain rights, shall not be construed to deny or disparage others retained by the people.

Article X. The powers not delegated to the United States by the Constitution, nor prohibited by it to the states, are reserved to the states respectively or to the people.

AMENDMENTS SINCE THE BILL OF RIGHTS
Article XI *(1798).* The judicial power of the United States shall not be construed to extend to any suit in law or equity, commenced or prosecuted against one of the United States by citizens of any state, or by citizens or subjects of any foreign state.

Article XII *(1804).* The electors shall meet in their respective states, and

---

31

32 **32. The first ten amendments grant basic human freedoms. The people have the right to freedom of religion, speech, the press, assembly, and petition. The states have the right to keep armed militias for protection. No individual can be forced to keep soldiers in his or her home against his or her will. And no government official can enter a person's home without showing reasonable cause that a crime has been committed.**

33 **33. All persons accused of a crime have the right to a fair and speedy trial. The government must formally charge someone with a crime before they can be brought to trial. Individuals cannot be tried twice for the same crime, and they cannot be forced to give testimony against themselves. In lawsuits of more than twenty dollars, the people involved have the right to a trial by jury. Excessive punishments cannot be given.**

34 **34. The people have rights that are not mentioned in the Constitution. The powers not given to the federal government are reserved to the states, or to the people.**

35 **35. A citizen of one state cannot sue another state in federal court.**

36

36. This amendment changed the way Presidential electors vote for the President and Vice-President. Now the electors vote for only one candidate in each office. If no candidate receives a majority of electoral votes, Congress decides the election. The House of Representatives selects the President and the Senate chooses the Vice-President. The Vice-President must meet the requirements needed for the Presidency.

37. These three amendments abolish slavery and protect the rights of all American citizens. They were passed following the Civil War. Any person who was born in the United States or who has been a naturalized citizen is a citizen of the United States. No state can take away the rights of a United States citizen. Many Confederate leaders were prohibited from holding office, but by 1872, most were allowed to return to political life. No United States citizen can be denied the right to vote on the basis of their race or color. The 19th Amendment changed this to include women as well. The 26th Amendment modified this to include all citizens over the age of eighteen.

36

vote by ballot for President and Vice-President, one of whom, at least, shall not be an inhabitant of the same state with themselves; they shall name in their ballots the person voted for as President, and in distinct ballots the person voted for as Vice-President; and they shall make distinct lists of all persons voted for as President, and of all persons voted for as Vice-President, and of the number of Votes for each, which list they shall sign and certify, and transmit, sealed, to the seat of the government of the United States, directed to the President of the Senate; the President of the Senate shall, in the presence of the Senate and House of Representatives, open all the certificates, and the votes shall then be counted. The person having the greatest number of votes for President shall be the President, if such number be a majority of the whole number of electors appointed; and if no person have such majority, then from the persons having the highest numbers, not exceeding three, on the list of those voted for as President, the House of Representatives shall choose immediately, by ballot, the President. But in choosing the President, the vote shall be taken by States, the representation from each State having one vote; a quorum for this purpose shall consist of a member or members from two thirds of the States, and a majority of all the States shall be necessary to a choice. And if the House of Representatives shall not choose a President whenever the right of choice shall devolve upon them, before the fourth day of March next following, then the Vice-President shall act as President, as in the case of the death or other constitutional disability of the President.

37

The person having the greatest number of votes as Vice-President shall be the Vice-President, if such number be a majority of the whole number of electors appointed; and if no person have a majority, then from the two highest numbers on the list the Senate shall choose the Vice-President. A quorum for the purpose shall consist of two thirds of the whole number of Senators, and a majority of the whole number shall be necessary to a choice.

But no person constitutionally ineligible to the office of President shall be eligible to that of Vice-President of the United States.

Article XIII *(1865).* **Section 1.** Neither slavery nor involuntary servitude, except as a punishment for crime whereof the party shall have been duly convicted, shall exist within the United States, or any place subject to their jurisdiction.

Section 2. Congress shall have power to enforce this article by appropriate legislation.

Article XIV *(1868).* **Section 1.** All persons born or naturalized in the United States, and subject to the jurisdiction thereof, are citizens of the United States and of the state wherein they reside. No state shall make or enforce any law which shall abridge the privileges or immunities of citizens of the United States; nor shall any state deprive any person of life, liberty, or property, without due process of law, nor deny to any person within its jurisdiction the equal protection of the laws.

Section 2. Representatives shall be apportioned among the several states according to their respective numbers, counting the whole number of persons in each state, excluding Indians not taxed. But when the right to vote at any election for the choice of electors for President and Vice-President of the United States, representatives in Congress, the executive and judicial officers of a state, or the members of the legislature thereof, is denied to any of the male inhabitants of such state, being twenty-one years of age, and citizens of the United States, or in any way abridged, except for participation in rebellion or other crime, the basis of representation therein shall be reduced in the proportion which the number of such male citizens shall bear to the whole number of male citizens twenty-one years of age in such State.

Section 3. No person shall be a Senator or Representative in Congress, or elector of President and Vice-President, or hold any office, civil or military, under the United States, or under any state, who having previously taken an oath, as a member of Congress, or as an officer of the United States, or as a member of any state legislature, or as an executive or judicial officer of any state, to support the Constitution of the United States, shall have engaged in insurrection or rebellion against the same, or given aid or comfort to the enemies thereof. But Congress may, by a vote of two thirds of each house, remove such disability.

Section 4. The validity of the public debt of the United States, authorized by law, including debts incurred for payment of pensions and bounties for services in suppressing insurrection or rebellion, shall not be questioned. But neither the United States nor any state shall assume or pay any debt or obligation incurred in aid of insurrection or rebellion against the United States, or any claim for the loss or emancipation of any slave; but all such debts, obligations, and claims shall be held illegal and void.

Section 5. The Congress shall have power to enforce, by appropriate legislation, the provisions of this article.

Article XV *(1870)*. **Section 1.** The right of citizens of the United States to vote shall not be denied or abridged by the United States or by any State on account of race, color, or previous condition of servitude.

Section 2. The Congress shall have power to enforce this article by appropriate legislation.

Article XVI *(1913)*. The Congress shall have power to lay and collect taxes on incomes, from whatever source derived, without apportionment among the several states, and without regard to any census or enumeration.

Article XVII *(1913)*. The Senate of the United States shall be composed of two Senators from each state, elected by the people thereof, for six years; and each Senator shall have one vote. The electors in each state shall have the qualifications requisite for electors of the most numerous branch of the state legislatures.

When vacancies happen in the representation of any state in the Senate, the executive authority of such state shall issue writs of election to fill such vacancies:

Provided, That the legislature of any state may empower the executive thereof to make temporary appointments until the people fill the vacancies by election as the legislature may direct.

This amendment shall not be so construed as to affect the election or term of any Senator chosen before it becomes valid as part of the Constitution.

Article XVIII *(1919)*. **Section 1.** After one year from the ratification of this article the manufacture, sale, or transportation of intoxicating liquors within, the importation thereof into, or the exportation thereof from the United States and all territory subject to the jurisdiction thereof for beverage purposes is hereby prohibited.

Section 2. The Congress and the several states shall have concurrent power to enforce this article by appropriate legislation.

Section 3. This article shall be inoperative unless it shall have been ratified as an amendment to the Constitution by the legislatures of the several states, as provided in the Constitution, within seven years from the date of the submission hereof to the states by the Congress.

Article XIX *(1920)*. The right of citizens of the United States to vote shall not be denied or abridged by the United States or by any State on

38. Congress has the right to collect taxes on people's income. Congress does not have to base this tax on each state's population.

39. This amendment changed the way Senators are elected. Before, they were chosen by the state legislatures. Now they are elected directly by the people. If a Senator cannot complete his or her term, the state's governor may appoint a temporary replacement until an election can be held.

40. This amendment prohibits the making, sale, and shipment of alcoholic beverages. It was later canceled by the 21st Amendment.

41. The right to vote cannot be denied on account of a person's sex.

account of sex.

Congress shall have power to enforce this article by appropriate legislation.

42 **Article XX** *(1933)*. **Section 1.** The terms of the President and Vice-President shall end at noon on the 20th day of January, and the terms of Senators and Representatives at noon on the 3rd day of January, of the years in which such terms would have ended if this article had not been ratified; and the terms of their successors shall then begin.

Section 2. The Congress shall assemble at least once in every year, and such meeting shall begin at noon on the 3rd day of January, unless they shall by law appoint a different day.

Section 3. If, at the time fixed for the beginning of the term of the President, the President-elect shall have died, the Vice-President-elect shall become President. If a President shall not have been chosen before the time fixed for the beginning of his term, or if the President-elect shall have failed to qualify; then the Vice-President-elect shall act as President until a President shall have qualified; and the Congress may by law provide for the case wherein neither a President-elect nor a Vice-President-elect shall have qualified, declaring who shall then act as President, or the manner in which one who is to act shall be selected, and such person shall act accordingly until a President or Vice-President shall have qualified.

Section 4. The Congress may by law provide for the case of the death of any of the persons from whom the House of Representatives may choose a President whenever the right of choice shall have devolved upon them, and for the case of the death of any of the persons from whom the Senate may choose a Vice-President whenever the right of choice shall have devolved upon them.

~~**Section 5.** Sections 1 and 2 shall take effect on the 15th day of October following the ratification of this article.~~

~~**Section 6.** This article shall be inoperative unless it shall have been ratified as an amendment to the Constitution by the legislatures of three fourths of the several States within seven years from the date of its submission.~~

43 **Article XXI** *(1933)*. **Section 1.** The eighteenth article of amendment to the Constitution of the United States is hereby repealed.

Section 2. The transportation or importation into any state, territory, or possession of the United States for delivery or use therein of intoxicating liquors, in violation of the laws thereof, is hereby prohibited.

~~**Section 3.** This article shall be inoperative unless it shall have been ratified as an amendment to the Constitution by conventions in the several states, as provided in the Constitution, within seven years from the date of the submission hereof to the states by the Congress.~~

44 **Article XXII** *(1951)*. **Section 1.** No person shall be elected to the office of the President more than twice, and no person who has held the office of President, or acted as President, for more than two years of a term to which some other person was elected President shall be elected to the office of the President more than once. ~~But this Article shall not apply to any person holding the office of President when this Article was proposed by the Congress, and shall not prevent any person who may be holding the office of President, or acting as President, during the term within which this Article becomes operative from holding the office of President or acting as President during the remainder of such term.~~

45 **Article XXIII** *(1961)*. **Section 1.** The district constituting the seat of government of the United States shall appoint in such manner as the Congress may direct: A number of electors of President and Vice-Presi-

42. This amendment changes the date for the President and Vice-President beginning their terms of office. The opening date for Congress was also moved. The amendment provides for what should be done in case something happens to the President-elect before taking office.

43. This amendment canceled the 18th Amendment, and made it once again legal to make and sell alcoholic beverages.

44. No person may serve more than two terms as President.

dent equal to the whole number of Senators and Representatives in Congress to which the District would be entitled if it were a state, but in no event more than the least populous state; they shall be in addition to those appointed by the states, but they shall be considered, for the purposes of the election of President and Vice-President, to be electors appointed by a state; and they shall meet in the District and perform such duties as provided by the twelfth article of amendment.

Section 2. The Congress shall have power to enforce this article by appropriate legislation.

Article XXIV *(1964).* **Section 1.** The right of citizens of the United States to vote in any primary or other election for President or Vice-President, for electors for President or Vice-President, or for Senator or Representatives in Congress, shall not be denied or abridged by the United States or any state by reason of failure to pay any poll tax or other tax.

Section 2. The Congress shall have power to enforce this article by appropriate legislation.

Article XXV *(1967).* **Section 1.** In case of the removal of the President from office or his death or resignation, the Vice-President shall become President.

Section 2. Whenever there is a vacancy in the office of the Vice-President, the President shall nominate a Vice-President who shall take office upon confirmation by a majority vote of both houses of Congress.

Section 3. Whenever the President transmits to the President *Pro Tempore* of the Senate and the Speaker of the House of Representatives his written declaration that he is unable to discharge the powers and duties of his office, and until he transmits to them a written declaration to the contrary, such powers and duties shall be discharged by the Vice-President as Acting President.

Section 4. Whenever the Vice-President and a majority of either the principal officers of the executive departments or of such other body as Congress may by law provide, transmit to the President *Pro Tempore* of the Senate and the Speaker of the House of Representatives their written declaration that the President is unable to discharge the powers and duties of his office, the Vice-President shall immediately assume the powers and duties of the office as Acting President.

Thereafter, when the President transmits to the President *Pro Tempore* of the Senate and the Speaker of the House of Representatives his written declaration that no inability exists, he shall resume the powers and duties of his office unless the Vice-President and a majority of either the principal officers of the executive departments or of such other body as Congress may by law provide, transmit within four days to the President *Pro Tempore* of the Senate and the Speaker of the House of Representatives their written declaration that the President is unable to discharge the powers and duties of his office. Thereupon Congress shall decide the issue, assembling within 48 hours for that purpose if not in session. If the Congress, within 21 days after receipt of the latter written declaration, or, if Congress is not in session, within 21 days after Congress is required to assemble, determines by two-thirds vote of both houses that the President is unable to discharge the powers and duties of his office, the Vice-President shall continue to discharge the same as Acting President; otherwise, the President shall resume the powers and duties of his office.

Article XXVI (1971). **Section 1.** The right of citizens of the United States, who are 18 years of age or older, to vote shall not be denied or abridged by the United States or any state on account of age.

Section 2. The Congress shall have power to enforce this article by appropriate legislation.

---

45 45. The residents of the District of Columbia have the right to vote in Presidential elections. The District has three electoral votes.

46 46. No person can be denied the right to vote in national elections for failure to pay a tax. In 1966, the Supreme Court extended this right to include state elections as well.

47 47. This amendment determines what should be done if something happens to the President. If the President dies or cannot continue in office, the Vice-President becomes President. This person then appoints a new Vice-President who must be approved by Congress. The Vice-President may also become Acting President if the President cannot fulfill the duties of the office for a limited time.

48 48. All United States citizens over the age of eighteen have the right to vote.

GLOSSARY

A

abolitionists people who believed slavery was wrong and tried to stop it in the U.S.

acquitted declared not guilty

adjourn to close a session, for a time

allies people united for a specific purpose

almanac an informational book published annually

ambushes traps

amendment change or addition to the U.S. Constitution

ammunition bullets and shells for weapons

annexed added on to its territory

Antifederalists people who believed in strong state government during the early history of the United States

apprentices persons learning a trade

arsenal store of arms

arson crime of purposely setting fire to property

assassin one who kills a well-known person

assemblies meetings of lawmakers

autobiographical about the story of one's own life

B

ballots tickets by which a vote is registered

ban an official order against something

barracks buildings soldiers live in

bayonet a long knife attached to the end of a rifle

Beecher's Bibles rifles shipped from New England by abolitionists

Black Codes laws passed by Southern states after the Civil War to limit the rights of former slaves

Board of Education elected or appointed group that directs a public school system

bondage being held against one's will; lack of freedom; slavery

boycotting refusing to deal with a nation, company, or organization in order to show disapproval or force a change

broadside poster featuring news

C

Cabinet officially chosen group of advisors to the president

candidate person seeking office

carpetbaggers Northerners who went South during Reconstruction to help blacks or to go into business

census an official count of people

chaplain minister, rabbi, or priest in armed forces

chattel moveable property, later a term for slaves

civilians any persons not active members of the military

civilization advanced stage of social development

clan group of families

colony settlement or community

column line of soldiers

command soldiers or area under an officer's authority

commission written order giving certain powers, duties, or rights

Committee of Correspondence a group of American patriots who worked to unite the colonies against Britain

communal shared ownership

compact agreement

compromise a way of satisfying both sides in a disagreement by which each side settles for less than it wants; mutual agreement

Compromise of 1850 Henry Clay's plan to deal with differences between slave and free states

confederation a joining together in an alliance

conquistador conqueror

Constitution the document that outlines the plan of government in the United States

continent one of the main bodies of land in the world

convert to persuade people to change their beliefs

cultures the way of life of a group of people

D

Daughters of Liberty women who boycotted British products during the Revolutionary war

Declaration of Independence statement declaring American colonial independence from Britain; also attacking British treatment of the colonies

Declaration of Sentiments statement attacking the treatment of women in the 18th century

delegates formal representatives

democracy government of the people

deserted ran away from duty

dictator ruler with complete power and authority

due process of law the set of rules for bringing a person accused of a crime to trial

E

economic depression severe reduction in business activity

economy financial affairs of a community

editorials statements of opinion in a newspaper or magazine

electoral college a group of people chosen by voters to elect the president and vice-president

Emancipation Proclamation the document written and signed by President Abraham Lincoln that freed all slaves living in Confederate states during the Civil War

emigrants people who leave one country to settle in another

empire a group of cities, states, or territories under the rule of one person

Enlightenment period of political questioning in 18th century Europe

equality having the same rights, privileges, and rank

European Americans Americans of European descent

executive person who enforces the law

exile long period living away from one's own country

exports goods sent to another country

F

faction group

Federalists people who believed in strong federal government during early history of the U.S.

First Continental Congress meeting of colonial leaders held in Philadelphia in 1774

fleet ships under one command

fort permanent army post

forty-niners people who moved to California during the gold rush of 1849

Free-Soilers group of Northerners who wanted to keep slavery from spreading into Western lands in the mid-19th century

Freedmen's Bureau an organization set up by Congress after the Civil War to help ex-slaves with jobs, legal needs, and education

Fugitive Slave Act a law passed in 1850 that made it illegal to help runaway slaves

G

Gadsden Purchase the purchase by the United States of the southern parts of Arizona and New Mexico

H

Hessians German troops hired by the British during the American Revolution

homespun cloth made of yarn at home

homesteaders people who claimed frontier property by settling there

House of Burgesses group responsible for making laws in colonial Virginia

hunter-gatherers people who move often to hunt and gather food

I

immigrants people who come into a new country or region

impeach to charge a public official with crimes or misconduct

imported brought in from another country

inaugural address speech made at time of being sworn in to office

indentured servitude an agreement to work a set number of years in exchange for passage to America

indicted charged with a crime

industrialization the process of developing large factories

infidels non-believers of a dominant religion

integration uniting racial and ethnic groups to function together

internment confinement

J

judicial review power of the U.S. Supreme Court to decide if laws are constitutional

judiciary branch of government that makes sure laws are constitutional; system of courts of law

jury a group chosen to make a judgment

justice of the peace judge who tries minor cases

K

Kansas-Nebraska Act law passed by Congress in 1854 that allowed settlers in Kansas and Nebraska to choose whether or not to allow slavery

L

legislature law-making body

liberals people belonging to a political party that favors reforms

literate able to read and write

loyalists American colonists who remained loyal to Britain

M

Magna Carta great charter sealed by King John in 1215 that guaranteed political liberty for the people of England

majority the group, party, or faction with the largest number of votes

Manifest Destiny belief held by many Americans in the mid-19th century that it was God's will that the U.S. extend its borders to the Pacific Ocean

merchant person who buys and sells goods

mesas flat-topped hills

Mexican Cession the land that the U.S. gained from Mexico in 1848; included all of present-day California, Nevada, and Utah and parts of Arizona, New Mexico, Colorado, and Wyoming

midwife person who assists women in giving birth

militia emergency army of citizens

Minutemen farmers in colonial America who trained to fight the British

missions headquarters of religious group setting up churches, schools, and hospitals

Missouri Compromise the agreement that made slavery illegal north of, and legal south of, a certain line

Monroe Doctrine a warning issued by President James Monroe in 1823 to keep European armies out of the Americas

Muslims people who believe in one God, whose name is Allah

N

nationalism a strong feeling of pride for one's country

Native Americans the first native peoples of North America including Eskimos and Indians

nomadic wandering from place to place

nonconformist person who follows own beliefs instead of what may be popular

nullify to declare illegal

O

oath pledge to tell the truth and keep promises

offensive an attack by armed forces

opinion what one thinks, formal statement

P

parallel imaginary line on the globe that runs in same direction as Equator

parliament a legislature

patriots people who are loyal and supportive of their country; 17th-century Americans loyal to the colonies

petition a written, formal statement requesting something

philosopher person who searches for wisdom and knowledge

plague a serious epidemic

plantations large farms or estates

plea request or appeal

political bias attitude in favor of or against a political issue, party, or person

political parties groups set up for the purpose of directing the policies of a government

popular sovereignty the right of people to decide an issue

preamble introduction

privateers privately owned, armed ships hired by a government

proportional representation a system in which a group (such as a state) is represented according to its population

provisional temporary

Puritans people who wanted to change and simplify the English church during the 17th century

Q

Quakers a Christian group called the Society of Friends, they believe in simple religious services and oppose war

R

Radical Republicans members of Congress during the Civil War who wanted to free the slaves immediately and favored strict reconstruction afterwards

radical someone who favors extreme changes in existing laws or conditions

ratified to formally have a law approved

raw material a natural product that is used in manufacturing

Rebels nickname for Confederate soldiers during the Civil War

Reconstruction the period from 1865 to 1877 during which the federal government controlled the states that had belonged to the Confederacy during the Civil War

redcoats nickname for British soldiers during the Revolutionary war

reformers people who try to improve quality of life

reforms changes

refugees people who flee a country during time of conflict

regiments large military units

repealed did away with a law

representatives people chosen to speak or act for others

republic a representative form of government; democratic nation

Republican party a political party formed by abolitionist and Free-Soilers in 1854 to keep slavery from spreading

reservation public land set aside for special use, especially land set aside for Indian peoples after European Americans occupied Indian land

riots violent disturbances of the peace

S

secede to leave, quit

Separatists people who wanted to separate from the Church of England in the 17th century

siege surrounding of a fort by an army trying to capture it

Sons of Liberty men who stirred up riots against the British before and during the Revolutionary war

spoils system an arrangement giving political supporters government jobs

strikes workers' refusal to work

subjects people owing allegiance to a monarchy

suffrage the right to vote

suit legal proceeding

surrender to give up

T

tariff a tax on goods sent from another country

Tenure of Office Act a law passed by Congress during President Andrew Johnson's administration that requires the president to get Senate approval before firing any members of the Cabinet

transcendentalists people who believe that each person has a divine spirit

Treaty of Guadalupe Hidalgo a law that set the boundary between Texas and Mexico at Rio Grande in the 19th century

Treaty of Paris Britain's recognition of American independence in 1783

treaty a formal agreement between nations

trial an examination of the facts of a case

truce agreement to stop fighting

tyrant a cruel and unjust leader

U

Underground Railroad secret escape route for slaves during the 19th century

utopia ideal place; perfect society

V

veterans people who served in time of war and survived

veto a refusal to approve

viceroy office similar to governor

W

Whiskey Rebellion an uprising of farmers in Pennsylvania who refused to pay new tax in the late 18th century

wilderness undeveloped land area

writ of mandamus court order to do a legal action

Y

Yanks nickname for Union soldiers

INDEX

A

Abbott, Edith, 50

Abolitionists and abolitionism, 25, 28, 90. *See also* African Americans; Freedmen; Slaves and slavery; beginnings of, 31-32; defined, 21; Douglass, Frederick and, 98-101; Dred Scott case and, 106-109; Harpers Ferry raid and, 110-113; increase in, 34-37; Kansas-Nebraska Act and, 102-105; North and, 91; Stevens, Thaddeus and, 175; Underground Railroad and, 94-97; women's rights and, 43-45

Adams, Franklin, 105

Adams, Harriet, 105

Adams, John Quincy, 4

African Americans. *See also* Abolitionists and abolitionism; Freedmen; Slaves and slavery; civil rights of, 4; Congress (U.S.) membership of, 178-181; discrimination against, 7, 34, 175; education and, 170; Reconstruction and, 166-169; Republican party and, 169; voting rights of, 164, 166

Agriculture, Spanish settlers, 65

Alamo battle (Mexican War), 54, 68-71

Alcorn, James A., 180

Alcott, Louisa May, 112

American Anti-Slavery Society, 36, 37, 43

American Red Cross, 161

American Revolution, Jackson, Andrew and, 9

American Society for the Promotion of Temperance, 28

A. M. E. Zion church, 25

Anderson, Robert, 119, 120

Annexation, 57, 71

Anthony, Susan B., 45

Antietam battle, 126, 129, 136-139

Anti-Slavery Convention (London, 1840), 43

Anti-Slavery Society, 28, 32

Appomattox Court House, 127, 152

Arizona, U.S. claims to, 59, 73

Army. *See* Civil War (U.S.); Military

Arts and literature. *See also* Culture; reform and, 32-33; transcendentalists and, 46-49

Atchison, David, 103

Atlanta (Georgia), burning of, 126, 148

B

Back-to-Africa movement, 21

Bagley, Sarah, 19

Bank of the United States, Jackson, Andrew and, 6

Baptist church, 25

Barton, Clara, 161

Battle of the Alamo, 54, 68-71

Battle of Antietam (Civil War), 126, 129, 136-139

Battle of Bull Run (Civil War), 126, 132-135, 141

Battle of Gettysburg (Civil War), 126, 129, 144-145, 146

Battle of New Orleans (War of 1812), 10

Battle of Vicksburg (Civil War), 126, 129, 144, 146-147

Beauregard, Pierre, 119

Becknell, William, 66

Bee, Barnard, 132

Beecher, Catharine, 31, 40-41

Beecher, Henry Ward, 103

Bill of Rights, slavery and, 25

Black Codes, 167, 168-169, 172, 176, 187

Blaine, James G., 179

Bloomer, Amelia, 30, 45

Booth, John Wilkes, 156-157, 158

Boundary changes, 86-87

Bowie, David, 70, 71

Bradburn, George, 43

Brady, Matthew, 143

Breckinridge, John C., 116, 124-125

Brooke, Edward, 180

Brooks, Preston, 104

Brown, John, 89, 93, 105, 110-113

Bruce, Blanche K., 165, 178, 179-181

Bull Run battle (Civil War), 126, 132-135, 141

Butler, Andrew, 104

C

Cady, Daniel, 42

Calhoun, John C., 6, 22, 80, 82-83

California; Gold Rush in, 55, 76-79, 85; Mexico and, 57, 75; slavery and, 79, 81-82; U.S. claims to, 59, 73

Canada, Underground Railroad and, 95, 96

Canals, 6

Carpetbagger, 166

Cartoons, 188-189

Catholic church, 69. *See also* Religion

Catlin, George, 32

Centennial celebrations, 184

Charleston, South Carolina, 118-121

Chattel, 35. *See also* Slaves and slavery

Cherokee people, 3, 7, 12-15, 70

Chesnut, James, 140, 141, 142

Chesnut, Mary, 140-143

Chickasaw people, 13

Children, women's custody of, 43

Chinese immigrants, 76, 77-78, 181

Choctaw people, 13, 140

Cholera, 61-62

Cities, freedmen and, 171

Civil rights; freedmen, 175-176, 176; slaves, 21, 25; women, 32, 36-37

Civil Rights Act of 1866, 164

Civil War (U.S.), 37, 102; aftermath of, 164, 166; Antietam battle, 136-139; battles of, 163; first Bull Run battle, 132-135; Gettysburg battle, 144-145, 146; Lincoln and, 127; military leadership and, 130-131; Sherman's march to the sea, 148-151; start of, 118-121, 126; strategy in, 129-130; surrender of South, 152-155; tragedy of, 128; Vicksburg battle, 146-147; women and, 161

Clay, Henry, 5, 59, 79, 80-83, 96

Clothing, bloomers, 30

Coffin, Charles Carleton, 145

Coffin, Lucretia, 43

Cole, Thomas, 46

Colleges and universities. *See also* Education; teacher training and, 40; women's education and, 43

Colman, Samuel, 60

Colorado, 75

Comanche people, 69

Compromise of 1850, 59, 82-83, 88, 91, 96

Concord, Massachusetts, 47

Confederate States of America, 118. *See also* Civil War (U.S.)

Congress (U.S.). *See also* House of Representatives (U.S.); Senate (U.S.); blacks elected to, 169, 178-181; civil rights and, 176; Freedmen's Bureau and, 171; Fugitive Slave Act and, 175; Native Americans and, 2, 7, 13, 61; nullification crisis and, 6; Reconstruction and, 166; slavery and, 21, 79, 103-105, 108; Supreme Court (U.S.) and, 109; tariff and, 5-6; Texas and, 71, 72, 73; violence in, 104-105

Conkling, Roscoe, 180

Constitution (Cherokee people), 12

Constitution (U.S.); Fifteenth Amendment, 173; Fourteenth Amendment, 168; presidency and, 124-125; slavery and, 25, 108, 115; Thirteenth Amendment, 37, 166, 167, 168

Cotton; cotton mills and, 17-18; slavery and, 83, 90-91

Cotton gin, 7

Covey, Edward, 99

Cowboys, Spanish, 64-67

Creek people, 7, 10, 13

Crockett, Davy, 70, 71

Culture. *See also* Arts and literature; reform and, 32-33; Spain and, 66; transcendentalists and, 46-49; westward movement and, 57

Currier and Ives, 121, 180

ILLUSTRATION CREDITS

2-3 (24). Manchester Historic Association, NH. Photo, E. Gould; 4. New-York Historical Society, New York City; 5. (Detail) *Canvassing for a Vote*, George Caleb Bingham, 1852. The Nelson-Atkins Museum of Art, Kansas City, MO. Nelson Fund; 7. (t) *International Indian Council*, 1843, John Mix Stanley. National Museum of American Art, Smithsonian Institution. Gift of the Misses Henry, 1908; 8. *The President's Levee or All Creation Going to the White House*, Robert Cruikshank. White House Historical Association. Photo, National Geographic Society; 9. Tennessee State Library and Archives, Nashville; 10. Library of Congress; 12. Robert Lindreux. Woolaroc Museum, Bartlesville, OK; 13. New Echota Historic Site, Georgia Department of Natural Resources, Calhoun; 16. Merrimack Valley Textile Museum, N. Andover, MA; 17. Massachusetts Historical Society, Boston; 19. Courtesy American Antiquarian Society, Worcester, MA; 20. *Sugar Harvest in Louisiana and Texas*, 1856-60, Franz Holzlhuber. Glenbow Museum, Calgary, Alberta; 21. Virginia State Library and Archives, Richmond; 22. Schomburg Center for Research in Black Culture. New York Public Library; 23. Virginia State Library and Archives, Richmond; 25. Thadeus Govan Photography; 28-29 (50). Burbank Camp Meeting. New Bedford Whaling Museum, MA; 29. National Library of Medicine, Bethesda, MD; 31. (t) By permission of the Houghton Library, Harvard University, Cambridge, MA; (b) The Metropolitan Museum of Art. Gift of I.N. Phelps Stokes, Edward S. Hawes, Alice Mary Hawes, Marion Augusta Hawes, 1937; 32. International Museum of Photography at George Eastman House; 33. Shaker Museum, Old Chatham, NY. Photo, Paul Rocheleau; 34. Library of Congress; 35. New York Public Library; 36. Massachusetts Historical Society, Boston; 38. Library of Congress; 39. *Punctuation Personified*, J. and B. Turnbull, Steubenville, OH, 1831. Rare Book Department, Free Library of Philadelphia. Photo, Joan Broderick; 41. The Schlesinger Library, Radcliffe College, Cambridge, MA; 42. Collection of Rhoda Jenkins and John Barney; 44-45. Women's Rights Historic Park, Eastern National Parks and Monuments Association; 46. The Cleveland Museum of Art. Hinman B. Hurlbut Collection; 47. The Bettmann Archive; 48. The Bettmann Archive; 51. Culver Pictures; 54-55 (84). *Emigrant Train Bedding Down for the Night*, Benjamin Reinhart. The Corcoran Gallery of Art, Washington, D.C.; 56. © C. A. Christensen. Courtesy of Brigham Young University Fine Arts Collection, Provo, UT; 57. Denver Public Library, Western History Department; 59. (Detail) *Indian Village*, Jules Tavernier. Thomas Gilcrease Institute of American History and Art, Tulsa, OK; 60. Paulus Leeser; 61. Kansas State Historical Society, Topeka; 63. Alfred Jacob Miller. Joselyn Art Museum, Omaha, NB; 64. *Gauchos in a Horse Corral*, James Walker. Thomas Gilcrease Institute of American History and Art, Tulsa, OK; 65. Historical Society of New Mexico Collections, The Museum of New Mexico, Sante Fe. Photo, Blair Clark; 66. West Side Main Plaza, San Antonio, *Texas*, William G. M. Samuel; On loan from Bexar County. Courtesy The San Antonio Museum Association, TX; 67. *Dona Mariana Grinding Corn*, c. 1885, Alexander F. Harmer. Seaver Center for Western History Research, Natural History Museum of Los Angeles County; 68. © Bill Reaves/Viesti Associates; 69. Texas Memorial Museum; 72. *War News from Mexico*, Richard Caton Woodville. National Academy of Design, New York City; 75. Carl Nebel, Illustration for *The War between the United States and Mexico* by George Wilkins Kendall, D. Appelton and Company, 1851. New York Public Library. Astor, Lenox and Tilden Foundations; 76. Oakland Museum; 77 (85). California State Library, Sacramento; 78. (Detail) International Museum of Photography at George Eastman House; 80. © National Geographic Society, Washington, D.C.; 88-89 (122). United States Military History Institute; 90. Library of Congress; 91. Library of Congress; 92. Temple University. Blockson Collection; 93. *Hauling the Whole Weeks Picking*, c. 1842, William Henry Brown. The Historic New Orleans Collection, Museum/Research Center; 94. Sophie Smith Collection, Smith College; 95. *The Underground Railway*, Charles T. Webber. Cincinatti Art Museum; 97. Schomburg Center for Research in Black Culture. New York Public Library. 98. *Frederick Douglass Series No. 21*, Jacob Lawrence. Hampton University Museum; 99. National Portrait Gallery; 100. National Archives; 101. Schomburg Center for Research in Black Culture. New York Public Library. 102. Kansas State Historical Society; 106. New York Public Library. Astor, Lenox and Tilden Foundations; 107. Louis Schultze, 1881. Missouri Historical Society, St. Louis; 108. *Old Kentucky Home (Life in the South)*, 1859, Eastman Johnson. New-York Historical Society, New York City; 110. Thomas Hovenden, 1884. The Metropolitan Museum of Art. Gift of Mr. and Mrs. Carl Stoeckel, 1897; 111. Boston Atheneum; 112. Courtesy James C. Holland; 113. Courtesy of the Pennsylvania Academy of the Fine Arts, Philadelphia. John Lambert Fund; 114 (123). Office of the Secretary of State of Illinois. Photo, Gregg Daniels; 115. Museum of American Political Life, University of Hartford, West Hartford, CT. Photo, Sally Andersen-Bruce; 117. © National Geographic Society, Washington, D.C.; 118. *The Flag at Sumter*, Oct. 20, 1863, C.W. Chapman. The Museum of the Confederacy, Richmond, VA. Photo, Katherine Wetzel; 121. Anne S. K. Brown Military Collection, Brown University Library, Providence, RI; 126-127 (160). *The Seventh Regiment Departing for the War, April 19, 1861*, Thomas Nast. The Seventh Regiment Fund, Inc; 129. Library of Congress; 131. Private Collection; 132. *General Bee at the First Battle of Manassas*, C. W. Chapman. Valentine Museum, Richmond, VA; 135. The Bettmann Archive; 136. Library of Congress; 137. *"Slavery Is Abolished..."*, c. 1865, Lewis Miller. Courtesy of Historical Society of York County, PA; 139 (161). American Red Cross; 140. Library of Congress; 141. Georgia Historical Society. United Daughters of the Confederacy Collection; 142. Portrait by Samuel Osgood. National Portrait Gallery, Smithsonian Institution. On loan from Serena Williams Miles Van Rensselaer; 143. Library of Congress; 144. Howard Pyle. © National Geographic Society, Washington, D.C.; 145. *McPherson's Ridge*, James Walker, from *The Civil War: Gettysburg*. Photograph by Larry Sherer © Time-Life Books, Inc. Courtesy The J. Howard Wert Collection; 148. Kean Archives, Philadelphia; 149. National Portrait Gallery, Smithsonian Institution; 150. Kobal Collection; 151. University of Georgia, Hargrett Rare Book and Manuscript Library; 152. *Furling the Flag*, 1872, Richard N. Brooke. West Point Museum Collection; 153. (t) Library of Congress; (b) Valentine Museum, Richmond, VA. Cook Collection; 156. (l) Chicago Historical Society; (r) The Kunhardt Collection; 157. The New-York Historical Society, New York City; 158. (t) Chicago Historical Society; (b) The Kunhardt Collection; 159. Illinois Central Railroad; 164-165 (186). Library of Congress; 166. Breton Littlehales; 168. Hill Memorial Library, Louisiana State University Libraries; 169 (187). Rutherford B. Hayes Presidential Center; 170. Courtesy Hampton University Archives; 171. U.S. Military History Institute. Photo, Jim Enos; 172. Western Reserve Historical Society; 173. G. William Holland; 174. Library of Congress; 175. Library of Congress; 176. Giraudon/Art Resource; 178. Library of Congress; 179. Library of Congress; 180. Mississippi Department of Archives and History. Special Collections; 182. The New-York Historical Society, New York City; 183. Museum of American Political Life, University of Hartford, West Hartford, CT; 184. Free Library of Philadelphia; 185. *Street Car Travel*, Edwin Haley. Historical Society of Pennsylvania; 188, 189. Thomas Nast.